WHY
YOU
SAY IT

WHY YOU YOU SAY IT

Webb Garrison

Rutledge Hill Press™
Nashville, Tennessee

A Division of Thomas Nelson, Inc.

Published by Rutledge Hill Press, a division of Thomas Nelson, Inc., P.O. Box 141000,
Nashville, Tennessee 37214.

Typography by Compass Communications, Inc., Nashville, Tennessee
Design by Harriette Bateman

Library of Congress Cataloging-in-Publication Data

Garrison, Webb B.
    Why you say it / Webb Garrison.
        p. cm.
    Includes bibliographical references (p.)
    ISBN 1-55853-128-9 (paperback)
        1. English language—Etymology—Dictionaries.

 PE1580 .G37   1992
 422'.03—dc20
                                                            92–26951
                                                            CIP

Printed in the United States of America

06 07 RRD 24 23

WHY
YOU
SAY IT

BEHIND EVERY WORD, THERE'S A STORY

Ambrose E. Burnside, a one-time manufacturer of rifles, became a colonel in the 1st Rhode Island Volunteers at the outbreak of the Civil War. When enlistment of his ninety-day regiment expired, Burnside remained in uniform, having been made a brigadier general by Abraham Lincoln.

He is the only man who twice refused command of the Army of the Potomac—only to accept that post under stern orders from his president. His daring but foolish attempt to cross the Rappahannock River in 1863 ended in a famous, or infamous, "mud march" during which Robert E. Lee's mocking Confederates pretended to offer help to place pontoon bridges for his troops. Removed from command, he was sent to Ohio. There he was the key figure in an unconstitutional punishment of a former U.S. congressman, whom he banished into Confederate territory.

At war's end, Ambrose E. Burnside served three terms as governor of Rhode Island, and was then elected to the U.S. Senate. Yet the most enduring memorial to a dashing and colorful soldier-politician is the descriptive term "sideburns," briefly described in these pages.

Numerous huge scholarly works, notably the 22,000-page *Oxford English Dictionary,* offer detailed accounts of the way speech has developed. Yet volumes produced by academicians are not easy to use. Neither do they appeal to millions of persons who every day employ hundreds of written and oral words and phrases.

Why You Say It is precisely what the title suggests: a collection of fast-moving accounts of expressions in wide use.

In 1955, Abingdon Press published a volume of the same title, with many similar emphases. This time, I have dug into a great many words and phrases not even in use thirty-six years ago. In addition, I have tried to take into account the new openness of our speech. Influenced by novels and television, today we think nothing of referring to a prostitute or a condom, for example. These and many other terms were taboo in polite circles until very recently.

This volume is offered primarily for your enjoyment, secondarily as an all-too-brief popular reference work. Delving into these pages, you'll find many stories that you will be tempted to introduce into your conversations. Please do so, any time you are so inclined!

Should you be called upon to provide material for a program, adaptations of accounts included here are suitable for many occasions. Note that the listings entitled "See Also" are suggestive, but by no means exhaustive; a quick glance at a few pages will yield other vignettes in the same category.

Space makes it impossible to compile listings of stories in all subject matter categories treated. If you care to do so, you may readily identify and use accounts relating to these and other special interests:

automobiles	horses
baseball	hunting and fishing
biblical words	medicine and health
books	music
Civil War words	mythology
con men	poker
cowboys	politics
farming	railroads
fashion	sailors and the sea
food and drink	science and technology
football	sex
golf	war

Here's hoping that you'll have fun discovering why you say some of the things that mark you as an individual, using inherited words and phrases in a fashion that is unique to you.

Webb Garrison
Lake Junaluska, N.C.

CONTENTS

CHAPTER 1

THE WORLD OF ENTERTAINMENT

> "Do you come to the play without knowing what it is?"
> "O, yes, Sir, yes, very frequently. I have no time to read playbills. One merely comes to meet one's friends, and show that one's alive."
>
> —Fanny Burney, *Evelina,* Letter 20

From the stage to the circus to the comic book, the world of entertainment has contributed to popular speech, while simultaneously drawing from it.

Sample words and phrases from this rich vein of speech will often help you "to know what the play is."

BARNSTORMER

BEHIND THE SCENES

BLOCKBUSTER

CAMEO ROLE

CHEESECAKE

CIRCUS

DONNYBROOK

DOUBLE TAKE

FANNY

FIRE-EATER

FLIP SIDE

GOON

GREEN-EYED MONSTER

HAM

HANDWRITING ON THE WALL

HEP/HIP

HIT

LIMELIGHT

MAKE A SCENE

MELBA TOAST/
    PEACH MELBA

OUT OF LINE

PAGEANT

PLAY SECOND FIDDLE

POOH-BAH

PRIMA DONNA

PULL STRINGS

RHUBARB

ROBOT

SLAPSTICK

TOP BANANA/
    SECOND BANANA

TWO TO TANGO

VAUDEVILLE

WHAMMY

SEE ALSO: Bandwagon, Chestnut, Dive, Doodly-squat, Gimmick, Hanky-panky, Hocus-pocus, Life of Riley, Mascot, Security Blanket, Well-heeled

Barnstormer

IN the early days of traveling theater, third-rate companies didn't get the best facilities. Many had to settle for almost any empty building. Some held one-night stands in barns.

Such a performing group didn't stay anywhere long. Entertainers stormed from place to place, sometimes having to wait for horses and cows to be moved out before a stage could be improvised.

A candidate for office who raced from one spot to another, addressing small crowds, had a lot in common with a theatrical barnstormer. From amateurish performers and hack politicians, the term attached to anyone who moves around a lot without getting much done.

Behind the Scenes

DEVELOPMENT of the theater proceeded rapidly during the long reign of England's Queen Elizabeth I. However, more attention was given to scripts and actors than to stage settings. Most performances took place before backdrops of simple curtains.

James I and Charles I encouraged free spending in the arts. Under their sponsorship, craftsmen began making elaborate painted slides and hangings for backdrops on a stage. Such pieces, which often represented landscapes, were known simply as *scenes*.

In many plays and operas, important action was not represented on the stage; instead it was simply reported to the audience. This was especially the case with murders and executions, which were often treated as having taken place between acts.

Patrons joked about the fact that many events occurred, not on the stage, but behind the scenes. Hence real-life action hidden from the public came to be described by the term born in the theater.

Blockbuster

ANY time a blockbuster movie or novel is released, lines are sure to form. Producers and publishers know that the glow won't last long, so they want to cash in while they can.

The earliest blockbusters stayed in the news for month after month during World War II. The original *blockbuster* was a high-explosive bomb that could level an entire block.

Eventually, anything that made a considerable impact, like a spectacularly successful enterprise or production, took the name of the most powerful bomb before the advent of nukes.

Cameo Role

SEASHELLS and gemstones often have several layers that include two or more hues. Long ago, artisans learned to take advantage of this factor by carving in such fashion that a raised central figure or figures is of different color from the background.

A cameo engraved in this way doesn't have to be rare and costly in order to be beautiful and prized. Many that are hawked on the streets of Rome and other European cities are inexpensively exquisite, though tiny.

Transferred to the world of entertainment, the name of small but lovely jewelry became the term for a bit part played by a notable performer. On the stage, in the movies, and in television, many producers vie for viewers by including cameo roles that feature persons with famous names.

Cheesecake

MEASURED by standards of their eras, some entertainers have been scantily clad since an early promoter first charged a fee to watch them. Until this century, however, deliberately un-covered flesh was seldom seen except in special places.

Photography and mass-circulation publications made near-nudity common, but not commonplace. Until recent decades, practically all subjects for this specialized form of art were female.

Especially in the case of a natural blonde or redhead, skin color is often remarkably close to that of a delicacy whose basic ingredient is cream cheese. It was natural—and inevitable—to compare flesh tones with food. That's why we use cheesecake to label big areas of bare skin and photos or performances featuring them.

Circus

LIFE under the caesars wasn't centered entirely upon war and conquest. Partly to keep common folk contented, rulers built in the capital city a vast sports arena. Shaped like a huge circle, or *circus,* Rome's biggest structure gained international fame as the *circus maximus.*

Males and females were separated at most public assemblies. Not so when they went to the *circus maximus.* There they mingled freely, and saw many lavish spectacles.

Long used to designate any structure built for sport or entertainment, the Roman name shifted from buildings to performances staged in them. When Phineas T. Barnum added acrobats and jugglers to long-traditional equestrian acts, the modern traveling circus was born.

Donnybrook

WHEN a fracas erupts in a crowded place, it's hard to be an innocent bystander. Such a spontaneous melee deserves a mysterious name, but why *donnybrook?*

Because the town of Donnybrook in County Dublin, Ireland, was for generations the scene of a yearly bash. In connection with a fair held there, revelers made it a custom to drink and celebrate so boisterously that authorities came to expect a rash of fistfights on the closing night.

About 1855, Donnybrook abolished the fair and put an end to

annual brawls. By then *donnybrook* was already in general use as a name for anything from a loud argument to a riot.

Double Take

HAVE you ever been stopped short by a subliminal glimpse of something and didn't believe what you saw? That common experience calls for a second and closer look—a double take.

Whether working on a set or in a studio, many a director has called for the camera to take another look at a snippet of action or a full scene. Every take is on trial until it meets the director's approval. When footage is judged unsatisfactory by an on-the-spot decision, a double take is in order.

Erupting from lingo of the entertainment world, *double take* has come to mean anything deserving a second, or better, look.

Fanny

FOR generations, a fanny belonged only to a female. In present-day usage, it is commonplace to use the label for buttocks of a male as well. It began as a sex-oriented word because of John Cleland's *Memoirs of a Woman of Pleasure,* a book published in England in 1749. Better known as *Fanny Hill,* many experts consider it to be one of the finest of all English-language exposés of life in a brothel.

Cleland's masterpiece created such a sensation that the name of his heroine became synonymous with the human posterior—and originally applied only to a shape resembling that which readers imagined belonged to Fanny Hill.

Fire-eater

IN many cultures, people have experimented with swallowing smoke and flames. European showmen of the 17th century managed to convince onlookers that they actually ate glowing coals.

Keen interest in the exploits of fire-eaters who flourished in that era led to wide use of their name in other circumstances. It was initially applied to bullies who were so fond of fighting that they willingly faced danger. Later the term was associated with any person quick and eager at work—going at it with the relish a performer showed in eating fire.

Flip Side

CHINESE think and speak of the working of opposite cosmic forces in terms of yin and yang. Americans, more versed in technology than in philosophy, say that every argument and each set of principles has a "flip side."

Though the expression is too firmly entrenched in speech to face an early demise, the technology that produced it is virtually obsolete. Tape cassettes wreaked havoc in the phonograph record industry; compact discs have sounded its death knell.

But in its heyday, the revolving platter ruled popular music in the western world. Practically every song that went through the top of the charts was accompanied by another that didn't rival it in popularity. Cut into the reverse face of a record, this musical hitchhiker was noticeably different from its companion. Which meant that practically every record had its flip side—a second recording that gave listeners a quite different impression from that produced by the first.

Goon

As a form of entertainment, the comic strip has shown unusual staying power. Black-and-white sketches, along with a few words, have held their own against the assaults of color television.

Artist E. C. Segar didn't exactly make his name a household word. But at the height of his career, from 1935–1938, a poll would have turned up mighty few American households unaware of his comic strip.

Practically everyone read *Popeye the Sailor* frequently enough to feel almost as though friends of the sailor man were next-door neighbors. That was the case with a lumpy looking hulk whom Segar called "Alice the Goon"—first drawn in 1919.

It took only a few frames of sketches to learn that the Goon was tough as well as rough. Borrowing from the funny paper in the Roaring Twenties, its devotees persuaded the world to call any hired thug a *goon*.

Green-eyed Monster

THEATERGOERS did not realize what a good thing they had when the plays of Shakespeare first hit the stage. But it took only a few encounters with his work to realize that he talked and wrote like no one before or since.

Casting about for a vivid way to describe jealousy, the Bard of Avon remembered that many cats have green eyes. Not necessarily correctly, he seems to have considered cats to be cruel and vindictive.

Therefore, in *Othello* (Act III), he called jealousy the green-eyed monster—comparing it with a cat that to a human appears to play with the bird or mole it has captured and is about to eat.

Ham

FOR decades, ham actors were seen only in theaters. Today, the appearance of a video camera at a picnic or family outing is enough to bring one or more hams in front of it.

Young or old, male or female, the ham bears a name derived from the minstrel shows popular in the 19th century. Here, black face performances by white entertainers were standard fare.

Many performers, perhaps most, used ham fat to remove black makeup. While on stage, some strummed instruments and sang "Ham's Banjo" or "The Ham-fat Man."

All of these usages were linked with performances of less than first quality. Consequently, any incompetent or unskilled actor came to be called a "ham."

Handwriting on the Wall

ANCIENT Babylon flourished under the rule of King Nebuchadnezzar. But his son and successor, Belshazzar, proved weak and profligate. Ignoring all standards, he once drank heavily from holy vessels seized from the Temple in Jerusalem. A mysterious hand appeared after this act of sacrilege and to the astonishment of the king wrote four strange words on the wall of the banquet room.

Only the Hebrew prophet, Daniel, could interpret the mysterious message. He boldly told the ruler that they spelled disaster for him and for his nation. Soon afterward Belshazzar was defeated and slain, just as Daniel said.

Religious dramas of the Middle Ages often included vivid interpretations of events in the ancient banquet hall. Viewers of such pageants sat enthralled as they watched the writing of the strange warning to a king. As a result, any threat of impending doom is still known as "handwriting on the wall."

Hep/Hip

IF you are really up to date about what is going on, ready to deal with whatever comes, an admirer is likely to laud you as being *hep*. Not a bad characterization, really. For that's a shorthand way of saying that you are in step with the times.

Ordinary folk picked up the terse descriptive term from early jazz musicians. In the 1920s when jazz hadn't yet won a wide following, players often staged parades as a way of attracting attention to an upcoming performance.

Much in the fashion of a military drillmaster, the head honcho insisted that the musicians keep in step. Jazz being what it is, it was easy to effect a verbal transformation: "Step! Step! Step!" became "Hep! Hep! Hep!"

A player or a fan of the radical new form of music who was hep was literally in step with the marching band. Constant use led to development of an alternative form, so that a person who's "with it" may now be either *hep* or *hip*.

Hit

AUTHORS and publishers, along with actors and producers and songwriters, want nothing so much as a hit.

That is precisely what a contestant engaged in a predecessor to baseball hoped to get when given an opportunity to swing a bat.

A good, solid hit on the playing field meant an opportunity to advance and maybe even to score. Consequently, onlookers and athletes applied the term to any enterprise that has a successful, popular following.

Limelight

LIGHTING was one of the chief problems of the early theater. In the time of Shakespeare, all available devices were crude and ineffective.

Actors, playwrights, and theatergoers were delighted when Thomas Drummond devised a new source of light in 1816. A cylinder of lime was heated to incandescence by a flame, and when placed behind a lens or in front of a reflector, the limelight proved to be intensely bright.

The brightness made it ideal for use in making a star performer more visible. As long as one remained in it, audience attention was riveted.

Competition for a place in the limelight soon became intense. Consequently, it came to label any conspicuous spot—whether flooded by one of Thomas Drummond's lights or not.

Make a Scene

EARLY playwrights had to take into account the physical limitations of small stages and the chore of shifting scenery by hand. As a result, they created divisions of fixed settings within an act, called "scenes." Numerous entertainers gained fame for their performances in particular scenes. Such episodes usually invited a display of strong emotion.

Many theatergoers re-enacted favorite scenes. Today we say a person who gives a theatrical display in everyday life is "making a scene."

Melba Toast/Peach Melba

ONCE in a generation, an entertainer makes such a splash that language is enriched. That was the case with Helen Mitchell, better known as Dame Nellie Melba.

After studying organ and piano in Melbourne, Australia, she made her operatic debut as a soprano in Brussels in 1886. Until her farewell performance 40 years later, her name was a household word. Reporters followed her everywhere; anything Dame Nellie did was news.

Because she liked and regularly demanded oven-baked slices of very thin bread wherever she traveled, you'll find Melba toast nearly everywhere. Her dessert choice was ice cream with fresh peaches, and it, too, was named for her: peach Melba.

Out of Line

ANYTIME you notice someone who is noticeably different from colleagues in actions or ideas, that person may be badly out of line without knowing it.

At least two areas of activity could have spawned the expression.

A military line is not only expected to be as straight as an arrow; each person in that line should move simultaneously.

Coordinated movement is even more important in a chorus line; a single kicker who is a few seconds off can make the entire line look ragged.

Which means that generally unacceptable ideas or behavior that peers judge inappropriate can make anyone, anywhere, out of line.

Pageant

EUROPE'S earliest public entertainments were often re-enactments of Biblical events. Lacking suitable buildings for performances, shows were held outdoors—on wheels. Big wagons used for these religious dramas held two-level stages attached to frames of heavy farm vehicles. From an ancient term for "to fasten," a wagon to which stages had been fastened was called a *pageant*.

Crowded with actors in costume, a pageant was guaranteed to attract an audience wherever it went. So many of these wagons-with-stages rolled into so many towns and cities that the word came to mean the kinds of drama enacted upon it.

Well established in speech, the entertainment word survived when pageants went into churches and theaters. Current popularity of outdoor dramas has put the pageant back into roofless settings—but not yet back upon medieval wagons.

Play Second Fiddle

MOST early viols, or fiddles, were small and high pitched. They were used along with the lute and timbrel as early as the 15th century. But the instrument didn't come into its own until Claudio Monteverde began using it in 17th century orchestral pieces. By the time first- and second-violin arrangements became common, the musician who played first violin was the most honored member of an orchestra.

Popular music followed much the same course as classical, with the person who played the first fiddle taking the leading role.

Even though he or she may not know one musical note from another, any person in a subservient role is said to play second fiddle—or follow behind.

Pooh-Bah

BEHIND the back of a VIP, some associates may refer to the dignitary as a great Pooh-Bah. This fun-poking title for an important person believed to be keenly aware of his or her importance sounds rather oriental, doesn't it?

That's precisely what a noted English playwright hoped theatergoers would think.

In 1885, William S. Gilbert and Arthur Sullivan offered what many consider their greatest comic opera, *The Mikado*. The setting of the piece required generous use of expressions that would sound as though they came from the far east. Gilbert coined Pooh-Bah, Lord-High-Everything-Else, as the special title for one of his characters.

Though not remotely like any term of respect ever used in China, *Pooh-Bah,* has such a distinctive quality that it entered general speech to designate any notable judged to be a bit of a blowhard.

Prima Donna

A PERSON doesn't have to be an entertainer in order to be known among colleagues as a *prima donna*. Anyone may gain the title, if others conclude that he or she is overly temperamental or conceited.

This usage is Italian, pure and unadulterated.

Literally meaning "first lady," it has been employed for centuries as a title of respect for the leading female member of an opera company. Like some stars of today, the prima donna was granted special privileges and perks, which, combined with rave reviews on her talent and beauty, could make her vain and demanding.

At least 200 years ago, many of our ancestors decided that it was better to have as little as possible to do with the first lady of a visiting opera company. Adopting the title bestowed on her at home, unchanged in spelling, they began using it in a derogatory sense. Once started, it soon became standard throughout the English-speaking world.

Pull Strings

ANYTIME a deal is pending, it helps a lot to have a friend who knows how to pull strings. We use this expression to indicate use of influence because string-pullers were among the earliest popular entertainers.

No one knows where the art of puppetry originated, but it reached an early peak in France. A veteran performer could make a marionette—or "little Mary"—execute movements so complicated that it seemed to be alive.

Most spectators knew that a showman pulled the strings that made the puppet bow or dance. Since hands of the puppeteer were out of sight, his actions were compared with behind-the-scenes manipulation of any sort and a long-lasting expression was born.

Rhubarb

A GOOD dictionary will tell you that *rhubarb* means a loud dispute or a noisy argument that may be a prelude to a fight. But the book won't give any hint as to why the name of a vegetable with edible stalks is attached to a squabble.

This usage arose from a common practice of stage and movie directors.

Simultaneous shouting of "Rhubarb! Rhubarb!" by numerous extras in a crowd scene creates an impression of angry chaos.

Actors who participated in mob scenes adopted the shouted word to name a loud fracas.

Robot

THESE days, you can hardly pick up a magazine without seeing a prediction that a robot will soon be doing much of your work. Some who peer into the future may not realize that the name of the mechanical worker or servant comes from the stage.

Karl Čapek, a Czech playwright, was among the pioneers of modern science fiction. Capitalizing on publicity given to mechanical guns during World War I, he wrote a play called *R.U.R.*

The action of the drama centered on a group of mechanized monsters who revolted against their makers. Abbreviating the Czech term *robota,* meaning "work" or "drudgery," Čapek called one of his imaginary machinemen a "robot."

His play proved a tremendous hit. Few dramas of the 1920s provoked so much discussion. As a result, industrialized modern culture borrowed from the world of entertainment and many languages adopted the word. Today we even have the science of robotics.

Slapstick

IT was common for an old-time stand-up comedian to do everything possible to milk his audience. When applause was scant and barely audible, such a fellow was likely to give a signal to an aide.

Thoroughly acquainted with the routine and knowing just when to expect the next punch line, the aide would step forward at the right instant. Before some onlookers knew what was going on, he'd give the wooden stage a mighty slap with a heavy stick or thick board. Some persons laughed and others frowned; anyone sleeping was awakened by the thunder of the slap stick.

So many performers made such heavy use of the slap stick that the name of the tool designed to put life into a dull routine attached to any broad farce or low-grade comedy.

Top Banana/Second Banana

A PERSON who is preeminent in a group or serves as its head is, of course, its top. But that term doesn't seem adequate to express some notions linked with leadership.

Tens of thousands of persons are believed to have attended a long-running burlesque in New York City. Its crowd-pleasing finale revolved about a bevy of girls whose gyrations led them gradually to form what seemed at a distance to be a huge bunch of bananas.

Naturally, a favorite performer was dead center at the top of the bunch when the bananas ceased to move. It was this head of a burlesque troupe, says undocumented but believable tradition, who caused us to laud any outstanding leader or wielder of unquestioned authority as a "top banana."

With a banana such as Jack Benny at the top, it was natural and logical to term his straight man, Rochester, the "second banana." From the stage and screen, the term entered general speech and is now used to designate anyone from the vice-president to the substitute coach for a Little League team.

Two to Tango

NO one is sure how a Latin American dance first zoomed to popularity in the U.S. Probably adapted from the beat of tribal drums in Africa, the tango in 2/4 or 4/4 time was found to be especially exhilarating by some who experimented with it.

Many dances lend themselves to solo exhibitions. Not so the tango. This aspect of what was once a novel form of entertainment was emphasized in a popular song of the 1930's that stressed: ". . . it takes two to tango!"

That made a vivid and emphatic way of saying that some

activities require two participants. So the dance-floor expression originally came into wide use as a response to accusations of sexual misconduct. Today it has become a defense for any situation in which no one assumes full blame.

Vaudeville

NEW techniques for capturing action on film brought about the demise of once-acclaimed vaudeville. Millions who never sat before a stage for a series of song-and-dance routines plus slapstick interludes have enjoyed re-creations of this form of entertainment.

Performances by Jimmy Durante and other notables owe this rhythmic title to a French valley that was home to a popular composer. Olivier Basselin's fast-moving satirical songs came from the Normandy town of Vau-de-Vire. Once they became all the rage in Paris, English-speaking patrons of the theater modified the name of the region to vaudeville and applied it to humorous compositions. These, in turn, passed their title along to any collection of short acts designed to keep onlookers' feet tapping and hands clapping.

Whammy

STRANGE as it may seem, the world of entertainment gave us *whammy* as a name for a potent spell or curse. Al Capp, creator of *Li'l Abner,* popularized this expression.

Millions of readers who regularly laughed at the goings-on in Dogpatch came to know each character in the strip.

Frequent appearances were made by the unappealing character. This creature of Capp's imagination knew enough about Indian lore to paralyze with a stare—a fearful glance that the cartoonist called a *whammy.* Once the term became familiar to readers, it was not unusual to see someone receive a double-whammy—a glance so potent that its recipient was frozen in his or her tracks.

CHAPTER 2

MANY WERE FAMOUS, OTHERS MERELY RICH

"Fame is not popularity. It is the spirit of a man surviving himself in the minds and thoughts of other men."
—William Hazlitt, *Lectures on the English Poets*

S ometimes by means of their names, often as a result of their achievements, famous persons in every field of endeavor have influenced our speech. So have others whose only claim to fame was wealth.

These stories are a far cry from the television program "Lifestyles of the Rich and Famous," and many of the words and expressions included here will be thriving when the TV program has been forgotten.

ACHILLES' HEEL
AMERICA
AMP
AX TO GRIND
BEST FOOT FORWARD
BLURB
BOMBSHELL
BOURBON
BRAILLE
CADILLAC
CHIPPENDALE
DECIBEL
DERBY
DIESEL
DON JUAN
DUKES
DUNCE
FISHING
FREELANCE
FREUDIAN SLIP
GREAT SCOTT!

HANKY-PANKY
HIGH-HAT
HIGH HORSE
JOSH
LET ONE'S HAIR
   DOWN
LIFE OF RILEY
LISTERINE
LYNCHING
MOLOTOV COCKTAIL
NICOTINE
O.K.
PANDEMONIUM
PLUSH
POINSETTIA
READ THE RIOT ACT
RITZY
SERENDIPITY
TANTALIZE
TYCOON

SEE ALSO: Birdie, Blowout, Blue Ribbon, Caddy, Chicken à la
   King, Circus, Cologne, Fire Bug, Golf, Hooker, Mascot,
   Plum, Poppycock, Real McCoy, Shampoo, Smoke Out

Achilles' Heel

REGARDLESS of how tough a person may be, careful study will reveal a weak spot somewhere. Such was the case with one of the greatest legendary heroes of Greek mythology.

In ancient times it was common knowledge that the water of the river Styx was potent—so potent that a baby dipped into it received supernatural protection. Skin touched by the water remained pliable, but was as tough as steel.

One mother decided to give her son a kind of immortality. Hours after the boy was delivered, she hurried to the river and dipped him into the mysterious water. That made Achilles invulnerable over most of his body.

But in the end, Achilles was killed during the Trojan War by a wound in his heel—the part his mother held when she dipped him in the river. Water didn't touch his heel, so the mythological superman had a small but mortal flaw.

Stories about that mother's son have survived after many centuries. As a result, any seemingly invincible person's weakest point is his or her Achilles' heel.

America

YOU probably learned in school that our nation—plus both New World continents—honors the memory of Italian navigator Amerigo Vespucci. But you are unusual if you learned from teachers the reason his name looms so large on the map.

Amerigo made several voyages to the West, and once spent a few days on the coast of Brazil. Writing about his adventures in 1503, he described western lands south of the equator as constituting a world Europeans had not even imagined.

Geographers took that description of the new world very seriously. Calling it "a New and Fourth Part of the earth's surface," they named it for the Italian explorer.

By the time other explorers found that Amerigo had made only minor additions to discoveries of Christopher Columbus, it was too difficult to get maps changed. As a result, the name of a mediocre adventurer covers most of the land surface of the western hemisphere.

Amp

AS a young teacher at the College de France, Andre Ampere made important discoveries about magnetism and electricity. His greatest achievement was highly technical: the discovery of fundamental properties of electrical currents.

Late in the 1880's, a world conclave of research scientists met in Paris. Probably because of his accomplishments and important discoveries, they decided to use his name as a label for a unit of electrical current.

In everyday use, the French surname was soon clipped in half. Now many a person can read a label and find out how many amps are used by an electrical appliance without needing to know how an ampere is measured.

Ax to Grind

INFLUENCE of *Poor Richard's Almanac* and other publications made Benjamin Franklin one of the most widely read of early American writers.

He is a central character in one of his own stories. In the tale, a young Franklin was approached by a fellow who stopped to admire the family grindstone. Asking to be shown how it worked, the stranger offered young Ben an ax with which to demonstrate. Once his ax was sharp, the fellow walked off, laughing.

Readers should beware of anyone who has an ax to grind, for they have a hidden motive.

Best Foot Forward

FOR a period of several centuries, European noblemen and wealthy gentry were greatly concerned about beauty of person. They affected ruffled sleeves, powdered wigs, black satin knee breeches, and full-length hose above buckled shoes.

Many of the idle rich were quite vain, and took pride in showing off a good pair of legs. Some went so far as to give preference to one leg as being more attractive than the other. Such a fellow wanted to make the greatest possible sensation at levees and balls. So he found a place where he could stand with his best-looking leg and foot in front, where it would attract many glances.

By the 16th century, a person wanting to make a good impression knew just what to do. He put his "best foot forward," and by doing so helped to create a phrase we still use.

Blurb

AMERICAN humorist Gelett Burgess was once more widely known than was Charles W. Fairbanks—the Hoosier who spent eight years as vice president under the shadow of Teddy Roosevelt.

Burgess, who was never more than a minute in any man's shadow, delighted readers and listeners throughout the 1920s and 1930s. Some of his gags were so preposterous that at first they were taken seriously.

Poking fun at techniques used by advertisers, Burgess prepared a dummy book jacket for use at a publisher's convention. He stole a sketch of a lovely young woman and displayed it prominently. Beneath the picture he put a brief endorsement of the book by "Miss Belinda Blurb."

His prank was so successful that the humorist is credited with getting an artificial word into the English language, single-handedly. Soon after Belinda Blurb's fake enthusiasm was circulated in 1907, any short but laudatory notice of a book, a record, a song, or a car came to be known as an advertising blurb.

Bombshell

GUNPOWDER sheathed in metal came into use long ago, but most early bombs were small and crude. Big and sophisticated ones, designed to be shot from cannon, were used in World War I. For the first time, a powerful explosive charge could be sent into enemy ranks.

Regardless of how close it came to its target, an exploding bombshell was an object of fearful admiration. It packed a punch like nothing else.

G.I.'s who lived through a hail of German shells came home with a new and descriptive label for an explosively attractive female. That's how Marilyn Monroe became famous as "the blonde bombshell"—though the term of admiration was also applied to numerous other celebrities.

Bourbon

MANY bourbon drinkers correctly associate it with Kentucky, famous for its manufacture. But roots of the name go far deeper than the middle of the 19th century, when the whiskey first attracted more than regional attention.

No one knows what experimenter in Bourbon County first came up with a distinctive brew that took the name of the county. It may have been brewed locally for years before it was mentioned in a *Knickerbocker* magazine story in 1851.

No one bothered to inform sippers who tried the unique beverage that a line of European rulers was responsible for its name. Various members of the French royal family of Bourbon ruled Naples, France, and Spain during a period that spanned 150 years. French-speaking settlers of Kentucky honored the family by giving the name to a county. Bourbon just happened to be the place where mash with at least 51 percent of corn was first used to make whiskey that took the county's name.

Braille

EVERY reader of Braille, along with most of us who don't have trained fingers, knows that the system of communicating by means of raised dots was devised by Louis Braille.

Born sighted, little Louis liked to play in his father's leather-working shop. It was there that he was blinded by an awl at age three. His parents sent him to a special school, where he learned to recognize huge embossed letters in books so big he could not lift them.

One day an army officer came to the school to demonstrate a system of raised dots and dashes. Since a message could be punched out in the dark, inventor Barbier called his system night writing. Though Louis was only fifteen, his imagination was fired. Within five years, he had improved and simplified the Barbier system. Braille's new unit of raised dots, three high and two wide, afforded 62 combinations.

It took decades for the system worked out by a 20-year-old to win acceptance. Once it did, Braille dominated communication of the blind until use of audio equipment became widespread.

Cadillac

THIS car perpetuates the memory of a man who otherwise might be nearly forgotten. Antoine de la Mothe Cadillac did not cut a very wide swath in his native France, but when the petty nobleman came to New World, he did a lot to hold the American west for his king. In the region that is now Michigan, he set up a trading post on a lake, now both named for him. Later he became governor of the immense Louisiana Territory.

Henry Ford's pioneer Detroit Automobile Co. was a small operation when it was acquired by new owners. They wanted a more aristocratic name for their business, so changed it to the Cadillac Company. Eventually it would become a unit of General Motors.

Now the car is a perennial GM favorite owned by plenty of big shots who are less important now than Governor Cadillac was then.

Chippendale

CHIPPENDALE furniture has been a perennial favorite since the 18th century.

Thomas Chippendale of London was one of those rare persons capable of putting inherited components together in order to come out with something strikingly new and different. He experimented with French furniture from the period of King Louis XV and much older Gothic designs. Not one to ignore beauty, he borrowed from Oriental styles as well. When the British artisan published his *Cabinet Maker's Directory* in 1754, he offered instructions for more than 150 styles.

Always using mahogany, Chippendale built so many kinds of beautifully carved and sturdy pieces that his name came to designate any and all furniture that resembles his handiwork.

Decibel

WHEN a neighbor's stereo reaches a decibel level that makes your ear drums throb, you can blame Alexander Graham Bell—after a fashion.

A Scottish immigrant who came to the U.S. as a teacher of the deaf, the inventor of the telephone also perfected the phonograph plus a sonic probe for locating bullets inside the body. In the process of doing these things, he devised a scale to measure electrically generated signals.

Dropping just one letter from his surname, Bell called his primary unit the *bel*. One tenth of a bel is a decibel. Originally used largely in electrical experiments, the unit of measurement was soon applied to sound as well.

Derby

ANYTIME you watch a TV short about the Kentucky Derby, actually attend the race, visit Hollywood's famous Brown Derby restaurant, or see a person wearing a dome-shaped felt hat, you pay verbal homage to a famous Earl of Derby.

Edward Stanley, twelfth English nobleman to bear the title, had the bluest of blue blood, claiming descent from William the Conqueror. A confirmed devotee of the racetrack, he launched a set of races for three-year-olds at Epsom Downs.

Male toffs, or swells, for whom the annual derby was the highlight of the year, typically wore bowler hats to the races. Americans adapted the horse race and the hat and named both for the earl.

Long the favorite headgear of U.S. males, the derby hat went out of style early in this century, while the Kentucky Derby is still going strong.

Diesel

EVERY neighborhood and parking lot includes some cars with diesel engines. On highways, you see a constant stream of big trucks powered by them.

Big or small, such a source of power bears the name of German mechanical engineer Rudolf Diesel. Working at the famous Krupp factory in Essen, where the biggest guns used in World War I were made, he concentrated on heavy-duty internal combustion engines. During a period of six years, beginning in 1892, he perfected the revolutionary new engine that took his name.

Don Juan

YOUR high school graduating class is unusual if it doesn't include at least one Don Juan. Surveys suggest that one young male in eight seeks renown as a lover—and gains it almost half the time.

Tall or short, dark or fair, the typical American loverboy can't be compared with Don Juan Ternorio. This legendary Spanish nobleman, said to have flourished in the 14th century, caught the attention of Mozart, among others.

No one knows where the composer got his data, but notes made for his *Don Giovanni,* say that the man whose name was given to the opera had 2,594 mistresses. He didn't make it to 2,595 because he was lured to a monastery. Monks who were furious that he gave the region such a bad reputation reputedly killed him— not in bed, but fully clothed and wearing even his boots.

Dukes

"PUT up your dukes!" is a challenge that echoes through the American saga from Revolutionary days until the present. Even on the frontier, the expression borrowed from the English was widely used. Yankees who borrowed the term probably didn't know that it was a tribute, of a sort, to a son of the king whose forces fought against our founding fathers.

Frederick Augustus, second son of King George III, held many properties and titles including earl of Ulster and duke of York and Albany. A sportsman, duelist, and commander of his father's army, he was so widely admired that bare-knuckle fighters dubbed their fists "dukes of York."

With the geographical designation dropped as it crossed the Atlantic, the pugilist's tribute was adopted by Colonials as, simply, *dukes.*

Dunce

IF you ever listen to a storyteller talking about school before the days of consolidation and buses, a dunce is likely to enter into at least one tale. Until modern times, few teachers hesitated to put a dunce cap on the head of a slow or rebellious student.

Generations of Americans followed or tolerated that practice. Few if any realized that a latter-day dunce took that title from a famous scholar.

Scottish-born John Duns Scotus founded the school of scholaticism called Scotism, which opposed the followers of Thomas Aquinas. Admirers and contemporaries in the 13th century called Scotus the Subtle Doctor.

Generations later in the 16th century, many scholars who revered him resisted new waves of learning. Their opponents ridiculed followers of Duns Scotus, or Dunsmen, frequently and loudly. So much noise was made that anyone judged incapable of accepting fresh ideas came to be called a *dunce*.

Fishing

GEOFFREY Chaucer is usually ranked among the world's most famous men of letters. His 14th-century *Canterbury Tales* had lasting influence upon literature of the English-speaking world.

Few of his admirers remember that he was almost as good a sportsman as poet. He spent so much time with his hobby that he introduced numerous sporting terms into his works. One of them, *fishing for information,* seems not to have been used in writing prior to his use of it.

Numerous writers later picked up the expression from Chaucer. Among them was diarist Samuel Pepys. On September 7, 1663, he jotted down a memo saying that he couldn't fish information from a friend.

The influence of these great writers causes us to say that anyone making an effort to catch a compliment or a secret or a good story is "fishing" for it.

Freelance

DOES your circle of acquaintances include a freelance artist or writer? Or maybe a musician or tax preparer?

Whatever his or her field of activity may be, the modern free-lancer is not on a payroll. Instead, services or products are offered directly to purchasers—often without a middle man.

The "lance" part of *freelance* harks back to the Middle Ages when knights fought with sword and lance. Most warriors had sworn allegiance to the king or lord of their realm. Others were roving soldiers or medieval mercenaries who operated on their own, offering their swords, lances, and services to the highest bidder. Freebooters arose a few centuries later, and these fellows outfitted their own ships in order to prowl the seas. Today, we call them pirates.

The term *freelance* was popularized by the novel *Ivanhoe,* published in 1819. Oddly enough, the book was written by a knight, Sir Walter Scott. *Ivanhoe* brought to us a term that is more poetic and versatile than "self-employed person."

Freudian Slip

MAYBE you keep such close watch of your tongue that you've never, never made a Freudian slip. If so, you're practically in a class by yourself. From time to time, most of us blurt out something that seems to reveal thoughts we prefer to hide.

Such verbal self-exposure owes its worldwide use and name to the founder of psychoanalysis.

Austrian neurologist Sigmund Freud was still studying in Paris at age thirty. Once he began seeing patients, however, he started developing new theories. Soon he said that every abnormal mental state involves repressed memories. Dreams, he reported in a sensational turn-of-the-century book, stem largely from repressed sexual desires.

Anyone interviewed by the great doctor or one of his early disciples was sure to say something that evoked an "Aha!" reaction from the analyst. That was inevitable, for everyday speech is saturated with sexual innuendoes and overtones.

A comment considered bland and innocent by a patient might be seen by Freud to indicate severe maladjustment. Hence any unplanned verbal revelation, not necessarily sexual now, is termed a *Freudian slip.*

Great Scott!

UNLESS you read a great many novels set in the past, you aren't likely to exclaim "Great Scott!" when startled. But you'll find that phrase in the pages of many a literary classic. It is there, some scholars believe, through influence of a long-time commander of the U.S. Army.

Vain Winfield S. Scott was disliked. Some subordinates resented the fact that he became a brigadier-general and a brevet major-general at age twenty-eight. Others claimed that he spent his time and energy strutting and swaggering instead of looking after his troops.

Nicknamed Old Fuss and Feathers before he ran for the presidency in 1852, he later became known as Great Scott. Picked up by civilians, that title spawned the exclamation that punctuated speech during the Gay Nineties.

Hanky-panky

WHAT on earth leads us to say that a person fooling around on a mate or other underhanded business is engaged in hanky-panky?

Strange as it seems, the expression is a logical one whose roots are easily traced.

In many eras, magicians learned to keep the eyes of observers off their doings by means of distraction. An umbrella or a coffin is a tried-and-proven source, as is a handkerchief, for that matter.

About 150 years or so ago, many a British master of fast movements swung a handkerchief with one hand to keep viewers from noticing what he was doing with the other. This practice was so common that use of a hanky came to be associated with clandestine activity. Maybe influenced by hocus-pocus, a rhyming word was added.

Presto!

Quicker than you can bat your eyes, hanky-panky came into being as just the right label for undercover doings.

High-hat

EVEN though an acquaintance may be bareheaded most or all of the time, he or she may act *high-hat* to you by failing to nod and speak.

Railroad builders, cattle men, miners, loggers, and other entrepreneurs made quick fortunes during the Gay Nineties in the United States. Many newly rich men spent lavishly on brownstone mansions, teams of trotting horses, and boxes at the opera.

A robber baron looked the part of the polished gentleman when he strolled about town sporting long tails and a high silk hat. But such a fellow was prone to snub former partners and boyhood friends. Such incidents occurred so frequently that anyone assuming superiority is said to high-hat others.

High Horse

WHEN a friend's arrogance gets on your nerves, you may react with, "Get off your high horse!"

Long ago, a person's rank was fairly clearly indicated by the steed he or she rode. Donkeys were used by peasants and serfs, and run-of-the-mill horses transported shopkeepers and petty gentry.

Big stallions bred and trained as chargers for use in tournaments and in war were reserved for the rich and famous. Before Columbus made his first voyage to the New World, England's pageants usually included at least one rider mounted on such a charger, or high horse.

Today a person figuratively perched astride a big stallion is likely to be so pretentious that it calls for a rebuke.

Josh

DO you have to deal with a fellow worker or family member who's prone to josh around? If so, don't feel that you're alone—habitual jokesters and pranksters are found everywhere.

Such a person keeps us from forgetting about Henry Wheeler Shaw. That name doesn't ring a bell? Then try Josh Billings—the pen name he used in newspapers and books.

Chances are that Shaw chose the Josh Billings byline because *josh* was already in limited use to mean fooling around or kidding. Elevated into national prominence by one of America's most popular literary clowns, josh has found a permanent place in everyday speech.

Let One's Hair Down

FOR decades, Paris has been the fashion center of the western world. Customs and sayings that originate there often become more firmly-rooted in England and in America than in their native soil.

Noted entertainers and wives of wealthy nobleman have long vied with one another in creating new and elaborate hair styles. It was once considered a serious breach of etiquette to appear in public without a coiffeur that required hours of work. Only in the intimacy of private quarters did beauties of the Napoleonic era relax by letting their hair down.

Moves toward pulling out pins and unbinding tresses came to be associated with relaxation. So any time inhibitions are discarded, we still say that a male or female lets his or her hair down.

Life of Riley

MOST people envy the lifestyles of the rich and famous. Stand-up comic Patrick Rooney exploited this feeling in a lilting song he wrote in the late 1880s.

Mr. Reilly, the central character of the Irish entertainer's song, didn't amount to much, but he was quite a daydreamer. Reilly imagined what he would do if he struck it rich in California.

Owning the railroads, he would buy no tickets. Having no need for money he would turn down jobs that offered to pay "a hundred a day." Best of all, he would take over the White House and sleep in the president's chair.

Though Reilly existed only in the imagination of Rooney, he voiced the feelings of multitudes who paid little attention to the spelling of his name. Having heard or read lines that described the way Reilly conceived of life at the top, people began to wish they could step into the Irishman's shoes. Decades later, folks would still give their right arms for a shot at the life of Riley!

Listerine

MOUTHWASH sold under the trademark Listerine is one of America's best-known medicinal products. But if a famous British surgeon had been given his way, it wouldn't be on the market.

Impressed by the findings of Louis Pasteur, Joseph Lister elevated antiseptic surgery to new levels. Contemporaries revered him so greatly that he became the central figure of a solemn ceremony. As a token of gratitude for his contributions to mankind, the son of a wine merchant was given a resounding title: First Baron Lister of Lyme Regis.

Ingenious Yankees adapted his name to label bottles filled with a mild antiseptic liquid. Listerine sold like hotcakes, so Lord Lister tried his best to make manufacturers change its name. Because he failed in that effort, millions who know little or nothing about him continue to rely on the only product that keeps his memory green.

Lynching

MOB violence is probably as old as mankind, but the American name for it is comparatively youthful. Two centuries ago, more or less, Captain William Lynch cut a wide swath through parts of Virginia. As magistrate of a kangaroo court, he heard brief testimony and then sentenced several Pennsylvania County ruffians to hang.

Lynch might have been forgotten, had not his exploits come to the attention of a literary giant. Writing in the *Southern Literary Messenger,* Edgar Allan Poe described the Virginia cleanup of crime as a *lynching.* He even published what he said was a pact drawn up by Captain Lynch's band.

Lasting influence of a famous writer caused mob violence to be known as a *lynching,* and *lynch law* designates the reasoning by which members of a mob arrive at a verdict.

Molotov Cocktail

YOU can't follow the news for more than a few weeks without hearing of an incident of violence involving at least one Molotov cocktail. Gasoline-filled bottles with slow-burning wicks have become staples in the arsenals of rebels and terrorists.

Vyacheslav Mikhailovich Molotov had nothing to do with devising the crude but effective explosive. The Finnish named it after him because he was the premier of the U.S.S.R. at the time, and they were seeking freedom from the communist regime.

Freedom fighters who faced soldiers armed with heavy equipment and weapons adopted the use of gasoline-bombs in desperation. Derisively, they reported that they tossed such explosives in honor of the Soviet premier whose regime they resisted. Since a homemade device consisted of liquid in a bottle, it seemed right to combine the Russian's name with that of a drink and call it the *Molotov cocktail.*

Nicotine

MUCH in the news since U.S. surgeons-general began issuing warnings about it, nicotine is a native American chemical. But its name has traveled around the world from France, where it was coined.

Jean Nicot, an early student of language, won appointment as ambassador to Portugal. While serving in Lisbon, he frequently talked with sailors who had made the long voyage to the New World. Around 1560 he obtained from some of them seeds of a plant unknown in Europe; from these seeds the first tobacco plants seen in France were grown.

When scientists began dimly to realize that tobacco includes a potent substance, whose nature was then unknown, they called it *nicotine* in honor of Jean Nicot.

O.K.

WHEN you're carefully scrutinized and pronounced to be O.K., you know you'll get an insurance policy, a promotion, or an extension of your credit. Anytime that happens, you can thank an often-overlooked president of the United States.

Admirers of Martin Van Buren, born at Kinderhook, New York, lauded him as Old Kinderhook when at age fifty-eight he made a bid for a second term in the White House. Running against war hero William Henry Harrison, it was to be an uphill battle.

Democrats of New York City formed a booster club and launched a campaign to raise money and win votes. On March 23, 1840, the city's *New Era* newspaper published an announcement: "The Democratic O.K. Club are hereby ordered to meet at the house of Jacob Colvin on Tuesday evening."

During a heated campaign that fizzled in the end, the president's abbreviated nickname popularized the rare New England phrase. Since then, the American-born political slogan has spread around the world.

Pandemonium

NEXT time you find pandemonium breaking out around you, maybe you can shut out some of the noise by thinking of John Milton.

Why Milton, rather than some other immortal poet, novelist, or playwright? Because he's the indisputable father of the label we apply to a chaotic uproar. Only a handful of persons have managed to coin a new word that has lasted. Milton was one of the few.

Writing of "the high Capital of Satan and his Peers" in his famous *Paradise Lost,* Milton combined the Greek words *pan* for "all" and *daimon* for "demon" into *Pandaemonium*—meaning literally "the place of all demons." His readers modified the spelling into today's more familiar form. Only a rare master of words could have thought of combining these five syllables in such rhythmic and evocative fashion.

Plush

LIFESTYLES of the rich and famous typically include a yen for whatever ordinary folk can't afford. So any scarce and costly commodity is likely to find a ready though limited market.

That was the case with a radically new kind of fabric developed in the 16th century. The nap of this cloth was even longer than that of velvet, a texture the French called *peluche* and the English shortened to *plush*.

Workmen and housewives had no use for the stuff; it was very thick and didn't wear well. But in wealthy establishments, it was seized upon as just right for garments of footmen. More than a few noblemen dressed their personal clowns in plush, so for a time it was known as *fool's cloth.*

Since only the wealthy could indulge in cloth more ostentatious than velvet, any establishment or thing notably costly or luxurious also came to be termed *plush.*

Poinsettia

IN the early 19th century, Joel R. Poinsett of Charleston, South Carolina, became our first minister to Mexico.

In Mexico City he was impressed by a native plant that turned red in December. Natives called it "flower of the blessed night" because it was often at its peak on December 25. Poinsett sent cuttings to the Smithsonian Institute and to Carolina friends. In honor of the diplomat, they called the imported flower the poinsettia.

The man who gave his name to a plant went on to become U.S. Secretary of War during the Van Buren administration. No one, least of all the central figure of the story, anticipated that the poinsettia would become *the* Christmas flower—annually bringing him honor throughout the world.

Read the Riot Act

NEARLY every frustrated parent and employer has been known to read the riot act. This in spite of the fact that a solitary culprit rather than a mob of rioters may be the target of wrath.

King George I of England had to deal with a house full of sometimes cantankerous children. But his real troubles were with his subjects. They created so much commotion that in 1716 he issued a proclamation. Any time twelve or more persons engaged in a demonstration, officers of the law were required to read a specified portion of the act and send the rioters home.

Only the very rash continued to push and shove or to yell after the king's edict was proclaimed. A fellow who ignored it could be sent to a penal colony for the rest of his life. In the early decades of the Georgian era, voices were lowered and fists were unclenched fast whenever the riot act was read.

Ritzy

OLD-TIME inns offered travelers a place to eat and to sleep, but little or nothing more. Toward the middle of the 19th century the rise of a new and larger class of wealthy persons created a different clientele. Promoters vied with one another in building elaborate hotels that included dining rooms about which patrons talked.

César Ritz, a Swiss-born hotelier, won international fame by attracting notables to one after another of his institutions in Paris, London, New York, and elsewhere.

As a posh establishment, the Ritz more than lived up to expectations of investors and travelers. That's why we've adapted a Swiss surname and use *ritzy* to label any establishment marked by costly elegance. The word is also used in reference to people and things of an elite, fancy, or sophisticated nature.

Serendipity

MAYBE you made a simply terrific accidental discovery of some sort in the past. If not, one or several unforgettable experiences may lie ahead of you. For there's nothing quite like making a great find you didn't anticipate and toward which you didn't work.

Horace Walpole was already internationally famous when he wrote a 1754 letter in which this melodic word appeared for the first time. He'd been reading an ancient fairy tale from Ceylon, earlier called Serendip. In the story, three legendary princes frequently stumbled across good things they did not anticipate.

The Three Princes of Serendip so excited the imagination of Walpole that he told Sir Horace Mann about it. To the veteran British diplomat, his correspondent suggested that serendipity enables a person who's looking for one thing to find something else entirely.

Adopted by Walpole's literary followers, the made-up term filled a gap in language. Especially among scientists and inventors, serendipity has paid big dividends so often that the world would be a great deal poorer without its effects.

Tantalize

MANY circumstances and events can produce a state of prolonged torment or anticipation. Receiving a tentative job offer without confirmation, seeing the previews for a new movie, and submitting an application that is left dangling are just a few of the many states of tantalization.

Tantalus, a minor figure in Greek mythology, made the mistake of talking too much; in the process, he exposed some of the secrets of the great god Zeus. As punishment, he was put into water up to his chin under a tree from whose branches the most beautiful and luscious fruits of Greece were dangled. When he reached for the fruit, the branch from which it was suspended moved upward beyond his reach. When he bent his head in order to quench his thirst, the water level dropped so that he could not reach it.

Frustration experienced by Tantalus caused his name to label any state of torment caused by inability fully to grasp something that seems within reach but is not.

Tycoon

IF given five seconds to name a modern tycoon, would you pick Donald Trump? Or does the late Sam Walton of WAL-MART seem a better choice for the title? Or perhaps you would think of Ann Cox Chambers of Cox Communications, one of America's wealthiest women.

Regardless of the financial or industrial tycoon who tops your personal list, that man or woman has only one attribute of the tycoon of old. That quality is power—raw and undiluted.

For the title we use so casually today was formed from Chinese words meaning "great prince." But the ancient Chinese never applied it to one of their own rulers. Instead, rivals located on a nearby island employed it when the Shogun of Japan was being described to foreigners.

All of which means that the modern tycoon, no matter how powerful his or her bankroll may be, doesn't quite sit on the throne occupied by a tycoon of old.

CHAPTER 3

FEATHERS AND FUR

"Animals are such agreeable friends—they ask no questions, they pass no criticisms."
                    —George Eliot, *Mr. Gilfil's Love Story*

Though they talk only in fables and fairy tales, birds and animals have had wide and lasting impact upon our speech. Have domesticated creatures with features and furs influenced your everyday use of words more greatly than have wild ones?

That's a tough question. Possibly these expressions will help you to answer it.

ALLURING
BADGER
BIGWIG
BOOTLICK
BUFFALO
CAPRICIOUS
CHICKEN FEED
CHUCKHOLE
DACHSHUND
EAGER BEAVER
FEATHER IN ONE'S CAP
FEATHER ONE'S NEST
FEISTY
FERRET OUT
GET ONE'S BACK UP
GET ONE'S GOAT
GOOSE BUMPS
GREENHORN
HAMSTRUNG
HIGHTAIL
HORSE AROUND
HORSE'S MOUTH/GIFT HORSE

JAYWALKER
JINX
LICK INTO SHAPE
MASCOT
MAVERICK
NO SPRING CHICKEN
PECKING ORDER
PIGEONHOLE
PLUG AWAY
RAIN CATS AND
  DOGS
RIDE ROUGHSHOD
RULE THE ROOST
RUMINATE
SMELL A RAT
SNIPER
STIFF-NECKED
TERRIER
UNDERDOG
WELL-HEELED
WET BEHIND THE
  EARS

SEE ALSO: Balled Up, Bark Up the Wrong Tree, Bats in the Belfry, Catbird Seat, Charley Horse, Cook One's Goose, Corner, Dogwood, Eagle, Full of Beans, Go Off Half-cocked, High Horse, Hold the Bag, Horse's Mouth, Hot Dog, Jaded, Jeep, Lay an Egg, Lion's Share, Loaded for Bear, Nit-picker, Old Stomping Ground, Out on a Limb, Possum, Skunk, Smelling Like a Rose

Alluring

ESPECIALLY in the world of entertainment, practically every female hopes to be described as alluring. If early use of the term means anything, this quality should be viewed with caution.

When English and European gentry were enamored with falconry, every owner of birds experimented with lures. Such a device consisted of a cluster of feathers to which food could be attached while a hawk was in training. Associating feathers with feasting, a soaring bird usually flew back to its owner when a lure was conspicuously displayed.

A lure's function was to attract a hawk's attention and induce it to return to its master. Hence anything or anyone tempting, fascinating, or enticing came to be described as *alluring*.

Badger

AT first sight, the badger seems to be one of the clumsiest little fellows ever put together. Short legs give the animal an ungainly waddle when it tries to run, but at close range it is a tough fighter.

For generations, it was considered great fun to put the waddling animal in a barrel, then encourage dogs to attack. Dogs barked lustily and nipped at their quarry repeatedly before moving in for a kill.

Persistent annoyance was the key factor in badger-baiting. So when a member of the family or a fellow worker sets out to badger you, the name of the game is low-level torment for what may seem to be hour after hour.

Bigwig

HAD not sheep been abundant in England until modern times, you might not include in your vocabulary a term from British legal practices.

Skins complete with wool were widely used in manufacture of

wigs. A judge could be distinguished from ordinary folk at a glance; his enormous powdered wig identified his office. Court officials were not the only persons who donned this special regalia, but they were often seen by members of the public.

A man who could decide the fate of another was clearly a person of great importance. Consequently, anyone in a position of authority came to be called a *bigwig*.

Bootlick

IN the Daniel Boone era, dogs were integral members of frontier households. Every family had one or two packs of hounds, a few bird dogs, and a watchdog. Often a few stray curs also hung around. Prized animals were well fed, but mongrels only got what the others didn't want.

Returning from a day in the woods, hunters often had bloody boots. Hungry curs, running up to them, would fight over the privilege of licking off the blood.

A human desperate for a favor may behave like a canine outcast and *bootlick* anyone considered likely to toss out a few scraps.

Buffalo

SPANISH conquerors of Mexico encountered an incredible animal in 1519. According to their description, the creature was "a rare Mexican bull, with crooked shoulders, a hump on its back like a camel and with hair like a lion."

Subsequent encounters with the "crooked-back ox" led amateurs to decide that it was kin to Asia's water buffalo. Naturalists rejected that idea and used *bison* to name the animal. They were too late to influence popular speech; many who flocked to the great American West hoped to get rich from buffalo pelts.

Capable of galloping at 45 miles per hour, the buffalo is the most ornery creature on the continent. Not only perpetually yearning for a fight, it is very hard to kill. Expert riflemen of early days sometimes put half a dozen balls into the head of an animal before touching a vital spot.

This most distinctive of American beasts can also be the most frustrating. As a result, we say we are buffaloed by anything that leads to bewilderment, frustration, or helplessness.

Capricious

WHEN you are forced reguarly to spend time with a capricious person, that trait may prove to be very annoying. Anyone who frequently indulges in impulsive changes of mind is hard to deal with. Italians of past generations wouldn't have challenged that verdict. Matter of fact, they coined the descriptive term as a result of watching goats in action.

No other domestic animal quite matches the goat in its tendency to switch suddenly from frolicking to butting heads. Many a goatherd noticed that animals seemingly intent upon grazing could be mating in a blink of an eye.

Called the *caper* by Romans, the animal's behavior led humans to label outlandish conduct as cutting capers. Italians who knew the goat as the *capriccio* adapted its name to describe a person subject to erratic whims and sudden willful behavior.

Chicken Feed

PIONEERS who pushed into the American West took their domestic creatures with them. Chickens were high on the list of favorites, for flocks could be brought through the winter on grain too poor for use in the kitchen.

Except for table scraps, inferior wheat and corn constituted the most common chicken feed. City slickers picked up the farm-born expression and applied it to copper and silver coins.

By the time riverboat gamblers became common, the label was being used to designate any small amount of money. One flashily dressed fellow who cleaned out a greenhorn complained that he had played all night for chicken feed—only $23.

Chuckhole

A GROUND hog of a type unknown in Europe once abounded in the region from Hudson Bay to South Carolina. Derived from a Cree word, settlers called it the *woodchuck*.

Powerful diggers, woodchucks usually sink holes in such a fashion that water will not run into them. Abundant almost everywhere but difficult to see from more than a few feet away, hiding places of woodchucks caused many a horse's leg to be broken. Even heavy wagons and coaches were jolted when a hole was hit.

Corduroy roads, followed by pavement and asphalt, put an end to hazards caused by the marmot. Far less common than 200 years ago, the woodchuck now hardly ever digs a hole in a road. But when traffic or weather damages asphalt or cement, the cavity formed is compared with the animal's little den and cursed as a *chuckhole*.

Dachshund

GERMAN breeders developed a queer dog with a slender body and tiny legs. It seemed only a curiosity until these features were found to be valuable. They gave the little fellow built-in advantages as a hunter of the badger, or *dachs*. Prized by sportsmen, the high-bred animal was known to them as the badger hound, or *dachshund*.

Until recent times, English breeders ignored the odd-looking animal. When they began to take interest, they treated it as an unusual pet rather than as a hunting dog. Nowadays, its distinctive build and good disposition have endeared it to hosts of owners, most of whom wouldn't know what to do with a badger if their low-slung hound should capture one.

Eager Beaver

IF you plunge into a task or show enthusiasm, someone is likely to call you an *eager beaver*.

That title of admiration, says folklore, comes from watching colonies of beavers at work. Some started gnawing trees and slapping mud into crevices with their tales right after sun up, frontiersmen swore. According to the same unimpeachable source, others took their own sweet time about joining the dam-building gang.

Observation by biologists has demolished this myth. There's no such thing as a beaver who's spectacularly eager. All members of rodent colonies are more or less alike—hard-working and skilled, but not markedly different in pace.

Realization that the four-footed eager beaver doesn't exist has not diminished the impact of the rhyming title. Often with admiration, sometimes with disgust, it is applied to any two-footed animal who seems more than eager to get started.

Feather in One's Cap

UNTIL modern times, ornamental feathers were more widely used by males than by females. Princes and noblemen vied with one another in finding colorful and expensive plumage with which to adorn their hats. Robin Hood, the prince of English outlaws, wouldn't have been seen in public without his feathers. Ostrich feathers constituted the special insignia of each Prince of Wales.

An unknown military leader hit upon the idea of using small feathers in lieu of badges of honor made by craftsmen. When a fighting man showed unusual gallantry, he was given a feather to wear in his cap.

By the time use of plumage was abandoned, language had been permanently affected. As a result, an honor or achievement of any kind is still called a feather in a person's cap.

Feather One's Nest

FOUR centuries ago, when this expression came into vogue in England, it was considered complimentary. For anyone who has ever watched a chickadee or a pair of wrens at work is conscious that the preparation of a nest is a big job. In order to be properly padded for babies, the nest must be lined with lots of feathers—not just a few.

Some birds are relatively sloppy builders; many are meticulous. One feather at a time is laid in place, often over a period of weeks. Well before the nest is ready for eggs, it is a marvel of craftsmanship directed toward a single goal—the welfare of babies.

It's true, of course, that some humans have little or no regard for colleagues. Such persons may feather their own nests without giving a thought to anyone else. But in the world of humans as well as that of flying folk, it isn't a bad idea to feather your nest as preparation for things to come.

Feisty

SOME persons, more or less lethargic by nature, hardly know how to make a come-back for a slight or a slur. Others, just the opposite, are so feisty that they seem to go about looking for opportunities to engage in spats and pick quarrels.

Members of the second category may not consider themselves dogged, but if speech means anything they're like some four-footed critters. For in the highly specialized language of Southern dialect, any quick-tempered lapdog is a fice.

At least in times past, the owner of a fice was likely to give it the best of food and a lot of attention. No wonder one of these pampered little animals was likely to have a temper with a short fuse!

Fice-like attitudes and reactions on the part of two-legged creatures warrants use of the label *feisty*—an indirect way of suggesting that a person is as snappy as a poodle.

Ferret Out

ONE of the strangest animals brought to Europe by Crusaders who had been in Africa made a good pet. But the newcomer to England and Europe was so fond of eggs that it was often caught stealing them. From a corruption of an old expression used to describe "a thief with fur," the egg stealer came to be known as the *ferret*.

Easily trained, the pink-eyed imported animal was widely used to hunt rats. Eventually it became both a serious pursuit and a popular sport to ferret for rabbits and other burrowing animals.

Charles Dickens' imagination was fired by the egg-stealer's name, so he picked it up and applied it to detective work. As a result, we say that a searcher for hidden things—not necessarily underground—is busy ferreting out secrets.

Get One's Back Up

IF a person or situation causes you to get your back up, you're likely to behave at least a little like one of man's favorite animals. As recently as the end of the Middle Ages, no household was complete without a cat. Both Puss-in-Boots and Old Tom Growler became immortal literary figures during this period.

Few common sights are more impressive than that of a cat strutting about on its toes, with its back arched very high. This feline stance is so common that a human in a state of fury was compared with such an animal before Spain sent her armada against England.

You may seldom or never make a noticeable change in the arch of your backbone. Nevertheless, when you show signs of rage or great indignation, your attitude is likely to cause you to be labeled with the expression that describes an angry cat.

Get One's Goat

A FAMILY member or fellow worker who has learned what button to push may get your goat at the drop of a hat.

Stable attendants were long convinced that the best way to soothe a high-strung racehorse was to give the animal a little companion. Not just any companion, but a goat.

Once the horse became accustomed to presence of the horned ruminant, it created an equine crisis to remove the stable mate. At least, that's the widespread oral tradition that offers to explain why a person who makes you angry or frustrated has laid hands on your personal goat.

Goose Bumps

ANY thrilling experience, from catching a glimpse of a movie star to attending the Kentucky Derby, may give you goose bumps.

Geese were important in the life of medieval Britain—so important that goose herds spent their lives tending flocks. Many owners plucked their geese five times a year, leaving them totally naked until new feathers appeared. When cold air hit such a bird, tiny muscles just under the skin would contract and create patterns of pimples.

The plucking of geese for feathers was common in Yorkshire until late in the last century, and is sometimes seen even today.

It doesn't take a draft to cause wee muscles of some humans to contract; emotion can do the job. Regardless of what triggers them into visibility, small and transient bumps on the human skin are so much like those of a plucked fowl that it's logical and natural to call them *goose bumps*.

Greenhorn

IF you include a greenhorn in an activity at which you're an old pro, be on the alert for mistakes and be patient in correcting them!

Tender new leaves in the spring often seem to be a shade of green that is seen during no other season. Because such growth is young and fragile, anyone or anything lacking experience and strength came to be labeled as *green*.

Experienced handlers of oxen could identify awkward young males at a glance; their horns were small and unscarred. Such a greenhorn wasn't ready for a job that required stamina and training. Neither are most human adolescents; though their heads have no bony protuberances, they are called by the name assigned to oxen with freshly sprouted horns.

Hamstrung

A PERSON who is hamstrung, or immobile and unable to do more than thrash about aimlessly, is worse off than someone who is simply unstrung.

Long ago, butchers and cooks discovered that tendons included within a ham are vital to movement of a pig. When hamstrings were accidentally or deliberately cut, the hamstrung animal could not run or walk. A convicted criminal who was punished by being hamstrung was permanently handicapped.

Long used in a literal sense, the label for an animal or person whose hamstrings were severed came to be applied to anyone who is rendered incapable of getting on with something.

Hightail

WHEN you move at top speed, whether running on foot or driving a car, you hightail it from one place to another.

That is because early cowpokes noticed the actions of wild horses. Herds of them, descended from steeds of Spanish explorers, once roamed the west. Always, a stallion served as lookout for these animals; at the slightest sign of danger, he would signal for them to take off at top speed.

Except for worn-out plugs, domesticated horses follow the

example of wild ones. When startled, they jerk their tails very high and burst into a gallop with a few strides. As a result of this equine trait, a person or vehicle getting off to a fast start is said to hightail it down the road.

Horse Around

MORE than any other large domestic animals, horses enjoy a vigorous frolic. Turned loosed in a pasture, two or three or more of them are likely to run and jump as well as nuzzle one another. Such horseplay is spontaneous, and seems to have little if any structure.

Every sizeable group of persons includes at least one who pays no attention to rules and precedents. Cracking jokes one minute and cutting capers the next, such a person likes to horse around— much like a stallion turned into a pasture with a couple of mares.

Horse's Mouth/Gift Horse

IF you get a tip straight from the horse's mouth, you know that your informant considers it to be absolutely correct.

In spite of the fact that horses talk only in fables and television programs, the expression is worth using. As early as the 16th century, equine age was accurately estimated by examination of the mouth. Physical appearance and claims of the owners may be deceptive—but the lower jaw of a horse tells all to a person who knows the pattern of tooth aging.

When deciding whether or not to put money on a nag, a race-track regular who gets a look at its teeth has accurate firsthand information about its age—secured straight from the horse's mouth.

The phrase "look a gift horse in the mouth" comes from this same practice. It was considered insulting to closely examine and inspect a horse that was a gift—as if you did not trust the donor to give quality.

Jaywalker

FEW North American birds are so loud and colorful as the blue jay. Now often seen in towns and suburbs of cities, the noisy creatures once avoided humans. Their prevalence in wooded regions caused any rustic to be derided as a *jay*.

Male and female jays who ventured into urban regions often found themselves confused. Not understanding patterns of movement, and sometimes ignorant of signals, they seemed to endanger their lives when they tried to cross streets.

Sophisticated city folk jeered at any erratic pedestrian as a jay in action. Hence *jaywalker* became the standard title of a person who crosses a street in a reckless or illegal fashion.

Jinx

BACK at the turn of the 20th century, there was a resurgence of interest in the occult. Some persons who didn't have much faith in horoscope readings went all out for fortune-telling by use of animals and birds.

One of the most popular of creatures for use in divination was the wryneck woodpecker—commonly known in much of the Southeast as the jinx. Many a person who paid good money for information from a jinx regretted having tried to peer into the future. Too often, none of the predicted good came about—while all the bad omens proved to be true.

This denouement was frequent enough to give the poor little woodpecker a bad reputation; disaster followed a reading by means of a jinx so often that the bird's name came to stand for bad luck.

Lick into Shape

BEARS figure in many ancient myths, appear in the sky as constellations, and are central figures in numerous superstitions. According to one belief, a cub is absolutely shapeless at birth.

The mother and father bear were thought to lick their newborn into shape with their tongues.

Persistence of the legend is due in part to the fact that few persons saw newborn cubs and lived to describe them. Still current during the century in which America was discovered, the superstition figured in several famous stories for children.

Totally without foundation but circulated for at least a thousand years, beliefs about bear cubs lead us to say that when we've mastered a difficult situation or made something presentable, we have licked it into shape.

Mascot

FRENCH composer Edmond Audran was all but unknown until he produced a hit in 1880. Audiences in Paris applauded his *La Mascotte,* titled after a provincial word for a witch. The central character had such good luck that opera goers knew it had to come from supernatural sources.

Offered throughout Europe, the title of the opera came to label any object or person bringing great good fortune. An early mascot might be a rabbit's foot or a four-leaf clover.

Gradually the vivid label was associated with animals and birds believed to bring luck. Schools, clubs, and sporting groups used them to represent their teams and bring good fortune. As a result, many an athlete who never attended an opera trusts in the feathered or furry mascot that helps the team to win.

Maverick

ATTORNEY Samuel A. Maverick migrated to Texas in the cowboy era of the early 1800s and built up a good practice. When one of his clients couldn't come up with cash, the newcomer from the east accepted some land in payment for his services. Soon he moved his herd to the Conquistar Ranch, near San Antonio.

Busy helping to fight Mexicans and win independence for

Texas, the attorney spent little time on his ranch. Since he didn't check up on them, lazy hands did not bother to brand his calves. By the time he sold out in 1855, unbranded cattle were running all over the place.

Neighboring ranchers who came across one of Maverick's animals seldom hesitated to brand it and run it into one of their own herds. No one knows how many cattle the greenhorn rancher lost in this way. But his naïve ways caused his name to enter speech as a word for a nonconformist or malcontent who bears no signs of belonging to a specific herd.

No Spring Chicken

ARCHAEOLOGISTS have found evidence that humans began keeping poultry at the dawn of civilization. Already ancient in the time of Julius Caesar, this type of husbandry spread throughout the world. Until recent generations, there were no incubators and few warm hen houses. That meant chicks couldn't be raised during winter.

New England growers found that those born in the spring brought premium prices in the summer market places. Sometimes they tried to deceive customers by offering old birds as though they belonged to the spring crop.

Wise buyers would protest that a tough fowl was "no spring chicken." As a result, the barnyard term came to designate persons as well as birds past the plump and tender age.

Pecking Order

OBSERVATION of the pecking order within your circle of friends or fellow workers will tell you who is really boss and who's actually on the bottom.

Biologist W. C. Allee gained fame from study of hens. Every barnyard flock, he found, has a clear pattern of social prestige.

Any hen pecks freely at those below her rank, but submits meekly to the pecking of those above her.

Male–female pecking occurs among humans, but in a flock of chickens no hen pecks a rooster. That means the barnyard term— apt and vivid as it is—is strained somewhat when applied to people.

Pigeonhole

ATTITUDES toward many things we use daily go through cycles. There is a period of excitement when something new is put on the market; then a replacement comes into vogue. As years pass, articles in attics and basements are seen as antique and valuable. That is when replicas come out.

Desks used by merchants and teachers and others have gone through every phase of this cycle. When it first became available, a piece with rows of rectangular compartments was an eye-catcher. Its little segments looked like holes in a pigeon roost, or côte. So a piece fitted with them was called a pigeon-hole desk.

Used for decades, then mostly discarded, replicas of the desk are now available. Of course, a good one will cost you a lot more than an original when it was new!

So many people sorted letters and bills and invoices and reports into pigeonholes for so many years that the noun was made into a verb of action. We use it to name any process of classification or as a symbol of putting something into a narrow slot.

Plug Away

GIVEN a long and perhaps monotonous job, one person may quit in disgust. Facing the same chores, another person will plug away, day after day, until the end is reached.

Speech compares anyone in the latter category with a run-of-the-mill horse. Unlike a splendid racer who gave everything it had for a limited time and then was put out to pasture, the plug horse sometimes devoted an entire life to pulling a hackney cab or a dray. After a decade of such work, an animal's steps were likely to be slow and plodding.

Probably named from typical noises made in walking, the plug horse had it all over the racehorse in one respect. A plug kept on going, year after year, until a contemporary racer's productive life was long surpassed. Which suggests that a person who plugs away at a task may eventually reach a point that a fiery enthusiast never glimpses except from a distance.

Rain Cats and Dogs

IF you're caught in a downpour accompanied by thunder and lightning and high wind, there is a good chance that you'll report having seen it rain cats and dogs.

These domesticated animals, and no others, are linked in speech with a furious storm. Some scholars think they know why. They point out that witches credited with causing storms often rode the winds in the form of black cats. And in Norse mythology, the god of storms was described as being surrounded by dogs plus their wild cousins, wolves.

Undocumented conjecture suggests that Norse mythology is the seedbed from which the modern phrase has grown. Another guess, equally plausible, is rooted closer to home.

Every furious gale, heard with a sensitive ear, sounds a lot like the sudden eruption of a dog-and-cat fight. Many householders used to keep half a dozen dogs and two or three sets of cats. Perhaps comments that the "storm sounds just like cats fighting with the dogs," were turned into the metaphor crediting heavy clouds with raining cats and dogs.

Ride Roughshod

IN your observation of others, you've probably seen a boss— or a spouse, a parent, or a child—ride roughshod over someone.

Even in the Space Age, that sounds like a terrible way to act; long ago it involved more than treating a person insensitively or brusquely.

Medieval blacksmiths who experimented with metal learned to make horseshoes of a special kind. Instead of the smooth metal oval used to protect the foot of a draft animal, a war horse might be equipped with shoes that had projecting points or cutting edges for better footing.

When horseshoes were turned into weapons, the course of empire was not altered; the devices never worked well. A rough-shod horse was likely to injure its rider's comrades about as frequently as his foes.

But to an injured man lying on the battlefield, the approach of a roughshod stallion was a fearful sight. As a result, any person who is vocally or physically brutal to an opponent already down is said to ride roughshod over the victim.

Rule the Roost

IF you know anything about Rhode Island reds or Plymouth Rocks, you have noticed that a flock—or roost—of chickens seldom includes more than one male. That is because a rooster comes out of the egg jealous and mean-spirited. He wants all of the hens and spring chickens for himself.

Bigger, stronger, and louder than females who make up his harem, Chanticleer literally rules every member of his roost—so effectively that his conduct gave rise to a phrase that conveys the idea of unchallenged control.

Ruminate

MANY domestic animals are equipped to gulp down forage rapidly, then chew it leisurely at a later time. These creatures are equipped with a "first stomach," or *rumen*, where food is held until it can be reworked by the teeth.

Wits had already quipped that a person who brings up remembered problems in order to rework them in the mind is like an animal that chews the same grass more than once. Once the expression based on the name of the first stomach came into vogue, anyone who meditated about a familiar topic was described as ruminating.

Smell a Rat

WHETHER or not you own a dog, chances are good that you've seen a pet suddenly begin whining, barking, and scratching at the floor or wall. When that happens, the dog may have smelled a rat.

Civilized man has had few enemies so cunning and persistent as the common rodent. Able to adapt to almost any climate and diet, the rat has been a nuisance since the Stone Age. For centuries, it was a common practice to give terriers and other rat-hunting dogs free run of palaces as well as huts. In the course of a quiet evening, it was not unusual for an animal to spring into action without an obvious cause.

If no other triggering effect could be found, the dog's behavior would be shrugged aside as caused by its having caught a whiff of a rodent. This occurred so frequently that when an event triggers automatic suspicion in a person, that person is said to have smelled a rat.

Sniper

ONE of medieval England's most common birds was the snipe. Wary and quick in flight, the fowl frequented marshes and swamps. The flesh was prized as a delicacy, but the birds were alert and fast. A hunter carrying bow and arrows found it difficult to get in range of his quarry.

This situation changed when firearms were improved in the

16th century. By lying in concealment and waiting until snipe came within range, it was easy to fill a bag with them.

A good sniper almost always shot his birds from ambush. As a result, the name of the bird hunter designates any solitary marksman or terrorist who fires from a place of concealment.

Stiff-necked

IN several ancient cultures, the ox was commonly used to plow fields and pull carts. Proverbially stubborn, these animals were hard to handle under the best of circumstances. When a sullen bull stiffened the muscles of his powerful neck, it was difficult or impossible to guide him.

Hebrews employed an expression meaning stiff-necked to identify persons as defiant and self-willed as oxen. This descriptive term was used both literally and figuratively in Scripture. As a result, it remains alive and well in speech long after use of ox power died in western society.

Terrier

LIKE many parts of Europe, old Normandy was rife with badgers. These animals made themselves nuisances by digging tunnels and building mounds. From a Latin term for earth, a badger's heap of it was known as a *terrier*.

Small, agile dogs proved adept at driving a badger from its underground fortress by digging into its *terrier*. As late as the time of Sir Walter Scott, English usually referred to the badger's nemesis as a terrier dog. Eventually clipped into a single word, the term for a skillful digger is now applied to many kinds of small canines—most of whom have never seen a badger's mound.

Underdog

SETTLERS who were pioneers on the American frontier were usually ready for a brawl. Many of them enjoyed fighting among themselves. Practically all made quite a sport of setting lean hounds upon one another.

Dogfighting has one significant factor in common with wrestling by humans. In both cases, it is a decided disadvantage to be on the bottom. That was notably the case in a backwoods dogfight. When one animal got the other down and started for its throat, some bystander had to intervene in order to save the life of the dog underneath.

Regular references to losses by canines on the bottom caused their title to be bestowed on any contestant—two-legged or four-legged—judged likely to be at a disadvantage in a struggle.

Well-heeled

IF someone comments that you are well-heeled, say "Thank you," regardless of the amount of money in your pocket. This compliment stems from cockfights of the Middle Ages.

Birds fought to the death, and some with good bloodlines were handicapped by short spurs. Owners learned to equip such a cock with a metal spur—or gaff. Strapped close to the heel of a fighter, it was even more lethal than a natural growth of bone and cartilage.

A bird equipped with a pair of gaffs was well-heeled, indeed—armed for quick victory. Since plenty of money is a major weapon in a business or industrial fight, anyone with ample resources came to bear the label of a fighting cock wearing gaffs.

Wet Behind the Ears

A PERSON wet behind the ears barely qualifies as a beginner. Compared with such a neophyte, a tenderfoot or greenhorn is an old pro.

Many newly born animals, wet from liquids in the womb, are slow to become fully dry. Some places, especially the indentation behind the ears, take the longest because they are not exposed to the air. The fur of animals like kittens and colts holds moisture, and stays damp until they are active.

A youth or an adult who knows absolutely nothing about a planned undertaking is a helpless infant in that field, or wet behind the ears.

CHAPTER 4

NAMES AND GAMES

"The only athletic sport I ever mastered was backgammon."
—Douglas Jerrold, *Douglas Jerrold's Wit*

Games, both athletic and not-so-athletic, have their special fascination. Part of it stems from the hope of winning— along with the fear of losing.

Regardless of whether or not you've ever been a devotee, poker may have influenced your everyday vocabulary more profoundly than any other game. But other games are in there rolling for your verbal allegiance as well.

ACCORDING TO HOYLE
ACE IN THE HOLE
BACK TO SQUARE ONE
BLUE CHIPS
BREAK THE ICE
CHIPS ARE DOWN
DOMINOES
DRAW THE LINE
DUCKS IN A ROW,
    GET/PUT ONE'S
FOUR-FLUSHER
GET A BREAK
HANDS DOWN
JACKPOT
KINGPIN

KNUCKLE DOWN
LEAVE IN THE LURCH
OFF THE WALL
ON A ROLL
OPEN AND SHUT
PASS THE BUCK
PLAY FOR KEEPS
RACK UP
RUSH PELL-MELL
SHOOT THE WORKS
SHOWDOWN
STAND PAT
START THE BALL
    ROLLING

SEE ALSO: Boner

According to Hoyle

LATE in the 17th century, whist became all the rage in England. Played with a deck of fifty-two cards, it was a forerunner of modern bridge.

Early players could choose between dozens of different kinds of play. There were so many varieties that Edmund Hoyle set out to bring order from confusion. His book of rules, which went through many editions, came to be accepted as the final authority concerning the game.

Anyone wishing to be sure whist was played correctly used Hoyle's book as a guide. Widespread over many years, this practice causes us to say we're proceeding "according to Hoyle" when we believe we are doing things correctly in any area of activity.

Ace in the Hole

STUD poker came into its own during the cowboy era. More than any other game, it separated cowpokes from their wages and miners from their dust. Complex rules govern the way in which cards are dealt, held, and played.

With other cards exposed so that opponents may see them, a lucky player sometimes holds an ace that is face down—concealed "in the hole." That card may be the pivot on which a game turns.

Any asset or source of strength, kept secret by its holder, is so much like a concealed playing card that it is an ace in the hole.

Back to Square One

ESPECIALLY during a group activity, it is common for someone to propose a return to square one. That is shorthand for suggesting: "Let's scrap all we have done, and start over."

Not a bad way to express the notion of giving up and making a fresh start. For the expression took shape during the pre-electronic era in which board games of many kinds were in use.

Several widely popular ones involved moving tokens in response to the throw of dice or drawing of a card. At the beginning of a contest, all tokens were placed at the same starting point—square one of the board.

A proposal about going back to square one meant scrapping the on-going game and starting a new one.

Blue Chips

BY the time poker became standardized, tiles were beginning to replace the earliest tokens—chips of wood. The color of the little cash substitutes was red, white or blue. Seldom made from wood in modern times, the value of a blue chip came to be ten times that of a red chip.

From table to table, monetary equivalents of chips can vary widely. Whether a blue one is treated as worth a dime or one thousand dollars, it outranks red and white ones.

Stock market investors who put their money into securities considered to be the most valuable pride themselves on holding blue chips—even though they may never have taken part in a game of poker.

Break the Ice

LONDON, Leningrad, and many other great cities grew strong and important as a result of being situated on rivers and channels. This geographical advantage was worth little, however, in periods of bitter cold. Even large ships could become ice-bound, making them useless for weeks.

Small, sturdy ships known as *icebreakers* were developed to precede traveling ships and make a way through the ice. Such work was preliminary to the central task of transporting goods through freezing water.

Every veteran boatman knew that he often had to break the ice before actually getting down to business. Consequently the water-born expression came to label any method of making a start.

Chips Are Down

EVERY confrontation sooner or later comes to a point at which the chips are down. Everything to be said has been said; everything that can be done has been done. A foreordained outcome will soon be made public.

At a poker table, when the final bets of a hand have been made, all the chips are down on the table. No more can be added, and none may be picked up until a winner is declared.

Finality at the table leads us to use the expression when an inescapable moment of decision is at hand.

Dominoes

AN Italian prisoner, forbidden to throw dice, may have been the inventor of a substitute game. It was played with twenty-eight pieces of wood, marked with spots representing all possible throws with two dice.

Soon devotees of the new game began making little tiles of ebony, covered with thin ivory. Such playing pieces reminded them of a special hood worn by priests. This heavy black garment, lined with white, was known as a *domino*.

After taking the name of the hood, "dice on tiles" swept through France and then across the channel into England. British players eventually used a plural form of the word, so *dominoes* became a favorite parlor game of the Edwardian era.

Most Americans have never seen a priest huddled in a domino, but many of them use English-style playing pieces that make dominoes a distant relative of shooting craps.

Draw the Line

A GAME that was the ancestor of tennis involved hitting a ball back and forth across a net. It required little equipment, since players used their hands to strike the ball.

Precise dimensions for the court had not been established, so play could take place almost anywhere. Having selected a level spot, contestants stretched a net. Then each stepped an agreed distance from the net and drew a line that was the visual boundary.

For decades, players knocked balls back and forth in impromptu courts. Through influence of the game, the act of drawing a boundary line came to name the establishment of a limit of any kind.

Ducks in a Row, Get/Put One's

PRIMITIVE versions of modern bowling were known many centuries ago. Pins of varied sizes and shapes were employed. Eventually they were standardized at fifteen inches in both height and circumference.

Originally called ten-pins, the equipment used in Europe was employed in the earliest American bowling saloons. The game was modified by introduction of a short, slender pin that was compared with a duck and, by extension, called them *duckpins*.

So many people reset so many pins in rows that one who completes a task is commended as having put his "ducks in a row."

Four-flusher

EVERYONE knows a four-flusher—a big talker whose deeds never match his or her words. These days, a person on whom colleagues bestow this title is likely to borrow without paying and may even engage in petty fraud.

That wasn't the case a century ago, when the title entered general speech.

At the turn of the 20th century, many a poker player let

opponents know he had four cards of one suit while carefully concealing his fifth card. If skillful in the art of make-believe, such a player might convince others to lay down their cards in the face of his straight flush.

Once the game was over, anyone who captured a pot by such a ruse revealed that his flush was "bob-tailed" and packed a lot less punch than he pretended. Influence of the poker table was such that any pretender was given the name of the *four-flusher*.

Get a Break

IN pocket billiards, or pool, the first shot of a game is the most important. No matter where it hits balls that have been arranged in the form of a triangle, the orderly arrangement is broken.

Skilled players know how to break in such fashion that the cue ball stops at an advantageous point. An especially good break can lead to a run of the table—every ball pocketed before an opponent has an opportunity to shoot.

Comparing any sudden advantage with a splendid first shot at the pool table, a person who receives a stroke of luck is said to get a break.

Hands Down

ANYTIME you score a victory without effort, you will win hands down—even if your hands were waving above your head at the moment of the finish.

Though firmly established, the origin for this phrase meaning an easy triumph is not clear. Some horsemen vow that it stems from the fact that a jockey may find his horse way out in front of the pack. That means the rider doesn't even have to lift his hands in order to guide his mount to a win.

Another theory gets "hands down" from the boxing ring. A prize fighter occasionally gets matched with a pushover. In such a bout, the stronger and more expert contender waltzes to victory after having barely raised his fists a few times.

You can pay your money and take your pick: a horse race that practically ends in a canter, or ten rounds in a ring during which the winner never works up a sweat. Either way, one contender will win hands down.

Jackpot

RARE, indeed, is the person who wouldn't like to hit a jackpot of one variety or another. To many a patron of casinos, the jackpot is much like a hole in one is to a golfer—only more so, if possible.

A big payoff as a result of hard work and ingenuity—or luck at a slot machine—owes its name to an intricate form of poker. In draw-poker, a person must have a pair of jacks or better in order to open, but has to ante regardless. If no one holds such cards, the pot grows larger and larger. Sooner or later, someone will rake in a pile of chips by hitting the jackpot.

Kingpin

DURING the second century, Germans perfected a game in which wooden pins formed the target for a rolling ball. Arrangement of the target varied until the number of pins was standardized at nine—with a king pin, sometimes decorated with a crown, standing taller than the rest.

The Dutch brought ninepins to New Amsterdam about 1600 and enjoyed it so much that authorities tried to suppress play. To get around the law, the size of pins was made uniform and a tenth one was added—and modern bowling was born.

Players no longer shoot for a center pin tall enough to be regarded as regal. Yet the label of kingpin is still given to anyone standing tall enough to play a decisive role in a club, association, or board of directors.

Knuckle Down

FACING a demand from the boss that you increase your productivity, you have two choices. You can put up a fight, or you can knuckle down to work like a veteran of the game of marbles.

Marbles are little round balls once made from the stone that gave them their name. Games played with them, popular for centuries, once came close to becoming the national pastime of England.

In many forms of play, each contestant is required to shoot from the exact spot at which his marble last stopped moving. That can't be done when a player's hand is upright, so it became standard to require that knuckles be against the ground before shooting. If a player seems tempted to move his marble, an opponent can demand that he "knuckle down."

Spreading from marble rings of old, the expression gained currency as a way of describing earnest application to a task of any kind.

Leave in the Lurch

ANYTIME you hopelessly outdistance a rival, he is likely to be described as having been left in the lurch. That's appropriate— for the expression was born in competition.

The French of the 16th century invented the game they knew as *lourche*. Few written records survive. Little is known about it except that large sums of money were frequently at stake in a game, which was somewhat like modern backgammon.

Widely popular for a period, lurch was abandoned and nearly forgotten. But before its popularity waned, it became synonymous with competitive states in which one player is far behind. In cribbage, for example, a state of lurch exists when one player has less than thirty-one points by the time a rival scores sixty-one.

Spreading from the gaming table, the expression survives long after the kind of play it names. Today a person left in the lurch is not in the running for an achievement, an honor, or a prize.

Off the Wall

WHY do we sometimes say that a really unusual piece of art work or a ridiculous plan is "off the wall?"

Because a wall is essential to several popular games, notably squash and handball. In them, as well as in racquet ball, a bounce from the wall is influenced by speed, spin, and angle. Even a veteran player cannot always estimate what direction a ball will take.

Like a ball bouncing at a weird angle, a plan or an activity may be so unpredictable that it, too, is described as being "off the wall."

On a Roll

ANYTIME you're congratulated as being on a roll, you are seen as unbeatable for the moment. Such a winning streak, regardless of the field of activity involved, takes its name from gambling tables.

Every crapshooter, beginner or veteran, yearns for the time when each roll of the dice will produce another in a long string of wins. A first throw of seven or eleven signals that this may be the instant at which luck will start.

Lots of persons have either experienced this work of chance or watched others profit from it. Consequently, anyone enjoying a great streak of luck is lauded as being on a roll—even though tumbling a pair of dice may not be involved.

Open and Shut

FEW card games have had a more hectic reign than faro. Sweeping to popularity about 1850, it became a major means by which prospectors were separated from their gold dust.

Standard play of the era included numerous complicated ways to place or raise bets. Novices were discouraged by these technicalities, so a gambling hall operator devised a simpler version.

In this modified faro, the pot was shut very soon after having been opened.

Veterans of the pasteboards preferred the older and more challenging game, and so turned up their noses at open and shut play. Spreading from gold fields into general speech, the expression from the faro table came to name any uncomplicated situation.

Pass the Buck

A PERSON who is inclined to pass the buck when pressed isn't likely to move up the corporate ladder very fast.

Neither is the buck passer the most likely candidate for winning a card game. For the buck used in such a game is a token, formerly a piece of buckshot, that indicates the position of the deal. In several kinds of play, the dealer has special responsibility. His opening wager will determine whether the pot is likely to be large or small.

A cautious fellow who wishes to avoid taking the initial plunge hesitates when the buck reaches him. At many tables, he's given the privilege of passing the buck so that the next player becomes the dealer.

Inevitably, anyone who evades making decisions or accepting responsibility of any sort is said to pass the buck. Very early in the life of the phrase, it became closely attached to politicians and officeholders.

Play for Keeps

HUMAN nature being what it is, differences in personality often emerge very early. When marbles were high on the list of favorite toys for children, many bouts ended by sorting them out so everyone could go home with the ones that were brought.

But there was another and a far more serious kind of play. Before starting it, opponents agreed that all marbles captured during competition would become the property of the winner. Any boy or girl who put a bag of marbles at risk was likely to have a little thicker skin than run-of-the-mill players—a competitor to be avoided by all except those also willing to play for keeps.

Rack Up

HERE is hoping that you will rack up enough years to qualify for a company pension or some other benefit tied to experience. When that happens, you're figuratively in the position of getting ready for a brand-new game.

For it is the arrangement of pool balls in a triangular frame that constitutes racking up. Once this has been done, the last game isn't nearly as important as the one about to begin.

Significantly, the expression meaning achievement or accumulation is strictly American. In England, pool has never displaced billiards—in which the triangular metal or wooden rack is not needed.

Rush Pell-Mell

WHEN you find yourself rushing pell-mell, in a big hurry but not having planned your stops, you act almost as though you were playing a game.

Borrowed by the English from the French, the game of pall-mall involved driving a boxwood ball with a mallet. This was done with the object of knocking the ball through a ring that was suspended at the end of a long playing surface. Pall-mall became so popular that many alleys were laid out for it in the suburbs of London. One of them later became the site of a street that took the name of the playing surface it replaced.

Because Pall Mall was a center of club life and major business houses, to which the War Office was later added, the street was always in confusion. Hurry became typical of those who had reason to ride or to walk along cobblestones of the street whose name natives pronounced as "pell mell."

Strangers who first laid eyes on bustling Pall Mall went away saying that it was unlike any other street they had ever seen. As a result of seemingly frenzied activity there, we say that anyone who runs around in circles is rushing pell-mell.

Shoot the Works

ANYTIME you decide to go whole hog, or abolish all limits, you are willing to shoot the works. Thoroughly respectable though the expression now is, it owes its existence to the gambling table.

Though far from sophisticated, the game of craps remains popular in the electronic age. A player willing to risk everything on one throw of the dice is likely to offer to "shoot the works." When that is done, there is no second chance; the game is over, and the little cubes have determined a big winner along with maybe three or more losers.

Showdown

IN many a search for truth or struggle for supremacy, a crucial moment comes when everyone is ready for a showdown. That means quick and decisive action—so final that there is no appeal.

Like so many other expressions that they've never been accurately tabulated, this one entered American speech straight from the poker table. A special kind of play is involved, of course.

Sometimes players will agree that in the next round, all cards will be dealt face up. Pure luck, not skill, determines the winner in such a case. Once the dealer has finished, a glance around the table will determine who holds the winning hand.

This version of poker doesn't have a great deal to recommend it. But showdown play has won enough followers to catapult its name into mainstream speech to designate a decisive confrontation or an act of bringing things into the open.

Stand Pat

SEVERAL common substances were long patted into shape by hand. This job took more skill than a person watching for the first time might think.

Dexterity involved in patting butter, dough, or potter's clay caused anything apt and clever to be called "pat."

Poker buffs borrowed the household term and used it to name an original hand not likely to be improved by drawing additional cards. An experienced player dealt the right cards would stand pat, or say no when offered more cards.

Whether in a business conference or a meeting of the PTA, a person who has never played poker can stand pat by refusing to budge or by resisting even minor change.

Start the Ball Rolling

CROQUET was one of England's favorite games during much of the 19th century. Annual matches at Wimbledon drew crowds that rivaled the size of those that now turn out for tennis tournaments.

One insurmountable liability contributed to its fall from favor: there is no way to organize a game so that each player has an equal chance to win. Given the first shot, an expert can often reach the goal before anyone else has had a chance to start.

Because of this factor it is all-important to be the first player. A coin is often tossed to see who gets to begin. During the era when croquet was king of the lawn, a person who took charge of any beginning borrowed from the game and said he or she would "start the ball rolling."

CHAPTER *5*

SPORTS TALK OFTEN FOLLOWS THE BALL

"I do not in the least object to a sport because it is rough."
—Theodore Roosevelt, *Speech,*
Cambridge, Massachusetts, February 28, 1907

R ough or gentle, so many sports involve the use of balls that talk about them centers in little spheres. But sports include bear baiting and wrestling, as well as others that do not rely upon balls. Our indebtedness to sports is so great that you're "out in left field" if you never use expressions born from planned struggle.

BALL

BELOW THE BELT

BIRDIE

BOGIE OR BOGEY

BULLPEN

BULL'S EYE

CADDY

DEADLOCK

EAGLE

FACE-OFF

FALL GUY

GAME PLAN

GOLF

HAYMAKER

JUMP THE GUN

KEEP AN EYE ON THE BALL

LEFT FIELD

ON THE BALL

PINCH HITTER

PLAY THE FIELD

REAL McCOY

RODEO

ROLL WITH THE PUNCHES

SCREWBALL

SOUTHPAW

STAVE OFF

TEE

THROW IN THE SPONGE/
  TOWEL

UP TO SCRATCH

SEE ALSO: Anchor, Badger, Ballpark Estimate, Beat Around the
  Bush, Bush League, Dachshund, Hands Down, Hit; Hook,
  Line, and Sinker; Inside Track, Keep the Ball Rolling, Pit
  Stop

Ball

MAYBE 600 years ago, a maker of "balles"—or things blown up—decided that intestines of animals were too flimsy. So he cut pieces of hide into strips and soaked them in alum. Stitched together until only a small opening was left, the new and novel leather piece was stuffed with boiled goose feathers.

A featherie, as golf's earliest ball was often called, was expensive; no artisan could turn out more than four or five a day. James Melville gained a monopoly in 1618 when King James I authorized him to seek out and confiscate balls made by his competitors.

Discovery of rubber and ways to process it put an end to the long reign of the featherie. But 19th-century achievements in technology marked only one important step in a ceaseless search aimed at improving balls that are all-important in golf, baseball, football, and basketball, and many other sports.

Below the Belt

RULES of boxing were informal and often irregular until modern times. Working with John G. Chamber, the 8th Marquis of Queensberry drew up a code that was adopted in the 1860s.

It was not acceptable, said the new rules, to hit whatever vital spot could be reached. Any blow directed to an opponent's groin would be ruled a foul.

Blows that landed in the outlawed area cost some oldtimers heavily, so newcomers to the ring became more cautious. Spreading into general speech, a verbal haymaker that violates accepted standards is said to have landed "below the belt."

Birdie

ADMIRATION for native birds caused early Americans to use their name as a way of expressing commendation. Any admirable person was likely to be admired as a "bird."

Golfers who used bogie to name a score of one over par chose birdie to indicate one stroke under par. Coined in the United States, the term later spread to England and Europe.

In the 1953 Masters, Ben Hogan's ball lay 60 feet from the cup on the 9th hole. When he sank a birdie putt, it proved to be one of the decisive shots of the tournament. Playing the same course years earlier, James Demaret scored six birdies in nine holes.

Regardless of the distance it covers, hearts beat faster when a birdie heads for the cup like a homing pigeon returning to its coop.

Bogie or Bogey

DR. Thomas Browne, secretary of the Great Yarmouth golf club, popularized an innovation. It added zest to competion, he said, for every player to compete with the "ground score"—or number of shots good players required for a particular hole.

Major Wellman, a retired army officer, hadn't played against ground scores of holes until he teed off with Browne. Soon he realized that his toughest opponent was not the club secretary, but the invisible standard. Trying to beat it, he remembered a song about "The Bogey Man."

Exasperated at failure to beat scratch, the military officer exclaimed: "Dr. Browne, both of us are really playing against Colonel Bogey!"

Colonel Bogey soon won a wide following, but U.S. players modified both the spelling and meaning of his name. Here, *to bogie* is "to lose a hole to Colonel Bogie by one stroke." On many courses in Britain, *bogey* labels the standard scratch score—or par.

Bullpen

LARGE numbers of civilians were placed under military arrest during the Civil War. Prisons were not large enough to accommodate everyone charged, perhaps, with "giving a hurrah for Jeff Davis."

To hold large numbers of prisoners, temporary stockades were built. Because such a structure resembled a cattle pen, and persons in them were as helpless as steers, it was called a *bull pen*.

Then the wartime place of detention gave its name to an area adjoining a playing field. While warming up, relief pitchers and other substitutes in the bullpen are almost but not quite as confined as steers waiting to be loaded on a train.

Bull's Eye

UNTIL it was outlawed in 1835, bull baiting was a major national sport of England. Always, some put their money on the dogs, while others preferred the bull. Just as present-day racing enthusiasts often put their money on a horse's nose, British sports were prone to put a crown on the bull's eye.

Since the coin equivalent to five shillings was roughly the size of an eye on which it was wagered, it took the same name. Targets developed for marksmen came to include a central black spot about the size of a shilling. Using the sportsman's label to designate the coin-size spot, the center of any target became it's bull's eye.

Caddy

EARLY golfers, some of whom were educated in France, were often assisted by cadets, or "young fellows," who carried their clubs. As the game matured, the label for a carrier of clubs became slurred in speech. Many a youth without a steady job was glad to work as a caddy.

That is how some golfing greats first walked the greens. Gene Sarazen was a caddy at Apawamis in Harrison, New York. John Bryon Nelson, Jr., "the mechanical man" of the 1930s, earned seventy-five cents a round as a caddy at Glen Garden in Fort Worth. Ben Hogan started at sixty-five cents a round, plus tips.

Future players may never see a caddy except in cup competition. But in pre-mechanized days a young fellow willing to carry bags was an essential ingredient to the elixir that is golf.

Deadlock

WRESTLING was a highly developed sport at least five thousand years ago. Sculpture from temple tombs near the Nile indicate that ancient grapplers used many of the holds still in vogue.

No one knows precisely when the sport became prominent in Britain. But by the time noblemen became engrossed with chivalry, many commoners were wrestling fans.

It was not unusual for a burly yeoman to make a special move. By means of it he could hold an opponent indefinitely, but was unable to force submission. Because it killed action, a hold of this sort was called a deadlock. Spreading from the ring, it came to label a stalemate of any kind.

Eagle

ONCE "Birdie!" became an exclamation, a name was needed for a score of two below par. Some players called a triumph of this sort "big bird."

To Americans, there's only one big bird with special symbolic importance. So locker room talk soon came to include "eagle."

It took a while for duffers to discover that a player who bragged about an eagle had not found a $10 gold piece. But a 1922 story in the *New York Times* cleared up the meaning of the new golf term. Editors played up an account of a match in which Von Elm lay in position for an eagle—then missed it by failing to drop a nine-foot putt.

British pros picked up the term and helped to spread it around the world. Regardless of native language, most players who shoot for the big bird these days know that it is a reminder of the eagle shown on the great seal of the United States.

Face-off

ANTICIPATING a confrontation and maybe hoping to avoid it, many a person gets involved in a face-off. This situation doesn't demand the presence of notables; it can develop between next-door neighbors or a pair of fellow workers.

Chalk this expression up to sports, rather than to meetings between world leaders.

As the start of a hockey game approaches, two players face one another tensed and poised. Each hopes to drive the puck when an official drops it between them. This hostile situation leads us to label any confrontation as a face-off.

Fall Guy

LATE in the last century, professional wrestling made a sudden spurt in popularity. Grunt and groan men fanned out from metropolitan areas and scheduled matches in dozens of small cities, often at agricultural expositions and county fairs.

Many if not most of the matches were fixed. One wrestler would agree to take a fall for a stipulated sum. His opponent would promise to handle him gently. But in order to make a match look good, the winner was often quite rough with the fellow who took the fall.

In sporting circles, it became common to speak of a loser as a *fall guy*. Firmly fixed in American speech by 1900, the sports expression came to indicate any loser, victim, or dupe.

Game Plan

PIONEER football teams took to the field with nothing better than a general strategy to be used against all opponents. That was evidently the case with the Cumberland team that was beaten 220-0 by hard-driving, pass-throwing Georgia Tech.

Many a team experienced disasters that post-game analysis suggested might have been avoided. As a result, alert coaches began scouting their opponents in order to assess their style of play. In the light of such analysis, strategy was tailored to specific foes. That is, every upcoming clash evoked a planned pattern designed to make the most of an opposing team's weakness.

This technique worked so well in sports that business leaders adopted it. Now a charitable organization planning a fund-raising campaign or a corporation about to launch a new product is almost certain to produce a detailed *game plan* long before the action begins.

Golf

YOUTHFUL King James II of Scotland wanted his subjects to be ready to go to war against England. Sporting events, he believed, required time that should be devoted to archery practice. So in 1457 he demanded of all citizens that "golf be utterly cried down and not used."

Scottish slang for "a stroke with the hand" probably supplied the name of the game prohibited by the ruler. But golf proved too stubborn, even for a king, and his edict was permitted to expire.

Decades later when James VI of Scotland became James I of England, he took the great game of his homeland to his new kingdom. Both the sport and its name became familiar to court followers as well as to noblemen. At least 375 years ago, many gave use of balls and clubs precedence over stag hunting—launching golf on its course to global conquest.

Haymaker

WHEN administered to a rival or competitor, a haymaker means that there won't be any more action any time soon. Though now linked with pugilism, the expression was originally rural.

A workman who exhibited skill and persistence with a scythe was termed a *haymaker*—because he made lots of grass ready to become hay. His repetitive motions produced the haymaker's jig, a folk dance in which his gestures were imitated.

Influence of the dance caused boxers to begin bragging about delivering blows as sudden as movements of a gyrating haymaker. Now the hoary term labels any blow good for a knockout—whether delivered in the ring or during a verbal bout around a conference table.

Jump the Gun

YOUR circle of friends probably includes at least one person prone to jump the gun any time plans are beginning to be made.

Foot races and other events that test speed and stamina are often launched by means of gunfire. A contestant who is tense and uptight, straining every muscle in order to get a fast start, is likely to jump into action at almost any sound or movement.

But a race track with a pistol-wielding official isn't the only place where a premature start can be made. Almost any group activity, whether cooperative or competitive, can provide an opportunity for someone to jump the gun.

Keep an Eye on the Ball

BALLS are basic to sports that range from polo to tennis. In all of them, a player whose attention wanders is likely to be signaled to leave the contest in order to warm the bench.

Especially in baseball, basketball, and football, it is a fatal error to lose sight of the ball for even an instant.

In the high speed game of life, whether in the home or workplace, every person is a first-string player. That means each and all should constantly keep an eye on the ball—or be keenly conscious of goals and objectives.

Left Field

UNLESS you are impelled to take part in a crusade, it might be a good idea not to give an impression that you are out in left field. At least in modern conversation, this piece of turf is reserved for oddballs and wackos.

Such characterization was appropriate in days when the phrase referred to territory rather than attitudes. Once in a while, a top-notch ball player would wander or drift far into the left field. That meant he had little or no chance to catch any ball hit down a main alley.

Fellow athletes made fun of a player found out in left field two or three times a season. Fans learned to give such a fellow the Bronx cheer when he started to move. Originating on the baseball diamond, the derogatory term entered general speech to label anyone markedly unorthodox.

On the Ball

WHEN you win an honor or achieve success against odds, chances are good that someone will say you have something "on the ball."

This term of commendation was coined by early fans of base-ball. Though it has much in common with rounders, long played in England, baseball elevates the pitcher to special prominence.

Pioneer hurlers discovered that they could deceive unwary batters by spinning the ball so that it didn't travel in a straight line. Their prowess caused the diamond-born expression to be used as a term of admiration for skill and proficiency displayed anywhere and any time.

Pinch Hitter

EVERY club and organization, along with practically all business enterprises, sometimes gets in a tight spot. Action is needed, and regular members of the team are reluctant to lead.

Regardless of the nature of the near-crisis, the situation calls for a pinch hitter—someone with highly specialized skills who will not be expected to do more than use those skills briefly.

In baseball, that describes the function of a substitute batter, called to the plate late in the game with runners on base. He may be awkward in the field and unable to throw anything but a slow, straight ball, but he is amazing with a bat.

Many situations have demanded pinch hitters for special tasks. As a result, the baseball term is applied to anyone called on to substitute for an entertainer or speaker who fails to make it to the plate as scheduled.

Play the Field

HORSE racing, "the sport of kings," attracts persons willing to take a risk. Anyone wanting some of the action, confident of having picked a winner, is likely to bet on only one animal.

Persons less sure or more cautious like to spread both risk and opportunity. Often that means placing a wager on half the horses in a race. With luck, winnings will be larger than losses when money is spread throughout the field.

Action in the realm of male-female relationships can be even more risky—and potentially more rewarding—than choices made at the pari-mutuel window. Here, too, some are bold enough to concentrate on a sure thing, while others play the field in order to hedge their bets.

Real McCoy

KID McCoy, now largely forgotten, was among the most colorful boxers of the 1890s. Outside the ring, he didn't look at all formidable. Persons who saw him for the first time often insisted that he couldn't possibly be the noted mauler.

Tradition asserts that mild-looking McCoy fired up when challenged to prove his identity. Barflies who refused to believe him were likely to wind up flat on their faces in the sawdust.

Kid McCoy's memorable demonstrations that he was the real fighter and not a look-alike created many legends. As a result, a person indisputably the authentic article is likely to be lauded as the real McCoy.

Rodeo

AT roundup time, cowboys of the Old West staged impromptu sporting events. In 1882 a Pecos, Texas, rancher offered $100 prizes in bronco riding, bulldogging, and roping. Yet these contests had no formal name until 1916. That is when a promoter turned to Spanish for "roundup" and sold tickets to his *rodeo*.

As a money-making sport, the rodeo spread throughout the world. By the time it reached Madison Square Garden in the 1940s, prize money amounted to nearly $100,000.

Today, a rodeo still rounds up big crowds.

Roll with the Punches

THERE is no way to go through life without being on the receiving end of a lot of punches. But you can try to deal with them as a skillful boxer does.

A beginner in the ring may try to slug it out with an opponent, hoping to catch sight of a haymaker in advance and dodge it. Many veterans insist that it is useless to try to avoid blows. Far better, they say, to reduce impact by bending or stepping to reduce the impact of an oncoming padded fist.

So if you adopt a pattern of rolling with life's punches, you find you can take a lot of punishment without going down for the count.

Screwball

CARL Hubbell, an all-time great baseball pitcher, started his pro career in 1923. Five years later he joined the New York Giants despite the fact that some sportswriters said no southpaw could last long on that team.

Carl's first big-league game was a disaster; opposing batters knocked him out of the box. Instead of sitting out the rest of the season, the Missouri native persuaded his manager to let him try a new throw he had developed. A ball that rolled off the outer side of the middle finger in a reverse spin looked as though it would be a curve—but behaved in opposite fashion.

Fans said there was only one thing to call a ball that behaved in such an erratic fashion. By the time the name of Hubbell's screwball was generally familiar, he had used it to strike out both Babe Ruth and Lou Gehrig in a single game.

Devotees of the diamond compared bizarre human behavior with that of a Hubbell ball that somehow broke away from a right-handed hitter. As a result, screwball is our universal label for a walking and talking oddball.

Southpaw

EVERY southpaw realizes that practically everything in modern life is geared for right-handed persons. There's a movement afoot to make some corrections, but an overwhelming preponderance of right-handedness makes progress slow.

All lefties owe the southpaw label to the influence of sports writer Finley Peter Dunne. Dunne captured a huge following during the 1880s and invented several new words, most of which didn't win general acceptance.

But he made a contribution to speech by calling attention to a feature of Chicago's great baseball park. With the home plate lined up directly west in the setting sun, it was the arm south of a line between the mound and home plate that a left-hand pitcher worked.

Dunne labeled such a player a *southpaw,* and the designation caught on. Wide use of it by baseball fans caused it to expand to name any left-handed person, not necessarily ever engaged in hurling baseballs.

Stave Off

WIDELY popular for many decades, the medieval sport of bear baiting was forced into partial eclipse. There simply were not enough animals to supply the demand. So a substitute sport pitted dogs against bulls. A big animal could disembowel a foe with one sweep of its horns, so tips were usually cut off. That enabled savage dogs often to get the better of it.

Once a bull was wounded, its owner liked to drive dogs away. This was not easy, since they were big and fierce. Most refused to stop tormenting a bull until given a smart rap with a staff or a barrel stave.

This occurrence was common enough to create a new phrase. It came to be roughly synonymous with postponement, since a fighting bull wasn't saved from death when his owner staved off a pack of dogs. A reprieve was brief; the bull would fight again and again, and ultimately be killed. By the 16th century, the notion of staving off was being applied to death or disaster of any kind.

Tee

FROM an old Scottish term, a wee pile of earth pulled together by a golfer or his caddy came to be called a *tee.* Little mounds of dirt eventually gave way to wooden tee-pegs that were whittled by hand and valued because they lifted balls rather than cushioned them.

Few pioneer clubs had rules governing the size of a tee. Many early players had elaborate ones that they prized so highly they tried to avoid breaking or losing them. Only with the advent of hard rubber and plastic has the tee become throw-away equipment.

Unique as a piece of sporting gear, the tee has spawned a vocabulary of its own. A person can "tee off"—or make a start—in a business venture as well as on the first hole.

Throw in the Towel/Sponge

BEFORE anyone thought of calling pugilism a science, sluggers went at one another helter-skelter. Even after bare fists were abandoned in favor of light gloves, victory was usually won by beef and brawn rather than skill.

Many a bruised and battered fighter found he could not get to his feet when he heard the signal for a new round to begin. Handlers of such a fellow knew that there was nothing to do but give up. So one of them would toss into the ring an article used to soak up blood—a towel or sponge.

Modern boxing is replete with rules designed to outlaw the brutality of the past. Even the lingo of the ring has become larger and richer. But in an era of instant replays for television, a person forced to give up at ringside or anywhere else is said to "throw in the towel."

Up to Scratch

EARLY bare knuckle prizefights were informal affairs. There were no rings; instead, seconds scratched parallel lines on the ground and action took place between them. At the beginning of a round, both fighters placed toes of one foot against a line.

Though the technical knockout had not yet been named, a mauler lost the bout if he was too battered to come up to the scratched line on signal. Today, a person may be unable to come up to scratch—or qualify for another round—in contests ranging from car sales to basketball games.

CHAPTER 6

THESE MAKE SENSE!

"It is better to understand little than to misunderstand a lot."
—Anatole France, *Revolt of the Angels*

Many of our everyday words and phrases make complete sense; they point to events and activities that are familiar and readily understood. Their development has been logical and orderly. Yet most of them have additional meanings that we employ without a thought because they are so familiar.

ALSO-RAN
AWOL
BACKLOG
BATS IN ONE'S BELFRY
BETTER HALF
BIKINI
BITE THE BULLET
BRAINSTORMING
BUSHED
CASH ON THE BARREL HEAD
CAUGHT RED-HANDED
COUNTDOWN
DISGUISE
EASY AS FALLING OFF A LOG
END OF ONE'S ROPE
FALLOUT
GAME
GRUBSTAKE
GUM UP THE WORKS
HAND-TO-MOUTH
HOTBED
LOCK, STOCK, AND BARREL

MAKE THE GRADE
MAKE THINGS HUM
MONKEYSHINES
MOONLIGHT
OLIVE BRANCH
ON THE BEAM
ON HOLD
OUT OF TOUCH
OUTLANDISH
PULL ONE'S LEG
RACK ONE'S BRAINS
READ BETWEEN THE
   LINES
READ ONE LOUD AND
   CLEAR
RUB THE WRONG WAY
SCORE
SPONGE
STUMPED
UP TO SNUFF
WHIPPERSNAPPER

SEE ALSO: Adam's Apple, Asleep at the Switch, Back Number, Blue Chips, Boycott, Bumper, Cold Feet, Cook One's Goose, Crawfish, Cut and Dried, Dead as a Doornail, Decibel, Diesel, Elbow Room, Fast Lane, Figurehead, Flip Side, Greenhorn, Half-baked, Haul Over the Coals, Hooker, Jackpot, Keep a Stiff Upper Lip, Knuckle Under, Lion's Share, Meltdown, Open and Shut, Pass the Buck, Pigeonhole, Play Possum, Poinsettia, Prima Donna, Pull Up Stakes, Right Down My Alley, Slapstick, Stuffed Shirt, Subdivision, Talk Turkey, Two to Tango

Also-ran

MANY horse races end when the first three animals cross the line. Others in the field follow, but the order in which they finish may not be announced.

Newspapers of the 19th century made readers familiar with animals that placed in major races. All three were frequently described, with their times, owners, and winnings listed. Toward the end of such a story, it was a common practice to mention many or all of the horses that also ran.

Presidential elections came more and more to resemble horse races with crowded fields. Greenback, Anti-Monopoly, United Labor, National Silver, and other new political parties were formed. In reporting results of an election, newspapers dismissed many an aspirant for the White House as an also-ran—one who was so far back in the field that his finish order wasn't computed.

By the turn of the century, the political term borrowed from the racetrack was being applied to a person badly beaten in any competition.

AWOL

THESE days, it's possible for one of your fellow workers to go "AWOL" or walk off the job without giving notice. Earlier, this form of conduct was limited to members of the military.

A fellow wearing the uniform of his country's army or navy or marine corps was never under any delusions about what he could and couldn't do. Discipline is basic to military life.

But many a buck private in the rear rank or brand-new member of a ship's crew simply walked off his base or vessel when the notion struck him. When discovered and placed under arrest—as he almost always was, sooner or later—he was listed on the roster as having been "absent without official leave."

The initial letters of the damning record, A.W.O.L., became the brand-new word, *AWOL*.

Backlog

FRONTIERSMEN faced a serious problem in regard to a source of fire. Matches were rare and flint and steel often failed in damp weather. So many pioneers tried to keep a fire burning without interruption for months at a time.

A big green log, next to stones in the back of a fireplace, would smolder for days. Dry wood would be laid in front of it to burn and the next morning the backlog yielded embers from which a new blaze could be started.

As a rule, the backlog was not used for fuel, although it could be pulled out and burned in an emergency. Today we call any sort of reserve a *backlog*.

Bats in One's Belfry

MOVIES and television programs that depict small town life a century ago are usually correct in at least one respect—the tallest structure in a village is the church. Its bell tower, surmounted by a steeple, is not enclosed. Rather, it is open so that the ringing of the bell may be heard afar.

Such a structure is about the closest manmade thing there is to a cavern—the natural sleeping place of bats. As night approached, their swirling and swooping seemed to indicate total and utter confusion.

A bewildered or befuddled person whose thinking was erratic was said to have "bats in his belfry."

Better Half

PURITANS and other zealots brought many religious terms into common speech. Doctrine said that the soul and body, together, make up a person. Since the spiritual self was considered more important, it came to be called the better half.

It took a genius to see new meaning in the old expression.

Writing in his *Arcadia,* Sir Philip Sidney applied it to the husband-wife union rather than the body-soul bond.

Long used to indicate either partner in the half-and-half match that is marriage, the inherited term was modified by male gallantry. For some generations, every husband with a spark of love has called the woman who makes up 50 percent of his life his "better half."

Bikini

IN 1947, the first swimsuit designed to reveal practically every asset of a woman's figure went on sale. Wondering what to call the daring garment, makers noticed that males who saw it for the first time reacted like it was an atomic bomb.

Scientists used the Marshall Islands in 1946 for a crucial experiment. Having moved 167 natives to Rongerik, "Operation Crossroads" head William H. R. Blandy used the Bikini atoll for tests of the atomic bomb.

Comparing the impact of the new swimsuit with world-shaking events in the Pacific, fashion experts called it the *Bikini.* Once that name was given to the explosive garment, the only change has been the dropping of capitalization.

Bite the Bullet

NEXT time you are caught between a rock and a hard place, with no good way out, you may decide to bite the bullet and push ahead. Sometimes that is the only alternative to calling things quits.

That was the case with many a Civil War casualty. Carried from the field with a mangled arm or leg, Billy Yank or Johnny Reb could not turn away when a surgeon with a bloody apron approached with a scalpel or saw.

With lives hanging in the balance, supplies of whiskey and other painkillers often ran out. That meant the best the medics could do for a fellow was to offer him a soft-lead bullet. Placed between the teeth, it did not give much, but it was better than nothing. It made amputation a little easier to bite the bullet instead of lying on the table screaming.

Brainstorming

ANYTIME you come up with a really new idea, it may be the product of individual or group brainstorming.

F. W. H. Myers, a distinguished leader of investigators, founded the Society for Psychical Research in 1882. His movement soon became the talk of the Western world. With initial study coming to focus upon telepathy, editors compared it with radio and suggested that brain waves make it possible. Engineers already knew that electrical storms affect many types of communication. That made it an easy step to compare a radio that acted strangely with an electrical storm in the brain.

Still far from understanding such states, we know that they somehow foster creativity and spontaneity. Which explains why brainstorming is regularly sponsored by some of our biggest research laboratories and corporations.

Bushed

WHEN you find yourself exhausted at the end of an unusually hard day, you may describe yourself as being *bushed*. If so, you can thank the early Dutch settlers in the New World for the colorful word.

Some of them came from the crowded Low Countries early in the 17th century. For a generation, thousands left their homeland every year. Wilderness land and uncleared forest tracts were given a special name by these settlers. English-speaking neighbors modified their word and began describing any dense region as *bush* country.

Even the hardiest of adventurers sometimes found bush so thick that it seemed to get the better of him. After a particularly difficult time trying to hack out a trail, a fellow was likely to protest that he was "bushed," or exhausted. Spreading from the frontier, the American-born term is now included in the vocabulary of ordinary folk as well as outdoorsmen and adventurers.

Cash on the Barrel Head

MANY a frontier saloon consisted of a lean-to shed, a couple of barrels of whiskey, and three or four stools. With barrels standing on end, a plank lying on top of them made a great counter. When the barkeeper had no sturdy plank, he was likely to use the top of a barrel as his counter.

With payment in advance the rule of the road, a patron wanting a drink was often told to put his coins on the barrel head. Failure to comply meant that, for at least one customer, the house suddenly went dry.

New fiscal devices mean that a purchaser can now offer a personal check, credit card, money order, securities, or traveler's check. No matter which is offered, anyone who pays before delivery is compared with yesterday's tippler and said to have put "cash on the barrel head."

Caught Red-handed

A COMMON felony of the past involved the butchering of another person's pig, sheep, or cow. Under legal codes that prevailed for generations, possession of freshly killed meat did not constitute proof of guilt. Only a man caught with the blood of an animal on his hands was sure to be convicted.

It was a waste of breath to plead for mercy after having been caught red-handed. That happened frequently enough for the expression naming guilt to survive long after most folk ceased to raise their own meat. Now we use it to indicate detection of an act of stealth—whether or not a law is violated.

Countdown

ABSOLUTE precision was the name of the game when the United States began to launch spacecraft. No meticulously timed earlier events made lasting impressions upon so many persons. Millions watched on television as a launch came near.

"Ten . . . nine . . . eight . . . seven . . . six . . ." With blastoff virtually at hand, every instant seemed to have been stretched—yet each new second saw the dramatic moment come closer.

Used earlier in tests of atomic bombs, the special system of counting made zero its end point rather than its beginning. Regardless of duration, any period of tense and expectant waiting now takes a Space Age designation as *countdown*.

Disguise

FOR 400 years after the fall of Rome, Europe was in turmoil. When stable political patterns were formed, rulers demanded strict conformity. Written and oral codes eventually prescribed every detail of a person's guise, or dress. Color, shape, and material of a guise indicated occupation, rank, and place of residence.

Medieval sharpers saw a golden opportunity to assume false positions. By putting on appropriate clothing and going to a strange district, a sharp-witted person could pose as a goldsmith, physician, monk, or even knight.

By 1350 imposters in false guise were so common that any masquerade came to be known as a disguise. Few persons adopted such an outfit unless they wished to become imposters or perpetrate hoaxes. Hence the venerable label took on sinister connotations still taken for granted except on Hallowe'en.

Easy as Falling Off a Log

DURING an earlier era in America the sport of logrolling was widely enjoyed. A common version involved logs on the surface of a pond or lake. Men rolled logs from one side to the other while managing to remain balanced.

To a city slicker watching this activity for the first time, it seemed ridiculously easy to master. Invited to try rolling a log, such a fellow almost always wound up in the drink within seconds.

A single dunking administered by a rolling log was enough to make a lasting impression. Anything that required no skill whatever came to be described as "easy as falling off a log."

End of One's Rope

EUROPEANS invented and used a number of elaborate devices designed to give a horse freedom to graze, but not to run away. Intricate hobbles and tethers seldom proved more effective than a length of rope, however.

With one end of a rope fastened to the bridle and the other to a post, a rider could rest while his mount filled its stomach. Many an animal moved to the end of the rope, then strained to eat grass barely within reach.

Like a tethered horse, a human who has exhausted all resources is at the end of his or her rope.

Fallout

PHYSICISTS who developed and tested early atomic explosives were a long way from fully understanding what they did. The power of a blast was obvious and measurable, but it took only a few experiments to discover unexpected aftereffects.

When the bomb was dropped on Hiroshima, Japan, much of the city was leveled. Simultaneously, minute particles of radioactive material went high into the air. Some were blown for many miles before they fell to the Earth's surface days later. In time, scientists learned that such fallout could be extremely dangerous or even lethal.

A situation may not really be over when it seems that it is. Sometimes there is fallout—aftereffects not anticipated at the time of the explosion.

Game

COCKFIGHTING, known since antiquity, surged to popularity in 12th-century England. Some schoolmasters permitted pupils to stage contests—on condition that dead birds be given to teachers. King Henry VIII added a cockpit to the grounds at Whitehall, and most major towns scheduled bouts at regular intervals.

Admiration for a notable gamecock led to a still-frequent usage in speech. Because feisty humans were widely compared with birds ready to fight, we describe a person of unusual courage as being *game*.

Grubstake

GRUB was in common use by the 11th century. At that time, it was a verb of action that referred to digging or breaking the ground. By 1600 it had become attached to food produced by grubbing; then it came to indicate food in general.

During the same period, bear and bull fights were common. Usually an animal was tied to a stake, then beset by dogs. Persons who wagered that the bear or bull would defeat the dogs were literally backing the animal who was at stake. So the wager itself was described as being "at stake."

Two ancient streams of speech met during the hectic days of the Gold Rush. Merchants often gave food to miners in return for a share in any future discovery. Since such a supply of grub was gambled as though it were at stake in a poker game, it came to be known as a *grubstake*.

Gum up the Works

VETERAN lumbermen who reached North America very early could hardly believe their eyes. It seemed impossible that a single continent could boast such a profusion and a variety of fine trees. One of them, the sweet gum, stretched in a broad belt from Connecticut to Missouri and from Florida to Mexico. Now often called the red gum, the tree is still a major source of lumber.

Aside from its size and abundance, the gum interested pioneers because of its fragrant resin. Lumbermen didn't like the stuff since it clogged up their saws. But venturesome boys discovered it was pleasant to chew, so they frequently went on gumming expeditions. After gathering a quantity of the sticky stuff, a youngster was likely to be daubed from head to foot. Gum was hard to wash from clothing and all but impossible to clean from hair.

Proverbial sayings came to include many references to the stuff. As a result, any person throwing a project into confusion is still compared with a resin-smeared boy and charged with having gummed up the works.

Hand-to-Mouth

IN 1586, Great Britain experienced a failure of grain crops. Thousands starved during a period of famine, and multitudes who survived became thin from hunger. Food was often so scarce that when a person managed to get a bit, he behaved like Kurdish refugees in 20th-century Iraq. As soon as a person had a piece of bread in his hand, he would thrust it into his mouth to make sure no one would snatch it away.

Hand-to-mouth existence was a fact of life until modern times. So many persons practiced it that we still use the phrase to label substandard living conditions.

Hotbed

WE include this term in everyday speech as a result of borrowing from practices of gardeners and farmers.

Long ago, it was discovered that seeds given a bit of protection will sprout earlier than those dropped into the ground without special attention. Even a thin cloth cover will raise the temperature of earth underneath it for several hours a day.

The earliest hotbeds were heated with fermenting manure and covered with glass—forerunners to today's greenhouses. They produced so abundantly that any institution or neighborhood yielding an abundant crop of like-minded persons took the name of the gardener's special seed plot.

Lock, Stock, and Barrel

WHEN you decide to put everything you have into an enterprise, associates are likely to comment that you're going for it, "lock, stock, and barrel." Anyone can take a half-hearted approach, but gumption is required for a decision to go all the way.

Muskets and rifles involved three major components: a carefully crafted lock, a stock made of wood, and a stout metal barrel. Each member of this trio was useless without the other two. Collectively, they came to indicate wholeness, completion, and later, unhesitating and unreserved action.

Make the Grade

WHEN you succeed in fund-raising or mastery of a new golf course, you "make the grade."

U.S. railroads had only forty miles of track in 1830. Expanding from that base, engineers found that the pulling power of an iron horse is greatly affected by the slope, or grade, of a track. When a train moves from a level section to a 1 percent grade, five times as much steam is needed.

A grade of 3 percent or more challenged the power of locomotives and called for a celebration when the top was reached. Hence anyone who overcame obstacles of any kind was lauded by railroaders as having made the grade.

Make Things Hum

ARE you a go-getter whose ideas and leadership can put a business or a cause into motion? If so, you belong to that rare breed whose members can make things hum.

Once the spinning of cotton moved from households into mills, the hum of machinery came to be a symbol of Yankee progress. There were frequent breakdowns, though, during which a mill fell silent. It took mechanical knowledge and management skill to produce the distinctive sound linked with productivity. Spreading from the processing of cotton, the mill-born phrase came to stand for proficiency in any type of activity or enterprise.

Monkeyshines

UNTIL recent decades, exotic animals viewed by the public were always kept behind bars. Even the famous zoological gardens of England and Europe made little or no effort to put inmates into their natural habitats.

Monkeys, crowd-pleasers from the time they were first exhibited, are dexterous and smart. Like humans, they are quickly bored by monotony. So when a knot of admirers gathered before a cage squealing with delight and tossing peanuts, a monkey responded by putting on a good act.

Jumping, swinging about the cage, chattering and often seeming to grin broadly, little showmen knew how to work the audience. Bolder antics meant more peanuts.

Because a person believed to be trying to win friendship or admiration was said to "shine around," antics of a monkey seeming to beg for acceptance were termed *monkeyshines*.

Moonlight

THESE days, many people decide to moonlight by holding down a second job in addition to a first one. Few descriptive terms are more appropriate than this one.

Its birth coincided with the advent of the forty-hour work week. Many employees accustomed to a fifty-six-hour week hardly knew what to do with the extra time; besides, they needed additional money.

Night afforded lots of opportunities to take on a second job, usually part-time. Now that industries and businesses operate around the clock, lots of persons working a second or third shift moonlight in broad daylight.

Olive Branch

EGYPTIANS began experimenting with a native shrub at least 4,000 years ago. Soon they produced varieties that yielded fine oil. As a result, the olive came into cultivation around the entire Mediterranean basin.

In the biblical story of the great deluge, a freshly plucked olive branch was the first thing to give hope to Noah and his shipmates. Soon this harbinger of good tidings was followed by a promise that the flood would never be repeated.

As a result of that memorable incident, an olive branch became a symbol of peace and good will. Even in lands far too cold for the evergreen tree with edible fruit, the expression born in Egypt is almost universally understood.

On the Beam

IT'S logical and natural for colleagues who see that you are headed straight toward a solution of a problem to say they're glad you are "on the beam."

Our earliest aviators had no guidance systems, and airports were not equipped to send radio beams into the air. Wilbur and Orville Wright and other pioneers flew strictly by the seat of their pants.

Introduction of guidance beams from the ground with receiving sets on planes worked a miraculous transformation. By using them a pilot could locate a beam and use instruments in order to follow it to a base.

Small wonder that a person or a plan or an enterprise not wavering from an objective is lauded as being "on the beam."

On Hold

A PLAN or enterprise described as being on hold comes from the use of modern telephones—exactly as might be expected.

It was a great day for American business when Alexander Graham Bell's invention became available with two or more lines and a special button. For the first time, "hold" meant that a conversation could be interrupted and kept alive while attention turned momentarily to another line or activity.

So many callers have been put on hold that the communications term expanded to mean any postponement or temporary suspension.

Out of Touch

LATE in the 18th century, many European military leaders moved toward use of tighter formations. Men were required to maintain rigid patterns even when on the march. As a practical way of regulating his space, the soldier in the ranks had to be sure that his swinging elbows would touch those of comrades on each side.

Whenever there was a gap in a line, it meant that some man was literally out of touch. Civilians adopted the military term and expanded its meaning to indicate any situation in which a person has lost contact.

Outlandish

NEARLY every body of speech reflects suspicion of foreigners, or casts aspersions on them. That was the case with

Anglo-Saxon English, which brought the Dutch word *uitlander* to British soil. By the 1600s, this word became *outlander.*

Costumes and customs from other lands can seem odd. As a result, any comment concerning an outlander was likely to produce a laugh. Henry Fielding took advantage of this when he wrote the famous novel, *Tom Jones.* In it, he jeered at a young woman whose clothing he described as being "outlandish."

This and other literary appearances gave respectability to the earthy old peasants' term. Unchanged in spelling since the 17th century, outlandish is now applied to anything bizarre or uncouth—whether it is of foreign or native origin.

Pull One's Leg

ANYONE who sets out to pull your leg will have a prank or practical joke in mind. Though the expression makes a lot of sense, its original meaning was far from funny.

Thieves operating in London's underworld didn't roll their victims until modern times. Instead, a mugger worked in partnership with a tripper-up. This rogue used wire or rope or a walking stick to trip pedestrians who ventured into alleys. Once a victim was prostrate, an accomplice of the tripper-up stripped him of valuables.

Since footpads really did pull the leg of a person in the process of tripping, their actions created a phrase used to name any mishap leading to stumbling. Over a period of centuries it came to be applied to the practice of making fun by causing someone to betray ignorance. This means that the victim of a modern tripper-up isn't likely to be robbed of a wallet or a purse—but may lose his or her temper.

Rack One's Brains

SINCE the beginning of modern times, Dutch craftsmen have been noted for skill and ingenuity. One of them invented a device used for stretching leather in the process of tanning. From terms conveying the idea of drawing out or stretching, it was given a name that later took the form *rack*.

Civil authorities borrowed racks from tanners and adapted them for use in questioning suspects. With wrists tied to one roller and ankles to another, a wretch who was stretched on the rack could literally be torn apart.

No other method of torture was more effective or more widely used. All civilized nations eventually outlawed the instrument adapted from the leather trade, but by the time it became obsolete it had made a lasting impression upon speech. Consequently, to rack your brains in search of an answer is a form of mental torture.

Read Between the Lines

SIMPLE methods of writing in code were devised long ago. Both Julius Caesar and Charlemagne sent battle reports in cipher. But the rise of cryptography as a science dates from the 16th century.

Rulers, diplomats, military leaders and business executives adopted the practice of writing in code. Some personal papers of England's Charles I were so obscure that they were not deciphered until about 1850.

To a person ignorant of the code, a secret paper was meaningless. Ordinary folk fascinated with this mystery concluded that the meaning was not in lines of gibberish, but in the space between them. Writing between lines with invisible ink strengthened this notion.

Except among intelligence agencies, interest in secret writing eventually waned. But language had already been enriched. Spawned from literal views of cryptographs, reading between the lines came to suggest the finding of inferences in any document.

Read One Loud and Clear

ANYTIME someone says he or she reads you loud and clear, complete understanding is meant.

Notoriously fickle in its early days, radio was prone to fade out for no apparent reason. When a two-way conversation was involved, common sense dictated that one party inquire of the other about receptivity. "I read you loud and clear" became the standard formula meaning splendid reception.

Significant always, this condition was all-important when a pilot was talking with a member of the ground control crew at an airport. Since communication is inherently slippery, face-to-face talk in which all parties read all others loud and clear takes place only occasionally.

Rub the Wrong Way

IF you are sensitive, it may not take much to rub you the wrong way. A thoughtless remark, a challenging look, or inattention to what you just said may be enough to do the trick.

Long ago, it took a different set of actions to spawn the expression.

Wealthy ladies of the Colonial era were proud of their wide-board oak floors. At least once a week, servants wet-rubbed and then dry-rubbed surfaces. Though simple and routine, these tasks involved running mops along the grain of the wood. A careless worker sometimes mopped across the grain, producing streaks on the floor. To her mistress, such cleaning was worse than none.

Vexation at a domestic who rubbed the wrong way was common enough to cause the housekeeping phrase to label clumsy or inept dealing with persons as well as with floors.

Score

LONG before pencils and papers were available for making memos, herdsmen of Britain devised a way to count their sheep. From an Old Norse expression naming a notch or tally cut into a stick, any group of twenty objects or animals came to be known as a score.

Shepherds may have counted orally up to twenty, then cut a notch before starting to number another batch. Well established by the 13th century, this usage was modified by sportsmen who made cricket a national pastime. As a result, whether recorded by notches in a stick or by electronic devices, total points made in competition constitute the score.

Sponge

TRADERS began bringing a few sponges to Britain before the beginning of written history. Yet for many centuries, the strange plant from the sea remained scarce except in warm coastal regions.

Exotic though it was, a sponge was customarily put to only one general use. It was ideal for wiping slates used by scholars in village schools. So it signified a significant upward step when a schoolmaster threw out his supply of old rags and began using sponges.

A person seeing one of these things for the first time usually marveled at its capacity to soak up water. As a result, the name of the schoolroom tool was applied to persons who excelled at soaking up the tavern keeper's liquids.

Such a two-legged sponge was usually down on his luck and addicted to wheedling gifts and loans. As a result, anyone who habitually avoids paying his own way is said to sponge off relatives and friends.

Stumped

TO U.S. pioneers who built cabins and barns of logs, trees they didn't need were a nuisance. It was difficult to cut and burn them in order to clear patches of land for farming—and stumps were even more troublesome than trees.

Frontiersmen frequently swapped work with one another in

clearing new ground. After a logrolling, it was necessary to have another gathering for the purpose of pulling up stumps.

Skilled workers prided themselves on knowing how to get big ones out of the ground. But it was not unusual for a veteran to admit defeat at the hands of a particularly stubborn stump. As a result, we say that a person is stumped when a job proves to be beyond his or her capabilities.

Up to Snuff

DURING the 17th century, Europeans developed a great passion for finely powdered tobacco, or *snuff.* So many Englishmen became fond of it that it was in nearly universal use among them. Users customarily grated tobacco on the spot. For this purpose, they carried around boxes that held coarse tobacco, with spoons and graters attached.

Advent of commercially ground mixtures brought an end to the use of individual snuff graters. But connoisseurs continued to pride themselves on being able to distinguish good from poor. A sharp fellow, not easily deceived, was said to be up to snuff—or able to discern quality at a sniff.

In popular speech, a negative form of the phrase came to label a simpleton or a gullible fellow. At first the new term was used literally. One derided as "not up to snuff" was considered an amateur at judging powdered tobacco. Soon the expression expanded and became a label of ridicule for any person or product considered to be less than discerning or below standard.

Whippersnapper

NO doubt you have noticed that any person who is called a whippersnapper is either a juvenile or a learner who is barely dry behind the ears. The full title addressed to such a person by the boss or used out of hearing is likely to be "young whippersnapper."

One of the easiest skills learned by a greenhorn cowboy is that of snapping a black snake whip. Decades ago, lots of fellows who could not bulldog a steer or rope a maverick prided themselves on being able to strut into a village while calling attention to themselves by snapping their whips.

Only neophytes, young fellows who did not even tote guns, followed this practice. But it was common enough to lead folk who never saw a trail herd's dust to adopt whippersnapper as just the right label for any brash but unskilled beginner.

CHAPTER *7*

DISTANCE LENDS ENCHANTMENT: WORDS FROM AFAR

"Far different do things appear far off
Than when we scan them close at hand."
— Euripides, *Ion,* about 419 B.C.

Many words and phrases are naturalized citizens, born and reared far from the streams of speech that produced the English language. Some have been polished so smooth by frequent use that they aren't immediately recognized as having come from a great distance. Were they not in our working vocabularies, everyday speech would be less colorful and precise.

ALIBI	HAUL OVER THE COALS
APPLE OF ONE'S EYE	HIGH MUCKETY-MUCK
ATLAS	JADED
BABEL	JUNK
BALLYHOO	KOWTOW
BANDIT	LUNATIC FRINGE
BLUE JEANS	MACHO
BLUE RIBBON	MEANDERING
BOYCOTT	PANIC
CHARACTER	PIPE DREAM
CHOW	SCAPEGOAT
COLOGNE	SHAMPOO
DRUG ON THE MARKET	SPILL THE BEANS
ELEVENTH HOUR	STEM-WINDER
GUNG HO	TABOO
GURU	WHITE ELEPHANT
GYP JOINT	YEN

SEE ALSO: Achilles' Heel, Alcohol, Bourbon, Braille, Cocktail, Corporation, Cut a Dido, Deviled, Dollar, Donnybrook, Dun, Dunce, French Leave, Gadget, Galvanized, Gringo, Harlot, Kingpin, Limerick, Moron, Prima Donna, Slush Fund, Tycoon

Alibi

COURTROOM practices are slow to change. Lawyers continued to use Latin long after it was abandoned in everyday speech.

A Latin term meaning "elsewhere" was standard in criminal cases for centuries. Many a defense attorney rested his case upon evidence that his client was *alibi* at the time of the crime.

Use of the centuries-old term was so common that it entered modern speech with no change in spelling and little in meaning. An accused person who is able to establish an alibi is almost like a citizen in the realm of the caesars who answered an accusation by saying he or she was elsewhere when the deed was done.

Apple of One's Eye

THOUGH your eyes have no structures that make moderns think of fruit, a person you love dearly is likely to be called the "apple of your eye." This age-old expression is a product of literary influence.

Round Pippin apples grown in early Israel reminded some folk of the pupil of an eye, leading to vernacular comparisons between the two objects. When this usage appeared in Scripture, it probably indicated something like "the apple-shaped organ that we see in the middle of an eye."

Supreme value of eyes is frequently stressed in holy writ. With fine shades of meaning lost in translation, English-language versions of Scripture include a number of references to the structure that ancients considered to be fruitlike. This usage caused anything extremely precious, regardless of shape, to be termed the apple of one's eye.

Atlas

ANYTIME you make detailed plans for a trip, you are likely to seek information from an atlas—using a volume whose name has traveled a long way through both space and time.

Greek mythology described Atlas, once one of the Titans who ruled the universe, as holding a flat earth upon his shoulders. Had he not held it firmly, verbal lore insisted, travel would have been impossible upon a vibrating earth. That idea caused geographers of later centuries to dedicate published collections of maps to the man who made travel possible.

With capitalization dropped and earth-bearing Altas largely forgotten, the name of the imaginary figure from the past now designates any book consisting primarily of maps.

Babel

OUR term for confused noise, in which individual sounds are difficult or impossible to distinguish, came to us from the Middle East.

Babylon, believed by some scholars to have been located in present-day Iraq, was known to ancient Hebrews as Babel. It was there, according to the Bible, that the people tried to build a tower to heaven so that their ruler could converse with God on his level. As punishment, Jehovah caused all the citizens to speak several languages rather than one.

The story of the city whose citizens suddenly found shouting didn't foster communication was preserved in Scripture. Persons who learned it came to use the city's name as a label for any chaotic uproar such as a hubbub or a hullabaloo.

Ballyhoo

THESE days, few potentially profitable new pharmaceuticals and no new models of cars come on the market without extensive ballyhoo. This name for attention-catching advertising seems as though it might have been coined on Madison Avenue.

On the contrary, advertising executives who resort to this practice may owe its name to events in faraway County Cork, Ireland. Tradition holds that residents of the village of Ballyhooly made a name for themselves by debating nearly every local issue as though the fate of the world depended upon it.

Located not far from Mallow, the town became known throughout the British Isles as a result of the way citizens talked on and on. Members of Parliament charged that some of the debates were as loud as goings-on in Ballyhooly, and tabloid newspapers eventually adopted the comparison.

With its final syllable dropped, the name of the noisy Irish town came to label any loud debate. Now it stands for the special kinds of noise made by candidates for public office and by purveyors of merchandise.

Bandit

UNTIL recent centuries, few European states had effective police forces. A man who ventured outside a city could depend upon little or no protection from officers.

In this situation, Italians discovered that banishment of a lawbreaker constituted a severe punishment. Brought before a crowd of residents, such a person was proclaimed to be a public enemy and was told that no town would give him shelter. He then had to leave the security of the walled city. Originally from the Latin *bandire* meaning "to proclaim," the subject of a formal proclamation was called a *bandito*.

Finding it difficult to survive alone, the bandito usually joined other outcasts. Bands of them lurked in the mountains of southern Europe. Forbidden to follow normal trades, they lived by robbery and murder.

English visitors to Italy listened to bandito tales and in the 16th century took the title back to the island kingdom. Used in a play from the stage into modern speech as a fit label for any armed robber.

Blue Jeans

MANY European cities once specialized in making a distinctive cloth of some kind. Heavy twilled cotton from Janua (modern Genoa) was called *jean* after its point of origin. In 1495, King Henry VIII of England bought 262 bolts of it. Jeans, or male garments made from jean, were prized because they didn't wear out quickly.

Undyed fabric was used for generations before a batch of cloth dyed blue was turned over to cutters and sewers. The resulting blue jeans quickly made undyed ones obsolete.

Today, trousers made from the Genoa fabric aren't fashionable until they have been bleached to remove spots and streaks of blue.

Blue Ribbon

PARTLY because blue dye of good quality was scarce and expensive, rulers of at least two nations elevated the color to prominence.

In France, induction into the ancient order of the Holy Ghost was the highest honor a knight could achieve. Membership in it was symbolized by a blue scarf that ordinary people were forbidden to wear.

English monarchs who wished to confer lasting honor upon a soldier or civil servant bestowed the Order of the Garter. A ribbon of bright blue constituted the order's badge.

Inevitably, judges of contests began awarding blue ribbons to persons who placed first. Whether or not a strand of fabric is used, anyone who wins or is awarded a blue ribbon knows that it signifies the highest possible honor.

Boycott

HAVE you ever participated in a boycott in which you refuse to buy certain merchandise?

Persons who engage in protests of this sort are following the example of Irish farmers. During the era of the famous potato famine, Capt. Charles C. Boycott was managing the estates of the Earl of Erne. When tenants couldn't pay, they were evicted.

Bands of County Mayo citizens got together and launched organized resistance. Merchants refused to sell to Boycott. He was hung in effigy and greeted with jeers when he appeared in public. Many of his employer's fences were torn down. Household servants were subjected to such harassment that they slipped away and sought other jobs.

This protest movement was so successful that Captain Boycott eventually left Ireland. Attached to organized protest movements, his name lingered in speech. By the time he had been gone twenty-five or thirty years, the Irish Land League launched boycotts against persons who didn't agree to its demands.

Such an imprint was made that the overseer's name has entered half a dozen languages to label refusal to deal with a business, an employer, a nation, or a line of merchandise.

Character

METAL workers of classical Greece developed a special tool used in marking. In time, such a character or instrument—whose name was altered in passing through several languages—came to designate any mark made by it.

Medieval courts made much use of characters. Convicted of murder, a person given penal servitude instead of the gallows was branded with the character "M." In the same fashion, an arsonist's forehead or shoulder bore the character "A."

Anyone branded by authorities was marked for life. One glance at a character told a stranger what offense had been committed.

As a result, the term indicating a branded letter came to stand for the sum total of a person's moral qualities.

Chow

YOUR appetite may not be big enough to make you a chow hound, but you probably join the rest of us in enjoying putting your feet under the table.

In many parts of the Orient you can't do that, of course. But chow has been available in China for centuries. Mandarins used more elegant words, while peasants employed chow to name any everyday dish—including dog meat.

Early explorers and adventurers had to eat chow, often with no idea of its components, in order to survive. They heard the word so often that they took it back to Europe as a label for food in general.

Chow-chow, also pure Chinese, seems to have been in use earlier than its abbreviation. When a servant performed a kowtow and said "Chow-chow!" that meant food prepared from a variety of ingredients was being offered. Since the delicacy was made from finely chopped ingredients, any chopped mixture on an American table may be offered as chow-chow.

Cologne

DO you prefer to whiff cologne rather than the heavier scent of perfume?

Pure air helped persuade the Roman emperor Claudius to chose a special site for a city. Named the Colonia Agrippina in honor of his wife, the place flourished. By the time it had become a beautiful German city of cathedrals, it was known as Cologne in England and France, and Köln in Germany.

An Italian merchant who lived there learned to make a light scent by adding alcohol and aromatic oils to traditional perfume bases. His Cologne water, or eau de Cologne, prompted dozens and then hundreds of perfumers to adapt his technique.

Drug on the Market

DYES and exotic foodstuffs were long given the same name as medications. A few European ports became famous as centers of trade in such drugs as Coventry blue, chocolate, tea, and sarsaparilla.

During periods of scarcity, imported commodities of this sort were in great demand. But when several cargoes of a single drug happened to reach a city simultaneously, the market became glutted.

Especially in the case of tea, periods of overabundance were frequent. From raw land to silicon chips, anything in such supply that it attracts few buyers is still called a *drug on the market*.

Eleventh Hour

FROM the Babylonians, Greeks and Hebrews adopted use of sundials whose faces were divided into twelve segments. Hours were counted from daylight to dusk, with darkness coming at the twelfth. A famous New Testament parable (Matthew 20:1-16) expresses the idea of lateness by saying some would-be laborers came at the eleventh hour of sunlight.

Western civilization later modified timekeeping so that twelve o'clock came to mark both noon and midnight. That means the sun is hardly halfway across the heavens at eleven o'clock in the morning, and has disappeared by that hour at night.

Force of the New Testament story is such that we still borrow from it. Despite the real position of the sun at the time, we continue to say that the eleventh hour is the last possible time to make a decision or to take action.

Gung Ho

MANY a gung ho sales trainer or sports fan manages to raise the level of enthusiasm of others. That is appropriate, since early usage of the ancient term involved groups of persons.

A few Europeans managed to get into China as soon as westerners began to be tolerated. All such visitors were awed by the Great Wall and other public works constructed by human labor. Big projects still under way employed vast numbers of coolies. At an overseer's signal, they shouted "Gung ho!" in unison in order to synchronize movements.

It became more popular in the west when it became a slogan adopted by the U.S. Marines under General E. Carlson in World War II. Less than fully understood, the Chinese phrase for "work together" was applied to actions of any enthusiast.

Guru

REGARDLESS of how you earn your living, it's likely that there is at least one nationally recognized guru in your field.

Since that expert may never have been outside the U.S., it seems a bit odd that we confer on him or her a centuries-old title from India. In that ancient land, it takes a lot of living for a person to become venerable—or *guru*.

Gurus swarmed into the U.S. late in the 19th century. Many proved to be charismatic leaders who attracted wide followings, and most were seemingly ageless. More interested in leadership skills than in age, we adopted the title and applied it to any outstanding authority.

Gyp Joint

IF you've ever been separated from your cash, with little or nothing to show for it, you may have been taken to the cleaners in a gyp joint.

Gypsies first appeared in England in the early 16th century, and were thought to be from Egypt because of their features. A person swindled by one of these wanderers was gypped—played for a sucker by an Egyptian, or gipsy.

In spite of the fact that some gypsies were honest and above-board, their name attached to a tavern or shop where customers got the short end of the stick. Such a spot has nothing to do with Egyptians, but is closely related to another establishment whose name sounds much the same. However, in the early days the clip joint was more highly specialized than the gyp joint.

Haul Over the Coals

IF you threaten to haul someone over the coals, the object of your suspicion or wrath is in for real trouble.

A tongue lashing is nothing compared to fearful ordeals faced by accused persons for many centuries. In the belief that God protects the innocent but permits the guilty to suffer, a trial often consisted of a physical test.

Frequently a suspect was forced to walk barefoot over a bed of hot coals. Burns brought an automatic verdict of guilty. But anyone who passed the heat test without injury was judged to be innocent. Onlookers at such a trial remembered it so vividly that its name attached to a severe test even if fire was not involved.

High Muckety-Muck

PRACTICALLY every organization, as well as every industry and business, has a "high muckety-muck." Lots of citizens also know someone who holds that unofficial title in financial or social circles.

Traced to its roots, this earthy phrase means simply, "A person who has plenty to eat."

It appears to have sprung from European attempts to under-stand the jargon of American Indian tribesmen. In periods of scarcity, only chieftains and their families had enough *muck-a-muck*, or native food.

Trying to imitate a vivid pattern of sounds, settlers seem to have garbled it. So the notion arose that a person becomes a high muckety-muck through importance—rather than through having a full belly when others are hungry.

Jaded

ENGLISH adventurers who first penetrated Iceland found it amazing. Nearly everything they saw added to their wonder—until they were shown a scrawny mare. At the sight of the puny native animal, they burst into laughter.

Travelers took home with them the Icelandic word for a mare and began to call any sorry, worn-out horse a *jade*. Some jades were foaled that way and couldn't help it. Others were once fine mounts that had been overworked and underfed.

In time, the Icelandic label transferred from a sorry mount to a weary rider. Even behind the wheel of a BMW, a person showing signs of exhaustion is compared with a hard-driven horse and described as *jaded*.

Junk

EUROPEANS are said to have laughed heartily when they got their first good look at an early oriental sailing vessel, or *junk*. Its flat bottom and high poop made it ridiculously clumsy in heavy seas. What's more, one of these queer craft was likely to be loaded to the gunwales with stuff no English or Portugese sailor would accept as a gift. Such strange and apparently useless cargo came to bear the name of the ship that transported it.

Junks were long ago replaced by steamers, generally western in design. Their name lives, however, as a label for any accumulation of worn-out and cast-off clothing, furniture, tools, auto parts, or other gear.

Kowtow

REQUIRED to be obsequious toward a foreman or supervisor, some persons will walk off the job. Others will swallow their pride and kowtow. Anyone who follows the latter course imitates, after a fashion, actions that were standard in China.

Jesuits and other explorers long ago penetrated the mysterious East. Newcomers learned that in order to stay there, they'd better observe some Chinese customs. One of the most important was the ritual of *kotow* (later Westernized to *kowtow*). In it anyone brought into the presence of a person of higher rank knelt in formal fashion and touched his forehead to the floor or ground.

Physical kneeling never quite caught on in present-day American business, industry, family or community life. But plenty of persons know what actions, words, and tones to use in performing a kowtow.

Lunatic Fringe

EXPANDING understanding of the human mind has led us to do away with long-established lunatic asylums. But the mind and its workings are far from being totally understood.

For countless generations, insanity was considered to be due to influence of the moon. Romans revered Luna as goddess of the sphere closest to earth, and credited her with enormous power. Her mood changes, reflected by what we know as phases of the moon, were believed to be responsible for many mental conditions.

Attributed to influence of Luna for many centuries, lunacy long labeled any significant aberration from what was considered to be normal. We now know that the moon seldom has anything to do with mental states. But since some persons who manage to function show signs of wobbling close to the edge, we continue to designate them as members of the lunatic fringe.

Macho

A SAMPLING of literature and newspaper clippings suggests that the macho has been around since day one of our republic. But the now-universal label did not make its appearance until this century. Two factors appear to have combined to push it into prominence.

Increased presence of persons from Mexico, Cuba, and South America helped Anglos become acquainted with frequently used Spanish words—including the label for a fellow who is belligerent about his masculinity.

Flow of nationals into the United States accelerated about the time the feminist movement began capturing headlines. Anti-feminist protest, of a sort, was strengthened by adoption of the non-English title. Lots of men who were already macho but did not know what to call themselves now had a great new title, and thus it entered mainstream American speech.

Meandering

ONE of the notable rivers of ancient times was the Maeander in Phrygia, now modern-day Turkey. Ovid, a famous Roman poet of the first century, used its name to symbolize any crooked path. He wrote: "The limpid Meander flows backwards and forwards, and meeting itself, beholds its waters that are to follow."

Long afterward, this and other passages from the poet and his contemporaries figured in the rebirth of classical scholarship. Persons who learned Latin by stumbling through Ovid had the crookedness of the Maeander impressed upon them for life. Small wonder, therefore, that by 1600 the name of a far-away stream was applied to twisting channels in general. Eventually the river's designation came to name any leisurely course.

As a result, we say that a person is meandering if he or she seems to weave and turn rather than drive straight toward a single goal.

Panic

SEVERE or mild panic is brought about by sudden mounting fear. Whatever its level, it perpetuates an ancient notion that something was wrong and might get worse.

Unusual sounds heard in the forest by Greeks were attributed to their god Pan. He was believed to be very mischievous and playful as the god of forests, animals, and nature in general. Noises attributed to him produced a special kind of breathless apprehension that Greeks called panic fear.

Our name for sudden and overwhelming terror has survived for centuries after Pan ceased to be a special source of fear.

Pipe Dream

SHOULD you come up with a really novel idea or plan, chances are that those who first hear of it will pooh-pooh it as a "pipe dream."

In its earliest decades, the pipe dream was so far out that it seldom made contact with reality. That's because it was produced by opium, brought to England and Europe by merchants who penetrated the Orient and began peddling the stuff yielded by some kinds of poppies.

Pipe dreams influenced several notable literary figures, with Samuel T. Coleridge being high on the list. But by and large, fantasies produced by opium were that and nothing more.

Scapegoat

VERY early, the black-coated domestic goat became important in Hebrew religion. On the annual Day of Atonement, it was customary for priests to cleanse people of guilt by "laying their sins on the head of a goat." Afterward, the animal was allowed to escape into the wilderness.

Early translators of Scripture were intrigued by the symbolism of the goat that was forced to escape. With the name of the sacrificial animal altered only a trifle, it became a household word.

Whether having two legs or four, black hair or white, any person or creature on whose head blame is heaped is compared with the animal of Palestine and called a *scapegoat*.

Shampoo

EARLY travelers in India were intrigued by a native custom. Sultans and nabobs had special servants who massaged their bodies after hot baths. From a native term for "to press," such a going-over of the body with knuckles was called a *champo* or *shampoo*.

Europeans were skeptical of its merits and sometimes afraid. One explorer said he wouldn't have taken the risk had he not seen several Chinese merchants shampooed before his turn came.

Outnumbered by a ratio of 40,000:1, every outsider—from merchant prince to soldier—learned to enjoy the luxury of a daily shampoo by servants.

Taken to England, the invigorating ritual quickly shrank to nearly nothing. Only the wealthy could afford to keep a professional bath attendant on the household staff. So by 1860 the once-exotic term named the operation of washing and rubbing only the scalp—usually without help.

Spill the Beans

EARLY Greek secret societies had strict membership requirements. A candidate for admission was voted upon by members, and only a few adverse ballots were required for disqualification.

In order to keep voting secret, white beans were dropped into a container by those who favored a candidate. Brown or black beans constituted negative votes. Only officials were supposed to know how many of these were cast. Occasionally, however, a clumsy voter knocked a jar or helmet over and disclosed its contents. It was embarrassing, to say the least, to spill the beans in this literal fashion.

While this is the accepted origin of the phrase, scholars are stumped as to how it entered the English language early in the 20th century. However, it is a popular phrase naming indiscretion in revealing information of any kind.

Stem-winder

NUREMBERG, Germany, may have been the birthplace of modern timepieces. It was there, around the year 1500, that coiled springs were first used to drive the works of clocks. Soon artisans learned how to use the new source of power in order to produce portable clocks known as *watches*.

Once these devices came into general use, there were no significant changes in manufacture for many generations. But in the aftermath of the Civil War, Yankee ingenuity found a way to eliminate the watch's winding key—essential up to that time.

Any Gay Nineties sport who had a fine watch that could be wound by a pin through the stem was prone to display it with pride. Such a timepiece was the subject of so much admiration and talk that *stem-winder* came to indicate anything or anyone considered to be first-rate. Likely soon to be made obsolete by digital and other new-fangled kinds, the gold-plated stem-winder remains alive in popular speech.

Taboo

EUROPEANS who ventured into the South Seas during early voyages of exploration were intrigued by colorful native customs. Some of the most puzzling were those that forbade passage or contact. Among the Tongans, it seemed that everywhere a seaman turned he was confronted by a priest who barred his way and muttered: "Tabu! Tabu!" (Forbidden! Forbidden!)

No forbidden object could be touched, or even examined from a distance, and a forbidden place could not be entered.

Famous explorer Captain Cook and other sailors altered the Polynesian term a trifle and returned home with the novel sound that expressed warning. Several classical and European words indicating caution were supplanted by the novel expression from the South Seas.

As a result, to speakers of numerous modern languages, anything forbidden is now likely to be termed *taboo*.

White Elephant

ONE of the rarest creatures in Thailand, once known as Siam, is the albino elephant. For centuries it was regarded as sacred. Virtually all white elephants were claimed by some member of a royal family, who could afford to keep it on exhibition for admiration of visitors.

When an ordinary citizen incurred the wrath of a blue blood, it wasn't necessary to find a way to squeeze money out of him in order to hurt him. Instead, the offender received the gift of a white elephant that he had to feed and could not work. Eventually, the British coined the phrase "white elephant" to mean a valuable item that is unwanted but cannot be given away.

Yen

SAILORS and other adventurers were among the earliest Europeans to spend any length of time in China. Some who managed to penetrate the forbidden land came home reporting that entry was easiest in the Peking region.

That part of China, they reported, was unusual in another respect. Everywhere a man went, he was likely to walk into a crowded room in which smoke was thick. It was hard to breathe in such an atmosphere, and the smoke seemed to have unexpected effects on a person who inhaled it.

Devotees of such smoke were afflicted with what speakers of the Cantonese dialect called *yinyan*—or craving for more of it. Anyone having yinyan was clearly subject to some powerful force.

Abbreviated in western speech, yen came to designate any strong appetite or passionate craving. Not until later generations was it generally known that the earliest and one of the strongest kinds of yinyan—or yen—resulted from smoking opium.

Today, a person who wouldn't be caught dead experimenting with opium may admit to having a yen for anything ranging from soul food to major league baseball.

CHAPTER 8

MONEY, BUSINESS, AND COMMERCE

"Business? That's very simple—it's other people's money."
—Alexandre Dumas, *fils, La Question d'Argent*

Business, flowing by exchange of money, doesn't tolerate foolishness. Therefore it would seem logical that the vocabulary of commerce would be straightforward and forthright, devoid of imagination.

Not so, as in other fields of endeavor, commerce borrows freely from any available source in order to form or to enrich a word or a phrase. Conversely, everyday speech often owes money and business a debt not noticed at a casual glance.

ACID TEST
BOTTOM DOLLAR
BROKER
CALCULATION
CHINAMAN'S CHANCE
CLIP JOINT
COLD FEET
CORPORATION
DOLLAR
DIDDLY-SQUAT
FALSE FRONT
FIASCO
FLEECE
GO HAYWIRE
HARD-BOILED
HAVE THE GOODS ON
LOOPHOLE

LOOSE ENDS, TO BE AT
MAKE ENDS MEET
ON THE CUFF, OFF THE
   CUFF
PAINT THE TOWN RED
PHONY
PIG IN A POKE
PRETTY PENNY
PROSTITUTE
PURCHASE
SCALPER
SELLING LIKE HOTCAKES
SILHOUETTE
SLUSH FUND
WASHOUT
WELCH

SEE ALSO: All the Way, Blue Chips, Bribe, Cash on the Barrel
    Head, Chicken Feed, Chips Are Down, Fork Over, Gyp
    Joint, High Hat, Monkeyshines, Plum, Rodeo

Acid Test

WANDERING peddlers, now supplanted by telemarketers, were once a familiar part of the European and American scene. A typical fellow carried a few household articles in a pack; if well established, he might drive a wagon with a variety of goods.

Many a peddler made his real money, not by sale of goods, but by purchase of old gold from persons he encountered. Even a veteran found it hard to assess the value of filled and plated articles by examination. But a positive test was easily used. After filing a shallow groove in a piece, the prospective buyer would touch it with nitric acid. Color reactions gave a reasonably accurate index to the gold content and hence the value.

Bottles of nitric acid were used on so many articles containing gold that any exacting trial came to be called an *acid test*.

Bottom Dollar

NOVELS and television dramas to the contrary, metallic dollars were never abundant in this country. During the first eighty years of U.S. coinage, only 8,000,000 silver dollars were struck. Less than 19,000,000 gold pieces were ever produced.

Most wealth was in terms of raw materials rather than in the coins of the realm. Even fur traders and buffalo hunters who swarmed in and out of St. Louis had comparatively few dollars from the mint. A typical hoard might include only a dozen or so.

Such a stack of coins never reached very high, and it didn't take skill or intelligence to know when a person came to the bottom. Because the bottom dollar was a signal to get back to a man's traps and guns, it came to symbolize the end of one's resources.

Broker

THESE days, a broker can't stay in business without substantial cash flow; money is the name of the game.

That was not the case with the earliest fellows given a version of the title. In medieval France, a tavern's tapster was responsible for broaching—or opening—casks of wine for resale. By extension, he became the middleman or agent who bought from one source and sold to another.

For generations, there were brokers of every imaginable kind; one or several specialized in every commodity on the market. With the rise of modern fiscal instruments, some began dealing in stocks and bonds. Brokers of this sort gradually came to be considered more important than those who dealt in sheep or iron or cotton.

Today's Wall Street executive who takes a client to lunch seldom functions as the title once intended. Instead, he or she is more likely to ask a waiter to open the bottle of wine.

Calculation

LONG ago, some Roman merchants built up large enterprises. A man's ships might sail all known seas, and his warehouse could bulge with staple goods and rare articles for the luxury trade.

Merchandise meant money, but the cumbersome system of Roman numerals made accounting difficult. This problem led to adaptation of a counting method used by children, who arranged limestone pebbles to form clusters standing for numbers.

These bits of limestone, or *calculi,* eventually named sliding spheres of the abacus—with which a skilled person can compute very rapidly. Centuries of transmission have brought about only slight modifications in the name of pebble-shaped counters that were central to Roman business. Computers have replaced limestone, but the process of calculation remains basic to Space Age commerce.

Chinaman's Chance

WHEN you are caught in a situation where you don't have a Chinaman's chance, you may as well call it quits.

We use that expression to indicate a zero chance because that is precisely what Anglos gave any oriental who ventured into gold fields in the American West. Unwritten codes stipulated that no forty-niner would sell to a Chinese prospector until he was dead certain that a claim wouldn't yield an ounce of precious metal.

Consequently, a Chinaman's chance is no chance at all—zilch, zip, nothing.

Clip Joint

IF you find yourself greatly overcharged at a place of public entertainment, chances are good that you have been lured into a "clip joint."

Until modern times, operators of shady pubs and dance halls accepted nothing except hard money—gold or silver. Coins made of soft metal were easily shaved—or clipped. A shrewd fellow could soon accumulate enough clippings to turn them in for a handful of newly-minted pieces.

The addition of milled edges to coins and the rise of printed currency threatened to put clip joints out of business. This dilemma was solved when operators learned to trim patrons instead of coins.

Cold Feet

IN rural Europe, a person with little money—hence unwilling to move toward a purchase—was often described as having cold feet. A gambler wanting out of a game could let it be known that he was dead broke by saying that his feet were cold.

With its fiscal roots forgotten, the ancient expression remains alive and well. Regardless of whether engaged in pursuit of a sweetheart or planning to change jobs, a person who suddenly withdraws from the action is labeled as having *cold feet*.

Corporation

QUINTUS Septimus Florens Tertullianus, better known as Tertullian, was among the best linguists of the second century. From Latin terms that meant the making of a body from components, he coined a new title for an established organization: *corporationem*.

Scholars of the 15th century discovered the ancient term and applied it to any organized group, such as the corporation of surgeons. But it was not until 1600 that English law provided for a such body to act as though it were an individual. That is, corporations became artificial persons created by charter and capable of living much longer than humans.

By Colonial times, organizations and land companies were encouraging investors to pool their resources in order to form corporations. As a result, a term born in Roman legal circles is one of the most common and important words of modern business.

Dollar

A SILVER mine opened in Bohemia in 1516 turned out to be one of the richest ever. So much precious metal was dug out that local jewelers couldn't use all of it. As a result, craftsmen made one-ounce coins from some of the Joachimsthal silver.

In commerce the novel coin soon became familiar as the thaler. So many thalers were circulated that the product of Bohemia became a standard unit of currency. English merchants eager for international deals stumbled over the name of the silver piece and wound up calling it "dollar." Dollars soon poured into and out of the island kingdom, but the coin was never made official.

Patriots who shaped our 1785 American monetary system wanted to be completely un-English. They devised a decimal system quite unlike that which made a guinea worth twenty-one shillings. Founding fathers scrapped both "pound" and "penny" and chose *dollar* to name a piece worth 100 cents.

Diddly-Squat

SOMETIMES a person has no opinion or feeling about an issue. Asked to take a pro or con stance, Andy Griffith might well respond: "I don't care diddly-squat; it makes no difference to me."

Strictly American in origin, that expression sounds suspiciously like a pair of modified barnyard terms—but isn't.

Carneys who traveled from town to town working one county fair after another developed their own private language. They had to do so in order to attract potential gambers who would pay for a chance at a gimcrack prize. *Diddle-e-squat* seems to have entered carnival talk to name money—often a nickel or a dime, since that was the going rate for a game of chance.

Frequently used to hide talk about a small amount of money, it was an easy and natural transition for the carnival term to indicate very little of anything. Only slightly modified, the expression may have entered general speech because it is just suggestive enough to seem bold and maybe vulgar. T-shirts boasting that "I CAUGHT SCROD IN BOSTON" have the same effect—to those who don't know that a young cod or haddock is known to fishermen as a scrod.

False Front

AMERICA has seen many periods of booming prosperity, but no other quite like the Gay Nineties. It was a period of quick wealth, free spending, and undiluted optimism. Many thought that such ills as depressions and wars had been conquered for good.

Inevitably, the mood of the era was reflected in the architecture of business. It became customary to build a commercial establishment in such fashion that its front wall extended well above the roof. Sometimes it extended upward for an entire story and was equipped with windows that opened on empty space.

So prevalent was the false front on Main Street that its name came to stand for pretense of any kind or for display of sham resources.

Fiasco

LONG ago, Venice became a great center of the glass trade. Her craftsmen developed the now-standard goblet made up of bowl, stem, and foot. They also imitated semiprecious stones in the color and texture of fine ware. Many pieces were so prized that royal inventories listed them along with gold and silver vessels.

In addition to costly ware, Italian artisans produced great quantities of the common flask—which in some dialects was known as a *fiasco*.

Flaws frequently developed in the process of turning out fine pieces. Glass was too expensive to throw away; even damaged, a hunk of it could be reheated and turned into a fiasco or two. So many inexpensive flasks were the result of bungling that the glass blower's term came to indicate any type of failure.

At least, that is maybe the most believable of half a dozen theories offered to account for the rise of a distinctive and elusive word.

Fleece

SEVERE winters have marked the British Isles since the region was first settled. Julius Caesar visited it very early, and may have been the first tourist to complain about the weather. Sheepskin and wool, widely used for clothing, also caught the attention of the Roman emperor.

From a long-lost word used by the earliest inhabitants, the English used *fleece* to name wool clipped from the backs of sheep. Most of it was consumed by producers. Not until the time of Queen Elizabeth did it become a major article of commerce. In business circles of the era, fleece was valued so highly that it often served as a medium of exchange.

It was inevitable that a trader who accumulated money by means of shady deals should be compared with a farmer stripping wool from a sheep. As a result, we still say that any sharper who preys upon the innocent and gullible *fleeces* his victims.

Go Haywire

MOSES P. Bliss launched a new era in agriculture and business when he patented a hay press in 1828. His power machine had many defects, but use of it was better than trying to tie loose bales of hay with string.

Demand for baled hay brought improvements that created bundles so firm they could be tied with wire. A major difficulty remained, however, as stiff hay wire easily became tangled or caught in machinery. At other times it would wind about legs of horses or snag clothing of workmen. When cut, wire sometimes snapped outward with enough force to cause an injury.

Until recent decades, production of hay in commercial quantities involved many accidents. As a result, we say that when a device or plan gets out of order, it "goes haywire."

Hard-Boiled

SHOULD you ever be called hard-boiled, don't fret that you are being compared with an overcooked egg. The descriptive term comes not from the kitchen, but from the frontier washhouse.

Homemakers of the era used lye soap that didn't get clothes very clean. Once a month, a fastidious woman boiled her wash in an iron pot in order to remove stains. Then she boiled the best pieces in starch made in her own kitchen.

Inevitably, Sunday shirts sometimes emerged from the wash with too much starch. A fellow who put on one of them was likely to joke that it was boiled so long it became hard. Passing from stiffly starched clothing, the wash-day expression attached to persons. As a result, hard-boiled men and women emerged as stock characters in the contemporary drama that we call business.

Have the Goods On

IF you have the goods on a friend or family member, explanations are worthless; it is an airtight case.

That situation occurred with some frequency in decades after the Civil War. Counterfeiters flourished, taking advantage of paper money issued to finance the war. Beginners at the confidence game tended to keep bogus money on their persons. A fellow arrested with the green goods in his pocket didn't stand a chance when hauled into court.

Police came to speak of any damning evidence, not simply counterfeit bills, as the *goods*. When authorities had the goods on a suspect, their open-and-shut case was unlikely to be damaged by a high-powered defense lawyer.

Loophole

IF you find a loophole in a contract or an insurance policy, it will constitute an escape route for one of the parties. This usage stems from a turn about in understanding of the name for what was once a special kind of tangible hole.

During the Middle Ages, architects and builders had to deal with the matter of defending a castle, once it was erected. Longbows, followed by crossbows, were formidable weapons typically used by both attackers and defenders. A narrow window, often oval at the top and wider at the inner side of a thick wall, was found to offer a difficult target from across a moat. At the same time, such an opening was big enough to enable defenders to fire at will.

This special form of loophole saved the hide of many a lord of the manor. When firearms made it obsolete, its name transferred to any opening that provides an advantage to one party in a dispute or an agreement.

Loose Ends, To be at

A BORED adolescent who decides to go hang out at the nearest shopping mall is "at loose ends"—not far from the original meaning of the expression.

During the days of the windjammers and other great sailing vessels, rigging grew increasingly complex. If ropes had been left free to ravel, a hopeless tangle would have resulted.

When other work was slack, sailors were put to work repairing loose ends of ropes. Many a captain was accused of ordering such a chore merely to keep his crew occupied. As a result, a person with nothing significant to do was said "to be at loose ends"—tying or taping untidy ends of ropes.

Make Ends Meet

FULL-RIGGED sailing vessels were equipped with a number of masts, each of which bore several sails. Since most pieces of canvas were raised and lowered separately, rigging involved hundreds of ropes. Many of these were movable, so were easily repaired when they broke.

Some ropes attached to lower edges of sails were permanently fixed. When such a length of hemp broke, frugal masters ordered sailors to pull ends together and splice them. In order to make both ends of a fixed rope meet, it was often necessary to strain and tug, stretching a piece of canvas to its limit.

Long used literally on the sea, we now apply the expression for "succeeding with difficulty" to anyone who makes both ends meet by managing to stretch his or her income to cover all bills.

On the Cuff, Off the Cuff

ELECTRONIC transmission of information now makes it difficult for anyone to treat debts casually. If a person has an outstanding obligation, a quick search is likely to reveal it. Today's transactions are a far cry from what they were a few generations ago.

So is easy credit. As late as the era of Theodore Roosevelt, many merchants seldom let people get merchandise without putting cash on the barrel head. Credit was so limited that a fellow operating a livery stable could keep his records on his shirt cuff.

Which meant that a drifter who lived "on the cuff" was adept at talking folk into extending credit without formality. Casual business transactions were common enough to cause anything impromptu to be termed "off the cuff."

Paint the Town Red

MANY a celebrating individual has set out to "paint the town red." So have lots of visiting conventioneers who would like to turn a convention into a spree.

Why this color, always, instead of a green or blue foray once in a while?

One theory links red with the flames of pioneer villages set afire by marauding Indians. Somehow, it seems inappropriate to compare the notion of a high-rolling good time with watching a cluster of houses burn to the ground.

A more plausible explanation suggests that fast action in red-light districts, or streets crowded with brothels, contributed to development of the phrase.

Red is the color of excitement in so many cultures that they cannot be counted. So it is at least an even chance that the

American who first spoke of painting the town red simply chose that expression as a way to express the notion of having a really exciting time.

Phony

WHEN you say that a piece of jewelry or a work of art is phony, you owe the label to early Irish sharpers. One of the favorite ruses of those bunco men was the "fawney rig"—given that name from Irish for a finger-ring.

A con artist using this stratagem put a ring, or fawney, in a public place. Sooner or later someone would come along and pick up the piece equipped with an imitation stone. Appearing from nowhere, the swindler persuaded or frightened his victim into paying him to keep quiet about the find. Making off with hush money, the sharper would leave the sucker holding a fawney that seemed valuable but was actually worthless.

So many persons were defrauded that anything fake came to be called *fawney*. The original Irish word was *fáinne*, in England it became *fawney*, and it was finally Americanized to *phony*.

Pig in a Poke

NEVER buy a pig in a poke; always take a look at merchandise before handing over payment, regardless of how great a bargain is offered.

That advice wasn't always heeded in early England, so many purchasers were stung by shrewd farmers. Until three months or so old, a young porker usually went to market in a heavy bag, or poke, that was carried over the seller's shoulder by means of a stick.

More frequently than we'd like to think, in "the good old days" a farmer's poke held a sick or deformed piglet, and sometimes even a cat, that was offered at a price below the market. If a prospective purchaser asked to take a look, the seller was likely to refuse to open his bag "because once little pigs get loose, they're almost impossible to catch."

Lots of folk who had a taste for pork and took a stranger's word actually bought a pig in a poke. Too often, a quick look inside the bag revealed that what seemed to be a good buy was money wasted.

Pretty Penny

PERHAPS you grew up in a region where the English influence upon American speech is still strong. If so, you may have heard relatives or friends who want something say of it: "I'd give a pretty penny for that!"

Since the ordinary one-cent piece is not especially pretty, the expression hints at a story.

Long ago, there really was a pretty penny—a gold piece coined in 1257, valued at twenty shillings. Subjects of King Henry III, who had the coin issued, didn't like it. Like the U.S. two-dollar bill, it wasn't well suited for commerce. So no additional gold pence were coined by later rulers.

For several centuries, a tradesman might occasionally see one of King Henry's pieces. In addition to their face value, they came to be prized as good-luck pieces. One of these shiny gold coins was both valuable and pleasing to the eye. So it became customary to speak of any prized article as being worth a pretty penny.

Obsolete so long that it is seldom found even in a valuable collection, the 13th-century coin retains a tenuous hold in American speech after more than 700 years.

Prostitute

IN the literal sense of the title, a prostitute is a self-employed person who offers merchandise for sale, with the only commodity on hand being sex.

Whether female or male, the title of such a vendor comes

directly from a Latin word meaning "exposed to sight for the purpose of sale."

Which may possibly help explain why bodily exposure is regarded by the typical prostitute as a trick of the trade.

Purchase

UNTIL modern times, there were no stores as we know them. Merchants occupied small booths that had no show windows or display counters. There was nothing resembling newspaper or TV advertising. Consequently a person wanting a specific commodity had to get out and hunt for it.

Every successful shopping expedition was a major or minor triumph. So many difficulties were involved that the process of searching became linked with actual buying. From an Old French term meaning "seeking ardently," it was called *purchasing*.

So many persons chased so much merchandise so fervently that the label stuck in speech. No longer signifying an act of searching zealously, it now implies that money will pass from the hands of the purchaser to the hands of the seller—unless both agree to use a plastic card.

Scalper

ANYTIME a scalper offers you a ticket at a high price, you talk with a person whose title has gone through several transitions.

An early word for a cup-shaped vessel led housewives of ancient Britain to call a shell-shaped bowl a *scallop*. Many vessels were much like the human cranium, so the rounded bone of the head took that name. Transferred from bone to the skin and hair that covered it, the old title became *scalp*.

Development might have halted had it not been for life on the American frontier, where some Indians scalped their foes. Fast growth soon led Chicago and other cities to become infested with men who bought unused portions of railroad tickets for resale. These traders in segments of tickets were compared with Indian braves who collected scalps.

Eventually the boom in transportation tickets came to an end. Passing from rail brokers to persons who speculate in tickets to sporting events and the theater, the name of a bloodthirsty trader became fixed as scalper.

Selling Like Hotcakes

NEWCOMERS to North America found one of its most versatile plants to be Indian corn, or maize. When dried and ground, corn yielded meal that made fine bread.

An unknown experimenter discovered still another use for cornmeal: batter fried on a griddle yielded a fluffy delicacy that was best while still hot. Frontiersmen said they preferred their hotcakes fried in bear grease, but town folk were partial to pork lard.

Whenever a Ladies' Aid Society put on a benefit, cooks found it hard to keep up with the demand for hotcakes. Their popularity and money-raising power was so great that by 1825 any merchandise that moved in a hurry was described as "selling like hotcakes."

Silhouette

ANY time you see a silhouette, the stark appearance of the black outline can serve as a reminder that its name was bestowed in mockery of a penny-pincher.

Étienne de Silhouette became controller-general of France in 1759. Selected because he was considered capable of solving the nation's financial troubles, he went to work with zeal. All of his money-saving proposals were unpopular, but his suggestion that government pensioners receive reduced allowances created a national uproar.

For generations, street artists had offered outline portraits at low prices. Since these represented an extreme example of economy in art, ridicule of the financier caused his name to become attached to them.

Slush Fund

SINCE refrigeration was far in the future, the food supply was a major problem during the great age of sailing. A seasoned ship's master wouldn't leave port without taking aboard as much salt pork as he could buy.

When fried or boiled, the all-important meat yielded grease in such quantities that special storage vats were used for it. Much waste fat, or slush, was used to grease timbers. But on many voyages the stuff accumulated faster than it could be used. Back home after months at sea, a vessel might have hundreds of pounds of slush.

Long-established tradition provided that when a voyage ended, slush was sold in order to buy extras for members of the crew. So widely familiar was this sea-going slush fund that its name attached to a sum of money diverted from an operating budget for extras such as bribery or corrupt practices.

Washout

EARLY U.S. prospectors liked to use water to separate particles of gold from dirt. Sluice boxes built close to streams permitted a man to process a great deal of ore. Where water was scarce, pans were in vogue. In either case, the miner expected water to remove earth and reveal gold.

Any time a claim started to play out, a forty-niner liked to open new diggings. That often meant leaving behind a bare sluice box from which all the gold had been washed. Many a box was washed so clean that any failure or calamity came to be known as a *washout.*

Welch

WHEN an obligation is loose, there is a chance that one party will welch on the other. Gambling debts are especially vulnerable, but a default can take place any time money is involved—especially at the racetrack.

Clearly disparaging even when used by Americans who have never been close to Wales, the expression took root at least 150 years ago. Like terms that disparage the French or the Spanish, this one grew out of hostility. Ideas behind it are reflected in a familiar children's rhyme:

Taffy was a Welshman,
Taffy was a thief . . .

These lines, along with a verb fashioned after Taffy's nationality, preserve longstanding English views. According to them, a fellow had better demand cash if he sells anything to a native of Wales or lets him try to pick a winner in a race. Otherwise, Taffy may be long gone—leaving nothing to cover his obligation.

CHAPTER 9

WHY DON'T FOLK SAY PRECISELY WHAT THEY MEAN?

"All speech, written or spoken, is a dead language until it finds a willing and prepared hearer."
—Robert Louis Stevenson, *Lay Morals*

The author of *Dr. Jekyll and Mr. Hyde,* Robert Louis Stevenson lived long before modern scientific study of communication. But from personal experience, he knew that a listener or reader has to interpret what he hears.

That process is usually so easy that it is automatic. But many a word and phrase seems on the surface to suggest something quite different from original connotations or the meaning found by "a willing and prepared hearer."

BEAT AROUND THE BUSH
BITTER PILL TO SWALLOW
BLACKBALL
BONER
BRAND-NEW
BY THE SKIN OF ONE'S TEETH
CARRY A TORCH
CARVED IN STONE
CHESTNUT
CRACKPOT
FIGUREHEAD
GET THE SACK
GO BY THE BOARD
HAVE ONE IN
  (OR THROW INTO)
  STITCHES
HEW TO THE LINE
JERRY-BUILT

KICK THE BUCKET
LAY AN EGG
LEAD-PIPE CINCH
LET THE CAT OUT OF
  THE BAG
NOSE FOR TROUBLE
PIKER
PLAY FAST AND
  LOOSE
PULL A FAST ONE
RED-LETTER DAY
ROGER
SCREAMING MEEMIES
SHORT SHRIFT
SHOT IN THE ARM
SIDEBURNS
SLIPSHOD
TALK A BLUE STREAK

SEE ALSO: Apple Pie Order, Bombshell, Bullpen, Chew the
    Rag, Clean as a Whistle, Double-Cross, Dukes, Eager
    Beaver, Face the Music, Feather in One's Cap, Fly-By-
    Night, Gaga, Give the Gun, Ham, Hamstrung, High Hat,
    Highball, Hogwash, Left Field, Life of Riley, Monkey
    Wrench, No Bones, On the Skids, On Cloud Nine, Pork
    Barrel, Put the Bite On, Putting on the Dog, Rain Cats and
    Dogs, Run a Hotbox, Shoot the Bull, Skeleton in the Closet,
    Tell It to the Marines!, Three Sheets to the Wind, Up to
    Scratch, White Elephant

Beat Around the Bush

NOBLEMEN and gentry who went in for the sport of boar hunting were glad for others to do the dangerous work. So they employed young males who fanned out through woods and swamps, making noise in order to beat animals toward the hunters.

The razor-sharp teeth of a big boar were lethal weapons no one wanted to encounter. Unarmed beaters frequently stayed out of dense clumps of undergrowth where a boar might be hiding. So many of them beat around the bush instead of going through it that their tactic came to label any evasive technique.

Bitter Pill to Swallow

ANY unpleasant news may be called a bitter pill to swallow. Figuratively applied to a wide range of situations, the expression was once painfully literal.

For centuries, a physician's pellet for use in sickness has been known as a *pill*. Honey and spices were about all that doctors had with which to try to mask disagreeable components. Bark of a New World tree, the cinchona, was effective in fighting malaria. But the quinine it contains is extremely bitter. Widely employed in the era before medications were coated, cinchona pellets caused any disagreeable thing to be termed a bitter pill to swallow.

Blackball

MEMBERS of some private clubs still vote on applicants for admission. Few, however, adhere to the time-honored custom of casting anonymous ballots by means of dropping marbles or balls into a hat or box.

When little spheres constituted votes, white or pink signified "yes," while black meant "no." In many instances, a single black ball caused a candidate to be rejected.

Clubs, fraternities, and sororities are today more likely to use an electronic device than a hat and a handful of marbles. Yet it may take only one negative vote to blackball an applicant.

Boner

OLD timers made fun of a person considered stupid by saying his head was so full of bone that there was little room for brains. Since a bonehead, male or female, was likely to be awkward, any glaring mistake came to be called a boner.

Gross errors on the baseball diamond may be called *skulls* or even *rocks,* but the majority of pros use the time-honored *boner* in speaking of them.

A classic boner pulled in 1908 cost the New York Giants a pennant. When a teammate drove in the winning run, Fred Merkle failed to touch second base. Johnny Evers of the Chicago Cubs signaled for the ball, touched second, and an umpire ruled that Merkle's apparent run couldn't be counted.

Brand-new

SAVED from a rectory fire, world-famous evangelist John Wesley called himself a "brand plucked from the burning." That way of designating a stick that is on fire, burning but not yet consumed, stems from *brand* once meaning "fire."

Intense heat was essential to artisans who shaped things made of metal, as well as to ceramic workers. A tool or a vase completed but not yet cool was just off the fire. That made it brand new—linked with brands of cattle by the fact that a branding iron worked only when hot.

Today workers and craftsmen produce a great variety of brand-new products that have never been close to an artisan's furnace.

By the Skin of One's Teeth

SINCE no tooth is covered with skin, why on earth do we say that when a person barely misses disaster, he has escaped "by the skin of his teeth"?

The expression comes from the Book of Job (19:20) where he describes his narrow escape: "My bone cleaveth to my skin and to my flesh and I have escaped with the skin of my teeth." With these words Job sought to show just how dire was his situation.

Retained in the famous King James version, the colorful phrase was pounded into everyday speech. Although we have no real skin on our teeth, Job's description is vivid, if exaggerated, and not likely to be replaced with a more accurate phrase.

Carry a Torch

TORCHLIGHT parades were common features of political campaigns in rural America. Accompanied by drums or other musical instruments, an evening demonstration was likely to be loud and colorful.

Only enthusiastic followers took part in such rallies. A fellow who carried a torch didn't care who knew that he was wholeheartedly behind his candidate.

It was an easy transition to move from describing a passionate political follower to speaking of an ardent lover. These days, many a man or woman will carry a torch for someone not interested in winning a political office.

Carved in Stone

IF you cite a long-prevalent social standard as a guide for present-day conduct, someone is likely to protest that it isn't carved in stone. Alive and well today, this saying is rooted in antiquity.

One of Scripture's most dramatic stories describes the encounter in which Moses received the Ten Commandments, or Decalogue. Artists typically depict the bearded prophet descending from a mountain carrying these important rules of conduct. They are carved into stone, so that no word—not even a single letter—can be altered.

Standards of behavior or inherited ways, compared with the laws received by Moses, may be dismissed as not "carved in stone." That is, they are far from timeless and are subject to change.

Chestnut

THE *Broken Sword* was once a smash hit in theaters of London. In the play, Pablo and Captain Xavier argue about things they both saw through the boughs of a tree. Pablo insists that the tree that obstructed their view was a chestnut. Xavier swears that it was *not* a chestnut, but a cork tree. Finally the exasperated Pablo smiles knowingly before exploding: "A chestnut; I guess I ought to know, for haven't I heard you tell this story twenty-seven times?"

Audiences roared so many times that lines from a now-forgotten play caused any musty joke or well-worn story to be called a *chestnut*.

Crackpot

CLAY pots were the most common household utensils for centuries. Since many were about the size and shape of the users' heads, the human skull was widely known as a pot.

Though it might be thick and strong, crude earthenware was likely to crack when dropped. Housewives compared damaged vessels with heads of peculiar or eccentric neighbors. That made it natural to speak of an odd person as wearing a cracked pot on top of his shoulders. Language then took another short step and anyone off the norm came to be known as a crackpot.

Figurehead

MANY early ships were painted or carved to display creatures designed to frighten sailors on enemy vessels. Such symbols were replaced by human figures placed over the cut-water when cannon made ships genuinely threatening.

A carved representation of a ship owner or nobleman was often the figure near the head of a big vessel. HMS *Marlborough,* a British warship, had as its figurehead "The Great Duke"—complete with long, curling hair and medals on his chest.

During the great age of sail, figureheads of many vessels were conventional representations of Victorian women. Such a carved dummy at the prow looked important but played no role in a ship's operation.

Today, lots of persons with important-sounding titles have no authority to make decisions. "Only a figurehead," say insiders who regard such a man or woman as being a lot like a wooden dummy.

Get the Sack

THESE days, an assembly line worker or an executive who gets the sack may receive severance pay plus a printed explanation.

As early as the 17th century, cloth bags were in literal rather than figurative use. Craftsmen and artisans provided their own tools as a rule, storing them in a sturdy sack.

When an employer was ready to dismiss a worker, it was common to hand him his tool sack. No explanation was necessary; the gesture meant "Put your tools in the sack, and get going."

As a result of this practice, a person who wouldn't know a drill from a tailor's needle is said to "get the sack" when fired from a job.

Go by the Board

"MAN overboard!" was the standard shout when a sailor was thrown into the drink by a lurching ship. Such an unlucky fellow went over the vessel's board, or side, in a matter of seconds.

High winds and big waves aren't the only source of catastrophe, though. In almost any activity, a sudden turn of events can lead to the abandonment of a cherished dream.

By means of a single vote, lawmakers or members of a management team or officers of a club can scrap a projected plan. Such action causes it to "go by the board" as abruptly as a seaman tossed over the board of his ship.

Have One in (or Throw into) Stitches

SPEECH of several early Teutonic peoples included a term meaning "to stick," as with the point of a knife. Passing through Old English it was modified into the form, *stitch*. All types of pricks and stabs took that name.

One characteristic stablike pain, caused by acute spasms of rib muscles, occurs after violent exercise. Though no wound is involved, a person may hurt almost as though stabbed. Athletes—especially runners—are still subject to pain from a stitch in the side.

Long ago, it was noticed that prolonged laughter may lead to stabbing muscular cramps. So the designation for a minor wound came to label pain triggered by excessive hilarity. To this day we say that an unusually funny episode can "have you in stitches" or "throw you into stitches."

Hew to the Line

CRUDE saws came into use sometime late in the Stone Age. Early specimens were made from bones and shells, and broke easily. Metal blades remained rare until the beginning of the machine age. As late as the 18th century, much heavy lumber was hand-hewn, and an expert with the adze was much faster than a sawyer.

For many purposes it was not worth the time and effort to turn out timbers that were straight and square. Beams in fine buildings were another matter, for these had to be reasonably uniform. To make such a piece, a craftsman had to stretch twine along a section of tree trunk and carefully hew along this guideline. Such labor was so tedious and exacting that in an era when lumber is no longer produced by hand, we continue to say that anyone who works under exacting standards is "hewing to the line."

Jerry-Built

A PERSON shown a hastily constructed home or office is likely to reject it as *jerry-built*. That may be because the language of the sea remains alive and well in the speech of landlubbers.

Gales often snapped some of the masts of sailing vessels. Sailors responded by rigging temporary poles in order to try to make port. In their lingo, a flimsy upright likely to crash on the heads of crew members was often dubbed an *injury mast*. Abbreviated to jury mast, the name of the hastily erected timber seems to have been slurred to jerry mast.

Landsmen borrowed the expressive term and applied it to anything flimsy that was put together hastily. Like the old-time sailors' jury mast, jerry-built housing is likely to deteriorate almost before the new has worn off it.

Kick the Bucket

UNTIL recent times, most slaughter of meat animals took place on the farm. Swine, sheep, and goats were comparatively easy to handle. Not so a steer that weighed one-half ton or more.

A special hoist was devised for use with heavy animals. With its hind feet tied to a rope, a steer or an ox was pulled toward a beam at the top of a three-legged frame. A heavy wooden cask or bucket was shoved under the animal to prevent waste.

Frequently the rope was jerked as pullers strained to get a carcass into position. This action threw the feet of the animal against the bucket, almost as though it were deliberately kicking.

By the time a steer or a prize hog kicked the bucket, its throat had already been slit. Consequently the farm expression came into use to name death in any form.

Lay an Egg

DID your sports team ever lay an egg? Chances are that it did.

That expression sounds complimentary. When a barnyard fowl produces an egg, the critter is appreciated for its achievement. Not so in the human world, especially the realm of sports.

In the game of cricket, you scored a "duck's egg" if you had no runs at bat because an egg resembled the shape of a zero. What better way to express the notion of "no score" than to say a team laid a duck egg or a goose egg?

It is no longer necessary to make zero points in order to "lay an egg." Any significant failure may evoke the expression that was once highly descriptive and self-explanatory.

Lead-Pipe Cinch

SOME urban ruffians of the last century used short lengths of lead pipe as blackjacks. Such a weapon assured its user that victims would be bruised or knocked unconscious. Wielding a lead pipe, a thug just couldn't fail to pull off a mugging.

While the name of the crude weapon was in the process of entering general speech, cowboys adopted a Spanish name for their all-important saddle-girth. Though small, the cinch was crucial. When properly fastened, it promised that a saddle would remain firmly in place.

Any type of cinch was better than an unsecured saddle, but one that positively would not slip was affectionately said to be as sure as a criminal's lead pipe. Through the unusual blending of urban lingo with cowboy talk, any undertaking whose accomplishment was dead certain from the start came to be called a "lead-pipe cinch."

Let the Cat out of the Bag

BRITISH tenants who farmed land belonging to gentry were supposed to turn over part of all they produced as rent. Many adhered to the letter of the law, but some sold suckling pigs, considered a delicacy and easily carried, without reporting the transactions. Frequently concealed in bags while being taken to market, black market animals were bought by butchers at bargain prices.

By the 18th century, shrewd farmers had learned that in a hasty illegal sale, it was easy to pass off a cat as a young pig. When a suspicious buyer insisted on seeing the merchandise before he paid, he sometimes found his doubts confirmed.

Today, a person with inside information may slip and give clues. Even though neither a feline nor a bag is involved, comrades are likely to chide the revealer of the secret for having "let the cat out of the bag." And a person who makes a hasty purchase without taking a look at merchandise is still said to have bought a "pig in a poke."

Nose for Trouble

AS noses go, those of most humans are second- or third-rate. Many wild animals depend on their sense of smell for much information about the outside world, as do most breeds of dogs. But for typical persons, the nose is simply an air vent in which organs of smell are located deep inside. Range of sensitivity to odors is extremely wide. Some persons react readily to scents that others cannot detect by deliberate effort.

Capacity to anticipate the coming of unpleasant events is an equally big variable. Unable to explain special sensitivity in this arena, common folk quipped that it must be due to keenness of smell. As a result, anyone regarded as having special ability to detect impending problems is admired as having a nose for trouble.

Piker

WHEN someone calls another a "piker," the label does not convey the meaning it would seem to have. For a piker was originally a person who walked along a turnpike built for carriages of the wealthy.

Many early American roads were created by private capital. In order to recover their investments, charter holders levied tolls for use of the turnpikes that were the luxury highways of their era. There were fixed fees for various types of vehicles, but persons on foot were usually permitted to go from town to town without payment.

Small wonder that a turnpike often carried a stream of vagrants. By association with the highway he traveled, such a freeloading traveler came to be known as a *piker*. With early associations forgotten, we use the term to label a cheapskate who does not pay his or her share.

Play Fast and Loose

CON men of 16th-century England learned how to arrange a length of string in a deceptive pattern. Laid on the ground or a bench, it seemed easy to put a stick into the string in such fashion that when the string was pulled the stick would be caught. Actually, "fast and loose" formed an optical illusion that never caught the stick.

Many a fellow who saw the setup for the first time wagered that he could cause the stick to be caught. Nearly always, though, a

pull by a practiced operator made the seemingly well-fasted stick
come loose.

Participation in the game that separated suckers from their
money spawned a new expression. As a result, any trickster or
cheat is described as prone to play fast and loose—often with a
lover or an employer, sometimes with a comrade or neighbor.

Pull a Fast One

SHOULD someone try to pull a fast one on you, take charge.
Look at details carefully and insist that sales talk or shuffled
papers be slowed down. If you don't, there is a good chance you
will lose.

That is probably what happened many times, during or soon
after the 1920s.

Many an obscure baseball pitcher seemed mediocre until a
moment of crisis. That's when he would pull a fast one—hurling
a ball at such speed that the batter would be caught off guard.
Another deception centered on movements of a dancer. Using a
confederate, or shill, many a sharpster shuffled clumsily for
maybe ten or fifteen minutes. When onlookers were persuaded to
wager about his skill, he would pull a fast one. That is, he would
move his feet so fast it was impossible to follow them.

Emulating the baseball pitcher who suddenly develops blister-
ing speed, and maybe the shuffle dancer as well, there are folks
who will try to pull a fast one—or get away with a smooth
swindle—in almost every area of activity.

Red-letter Day

EVEN if your engagement calendar is an arrangement of
black lines and numbers against a white surface, it is likely to
include a red-letter day or two.

We use that label for the start of a vacation, a birthday, or a holiday because calendars were once produced by hand—and were seldom seen except in monasteries and convents.

Scribes who prepared ecclesiastical calendars fell into the custom of emphasizing saints' days and feasts by listing them with ink made from ocher—a mineral oxide of iron. A quick glance at a calender hanging on the wall of an abbot revealed days numbered in red. Since each of these involved both anticipation and preparation, its name attached to secular observances or days that are special for personal reasons.

Roger

WHEN you ask if you have made yourself clear, instead of being told "Of course I understand!" you may get a one-word response: "Roger."

On the surface, there seems no reason why this name rather than, say, Harry or Mabel, should be used to mean "O.K.—I get the message."

Development of the usage was complicated, but wholly logical. For pilots in Britain's Royal Air Force found it a bit stilted as well as awkward to acknowledge a message by responding "Received." As "Roger" was used to represent the letter "R" in radio transmissions, it was natural to adopt its use instead of the less clear response of "Received." In conversation with civilians, pilots began using their special response to indicate "Yes" and "I know what you mean." Since general speech had no precise equivalent, the air-born word that fills an empty slot is now almost universally used and understood.

Screaming Meemies

SCANNING your working vocabulary for just the right words with which to speak of severe jitters, there is a good chance you may describe this state as a case of "screaming meemies."

If you use that expression occasionally, or hear it from others, you are indebted to German makers of weapons. During World

War II, many an American doughboy was startled half out of his wits at a never-before-heard sound halfway between a scream and a wail. This sound pattern, never forgotten once it was heard, was a byproduct of special artillery shells. Allied fighting men used a word that echoed the sound. As if that were not enough, many who heard it retreated into nervous hysteria that took the same vivid title.

As a result, the screaming meemies remains a familiar and dreaded condition long after screaming shells of World War II vintage became obsolete.

Short Shrift

HAVE you ever been accused of giving short shrift to instructions from a superior or a lecture from a relative? If you are guilty of having yielded only quick and perfunctory attention to something, you are not giving short shrift in its original sense.

From an Anglo-Saxon term for receiving confession, shrift named a common activity of priests—hearing of confessions and giving of absolutions. This could be long and tedious in the case of a person with a badly bruised conscience.

That must have been the case with many lawbreakers. But authorities were often more concerned with schedules; when a head was to be chopped off or a noose was to be fitted, the sheriff wanted the show to come off on time. That meant the final confession of a condemned person had to be brief. Hasty confession followed by fast pronounciation of absolution constituted not a normal rite but a short shrift.

So when someone gives you short shrift, you receive time and attention of duration and quality about like shrift yielded to a felon only minutes away from execution.

Shot in the Arm

NEXT time you receive a sudden infusion of energy and enthusiasm there is a good chance that you will tell others you got a "shot in the arm." To law-abiding citizens, the idea expressed is so general that it crops up every day in the best of circles.

Mood-altering drugs injected by means of a hypodermic needle were first used by physicians. Some employed them, along with adrenalin and other natural stimulants, in everyday practice. A patient suddenly stimulated, without knowing the nature of the drug received, was likely to call the experience a "shot in the arm." Under such circumstances, the boost in confidence or energy was therapeutic, legal, and commonplace.

Sideburns

CIVIL War General Ambrose E. Burnside was almost as dashing a figure as was George Armstrong Custer. In most public appearances, he sported a hat so flamboyant that it took his name. Defying established custom, Burnside shaved his chin smooth while displaying a full mustache and side bar whiskers.

Thousands of men wore Burnside hats and adopted the Burnside style of facial hair. But reversal of syllables is a common form of word play. Many a dashing fellow who prided himself on his lovely burnsides enjoyed turning the name around. Inverted in popular speech, whiskers that imitated those of the general's became sideburns.

The vogue for side whiskers has waxed and waned. Since then, the colorful name adapted from that of a general has been used to designate any patch of hair in front of a man's ears.

Slipshod

AT least as early as the 15th century, house slippers came into vogue. Made without heels or fastening devices, they did not damage floors and seemed to be easy on the backs of the wearers. Thin felt was the standard material used in making them.

Slip-shoes, as they were widely called, were designed strictly for indoor use. But careless persons often kept them on their feet when walking near their homes, or even on longer excursions. By 1580, it had become proverbial that a shameless person would go slip-shod to worship.

Many persons who wore slip-shoes into public places were careless about their appearance. As a result, we still use *slipshod* to designate anyone who is slovenly in appearance.

Talk a Blue Streak

Tall tales were the stock in trade of early American yarn swapping at the general store or tavern. Possibly from the influence of lightning, often having a bluish hue, fast movement was widely known as a *blue streak*.

What, if anything, moves as rapidly as the human tongue?

An excited person can jabber almost as fast as lightning stabs through the skies. But rapid speech is no more exhausting to listeners than is the slower-paced chatter by someone who talks endlessly. A person indulging in either speech pattern will talk a blue streak as long as even one listener occasionally nods understanding.

CHAPTER *10*

THE GREAT OUTDOORS

"Believe one who knows: you will find something more in
woods than in books. Trees and stones will teach you that
which you can never learn from masters."
$\qquad$ —St. Bernard of Clairvaux, *Epistles*

Our ancestors lived much more of their lives outside than
we do. They took many colorful examples from nature
and passed on to us a linguistic heritage rich in references to the
great outdoors.

BALLED UP
BALLPARK ESTIMATE
BARK UP THE WRONG
  TREE, TO
BAWL OUT
BITE
BROWSE
BUILD A FIRE
  UNDER SOMEONE
BUSH LEAGUE
CATBIRD SEAT
CINCH
DOGWOOD
FIELD DAY
FIREBUG
FLASH IN THE PAN
GET A RISE
HEDGE
HOOK, LINE, AND
  SINKER
HORSEPLAY
HUSKY
ILL-STARRED
LION'S SHARE
LOADED FOR BEAR

OLD STAMPING
  GROUND
ON CLOUD NINE
ON THE SKIDS
OUT ON A LIMB
PESTER
PLAY HOOKEY
PLAY POSSUM
REDNECK
RIDE HERD
RIDE SHOTGUN
SKID ROW
SKUNK
SMELLING LIKE
  A ROSE
SNOW JOB
STRING ALONG
SUCKER
TALK TURKEY
THROUGH THE
  GRAPEVINE
THUNDERSTRUCK
TUXEDO
UP A CREEK
UPSHOT

SEE ALSO: Blow Off Steam, Bury the Hatchet, Crawfish, Easy as Falling Off a Log, Feather One's Nest, Fishy, Go Off Half-cocked, Greenhorn, Jaywalker, Jinx, Land-Office Business, Mossback, Not Worth a Hill of Beans, Peter Out, Pull in One's Horns, Ramrod, Seedy, Smokey, Southpaw, Stool Pigeon.

Balled Up

EVER see a presiding officer or a committee chairman get all balled up? That's likely to happen when someone tries to handle a red-hot issue without reading up on parliamentary procedure.

The CEO of the moment may find himself in a fix about like that of a horse who's spent most of the day trudging through snow. By nightfall, the nag's shoe will have accumulated so much snow—packed into a hard ball of ice by its weight—that it is prone to slip and fall.

Does such an animal sound like some confused and incompetent leaders you know? If so, it's not a new condition. In 1920, F. Scott Fitzgerald had a befuddled character confess to being all balled up, having misjudged the meaning of the fellow who called the signals. Of course, this fellow may never have seen a balled horse—but could have been familiar with a tangled mass of string wadded into a ball.

Ballpark Estimate

WHEN you talk to your accountant about the bottom line on your tax return, you want an exact figure—not a ballpark estimate.

In the days when all baseball games were played in the open air during daylight hours, newsmen would have liked to know precisely how many fans showed up for a given game. But they seldom found out because owners and managers were cagey and it was hard to get a precise head count. Besides, publicity about a low turnout might keep people away from the next game.

It became standard practice to give a very broad estimate— plus or minus a few hundred or a few thousand—when asked about the size of the gate on Saturday afternoon. Influence of what has long been billed as America's national pastime made the *ballpark estimate* our standard label for any rough count.

Bark up the Wrong Tree, To

EARLY settlers in what is now the United States discovered a new prey for hunting. Raccoons and possums were abundant, and could be hunted with nearly any kind of dog. When first pursued, a 'coon would run through the underbrush. But as dogs neared, the animal would climb the nearest tree. Barking and jumping underneath, dogs tried to keep their quarry at bay until hunters came to make the kill.

Sometimes, however, a shrewd animal played a trick. After climbing a tree, it worked its way through branches and across other trees to freedom—leaving dogs barking under an empty tree. This outcome of a hunting expedition was common enough to cause us to say another person is mistaken by commenting that he or she is "barking up the wrong tree."

Bawl Out

SHOULD you ever bawl out a delivery person or a sales clerk, your actions may remind someone of a really ornery creature.

Handlers vow that the domestic bull is the most persistent and belligerent animal on earth. When a big fellow is angry, he is mad at everybody and everything. In the Old West, every cowboy knew that when a bull was rounded up, he was likely to bellow for hours.

Angry noise made by animals was so common that a cattleman who berated another was compared with a bull and said to bawl out the other. Long a part of ranch talk, the term was popularized by writer Rex Beach. It caught the public imagination and soon swept the country as a vigorous way to describe a vocal display of anger.

Bite

IN 1644, Isaak Walton retired and spent much of his time in England's countryside. At age sixty he wrote *The Compleat*

Angler, a volume about fishing. Walton's classic passed through five editions in twenty-five years, then was enlarged by chapters on making flies and fishing with them.

Typical run-of-the-mill sportsmen, though aware of what was offered in the book for anglers, continued to depend upon coarse bait and crude hooks. In order to be caught, a fish had to swallow the bait or clamp down on the hook firmly enough to fix it in the mouth.

Practical jokers saw an analogy between catching fish and hooking human victims, as did confidence men. They began to say that in order to deceive a fellow successfully, he must be persuaded to bite on bait of one kind or another. By 1750, the expression born on riverbanks of England had entered standard speech to name any response to trickery.

Browse

MULTITUDES of persons like to browse among the offerings of a shopping mall or titles available in the local library. If you are among these, you emulate—after a fashion—actions that once took place only in open air.

In seasons when grass was in short supply, hungry domestic animals of Europe often nibbled leaves and twigs. From an old expression naming a tender young shoot, or growth, an ox or sheep that filled its stomach with such stuff was said to *browse*.

Merchants became irritated because folk often spent more time looking than buying. Half-hearted shoppers were compared with a cow moving from shrub to shrub, and the outdoor label attached to actions of any person who takes a nibble now and then without pausing for a hearty fill.

Build a Fire Under Someone

A MULE, half brother to the horse, is among the sturdiest work animals. But in and out of season, he is likely to be ornery and stubborn. When all four legs are spread apart, an animal can take so firm a stand that neither coaxing nor beating will make him budge.

Cotton belt farmers adopted a desperate course of action. When everything else failed, a small fire was built under the mule's belly in hopes that once in action the animal could be guided and kept moving.

This expedient figured in many yarns and jokes. It probably wasn't tried nearly so often as earthy tales suggest. But occasional actual incidents and numerous stories brought a new phrase into speech. Regardless of what is actually intended, a person may borrow from the lingo of the mule-skinner and threaten to build a fire under the person he hopes to stir into movement.

Bush League

ANY sparsely settled area aside from a desert is likely to abound in bushes and trees. Not simply in modern times, but for many centuries, urban dwellers have been prone to look down their noses at bush country.

Small cities located in such regions cannot pay the freight in order to have major league baseball teams. A minor confederation is the best that such a place can afford.

Spreading from baseball talk, even if located in the heart of Manhattan, a small enterprise is likely to be disparaged as *bush league*.

Catbird Seat

ANYTIME you are in complete control of a situation you are sitting in the "catbird seat."

That was often the case with persons who tried their luck at pioneer sportscaster Red Barber's poker table. When he was sure that there was an ace in the hole, whispered that he was sitting in the catbird seat.

Red's memory of tales heard in youth may have influenced

him. Tall tales transmitted orally in the Southeast praise the catbird as being the smartest of all wild feathered creatures.

Intrigued by his poker-playing friend's vivid expression, James Thurber called one of his famous stories "The Catbird Seat." Introduced into everyday speech by Thurber, the phrase has proved so resilient that no one describes a position of advantage as a bluebird's seat or a redbird's seat.

Cinch

CITY-BRED adventurers who flocked to gold fields in 1849 encountered many strange customs. Not the least of these was the use of a novel saddle girth for horses. Instead of using English-style belly bands with straps and buckles, Mexicans of the southwest employed twisted ropes running between two rings.

Such a piece of gear, called a *cinch,* was far more adjustable than any equipment familiar in the East. A rider who knew how to fasten a Spanish cinch could lace a saddle so that it stayed in position all day. Clumsy buckles had to be adjusted frequently. Such is the holding power of the cinch that its name is employed to stand for any sure thing.

Dogwood

DURING April, much of the southeastern United States is decorated with the glorious white and pink of flowering dogwoods. A Smoky Mountain tale would have you believe that the tree owes its name to bloodhounds.

These animals, according to a story usually told with a chuckle, were highly prized during pioneer days. They seemed to realize that they were no ordinary dogs, for some of their habits were peculiar. Among other things, a male wouldn't lift his leg against just any tree or post—he would use only the variety that scientists call *Cornus florida.* The legend says that so many bloodhounds relied on this tree that mountaineers called it *dogwood.*

There is not a word of truth in that explanation. Dogwood gets its name from the fact that lots of old-time folk remedies made use of bark from the tree. Dried and ground before being included in an emulsion, the stuff was considered the best of all concoctions with which to rid a dog of fleas. So much bark was applied to hides of canines that the tree from which it came is known as the *dogwood*.

Field Day

ONCE in a while everyone ought to enjoy a field day. It makes little or no difference what goings-on are involved; romping around and having things pretty much as you want them is a special kind of self-rewarding activity.

That is what members of fraternities, sororities, and civic clubs discovered long ago. Instead of sticking strictly to routine, many groups of this nature announced that two weeks from Saturday every member would spend the day outdoors. Rivals were challenged to set the day aside, too, in order to compete in games and sports.

Canny leaders often arranged things so that it would be difficult or impossible for a really tough set of opponents to be on hand at the time selected. This meant that sponsors could cavort through the field day, having things their own way and gloating at winning easy victories.

Firebug

GNATS, flies, and other insects have pestered outdoorsmen for centuries. Sparsely settled frontier America seemed to be a special haven for them. Swarms of bugs could drive a hunter, farmer, or homemaker nearly crazy.

An extremely enthusiastic person, almost obsessed, was compared with a persistent insect and called a bug. Tariff bugs of the

South, denounced in 1841, were as zealous as computer bugs today.

No other human who acted as single-minded as a buzzing fly was so dreaded as the firebug. This label for an arsonist was current soon after the Civil War. Mark Twain helped the label gain wide acceptance when in 1881 he described a character as a "counterfeiter, horse-thief, and firebug from the most notorious nest in Galveston."

Flash in the Pan

EARLY Americans hunted game under conditions that would baffle many modern hunters. Their greatest handicap was the inefficiency of crude flintlock guns. When a trigger was snapped, friction between flint and steel might produce a good spark—and might yield none.

Even a strong spurt of flame didn't guarantee that a gun would fire. It was equipped with a shallow pan in which a trail of powder led from flint to charge. A jolt or a period of dampness could render the thin line of powder ineffective. In such cases, the flash of light from the pan was not followed by detonation of a charge. Such a flash in the pan was experienced so frequently that we use the weapons term to stand for any quick and dazzling failure.

Get a Rise

SOMETIMES a casual comment from you will get a rise from a listener. A quick retort may run the gamut from minor vexation to high-level indignation. Whatever the response, if it is accompanied by reddening of the face and neck, you may be sure you have hit a tender spot.

But, you don't have to be fishing for a heated comeback in order to get one. It can be triggered by a perfectly innocent remark.

Rapidity of response in such a situation is similar to a hungry fish rising to the bait. A human whose emotions are aroused by a sentence or a phrase or even a single word rises to it like a bass going for a fly.

Hedge

THROUGHOUT much of northern Europe, early farmers planted bushes and shrubs to serve as fences and boundary lines. Anglo-Saxons were partial to hawthorn, a row of which they called a *hege*. It was a mark of caution to plant hawthorn around a field, or hedge it.

Eventually the name of the barrier came to be used in connection with many kinds of safeguards. As a result, we say that a person who wagers on several horses rather than only one hedges his bet. Many a person manages to hedge by avoiding direct promises and unqualified commitments.

Hook, Line, and Sinker

DURING the colorful era when stories circulated largely by word of mouth, tall tales were popular and prized. Many fishermen tried to impress cronies by telling about a hungry one that didn't stop with the hook, but gulped down the line and sinker as well. A tenderfoot from the east was likely to bite on almost any yarn. Compared with a ravenous fish, he was ridiculed as swallowing the tale, "hook, line, and sinker."

By the time civilization settled the frontier, the phrase had crossed the Atlantic from east to west. On both sides of the ocean, it is just right to label gullible and uncritical listening.

Horseplay

DURING many centuries, horses were rare and expensive. Some knights actually did dash about Europe on spirited chargers. But oxen and donkeys were the most abundant and familiar beasts of burden.

Rarity of horses meant that it was quite an experience to see one of them frisking about a field or wallowing in dust. A big animal who lay on its back with all four feet flailing was obviously having a good time. So was a pasture mate who ran up to another in order to nuzzle.

Rough wallowing of a stallion and gentler romping of a mare was compared with boisterous action of humans. As a result, since the 16th century we have used horseplay to label rowdy and prankish behavior—indoors as well as outdoors.

Husky

EARLY explorers in the far north thought that natives called themselves *Huskemaws*. The English who visited the region applied the abbreviated word *Husky* to many things they found there, including the Husky dog.

Eventually the people came to be known as Esquimos, and later Eskimos. But the older title, *husky,* clung to the native canine. Since a husky is notably powerful, its name was used to designate sturdiness in general.

Harriet Beecher Stowe, author of *Uncle Tom's Cabin,* picked up the term and used it in an 1869 story. Adopted into general speech, the mangled Esquimo word is now applied to any stalwart person—who may or may not be pleased at being compared with a sled dog.

Ill-starred

STARS have fascinated people since the beginning of civilization. Ancient seers who watched them decided that they affected everything on earth. Babylonians developed astrology as a science, then passed it along to the Greeks. As late as the time of

Columbus, students of the stars had great influence at many European courts.

Each star was considered to affect the destiny of nations and of individuals. Elaborate star maps were consulted at the birth of children in an attempt to discover their futures.

Deep and pervasive belief in astrology affected both actions and speech. A person who met disaster was long prone to blame it on the heavens and describe himself or herself as being "ill-starred"—or fated to have bad luck.

Modern astronomy has shown that stars have no direct influence upon the course of events. But ardent believers ignore logic. Influence of astrology often leads us to say that an unfortunate event or set of circumstances is ill-starred.

Lion's Share

WHEN a bonus plan or vacation schedule is announced, it may not be equitable. Sometimes two or three people get the lion's share of the package.

In one of Aesop's fables, a lion, a goat, a sheep, and a heifer go hunting together. When a splendid deer is killed, the lion divides the venison into four equal portions. Then he seizes three for himself and suggests that his comrades may divide the fourth—if they dare.

Even when someone other than the boss of all the animals does the dividing, the one who gets the biggest portion automatically gets the lion's share.

Loaded for Bear

IF you ever face a situation of conflict in which you will be up against a tough and seasoned opponent, you had better try to be "loaded for bear."

Why bear, rather than wolf or deer or moose?

Because hunters of the frontier era found bears to be their

toughest quarry. Nothing in nature is more dangerous than a full-grown bear, wounded by a shot that failed to kill.

Tiny pellets packed into a shotgun were adequate for a squirrel or a rabbit. When a person went after a twelve-point buck, he loaded his gun with buckshot. And for the fiercest creature of the American wild, he stayed home unless he was loaded for bear.

Old Stamping Ground

ONCE abundant, the prairie chicken or pennated grouse is famous for its behavior. Many early settlers watched males gather at dawn on knolls. Performing an elaborate courtship dance, they made a loud booming noise while strutting and stamping about. Throughout Indiana and Illinois, many gathering places were worn bald by the feet of birds telling the world that they wanted mates.

Courtship spots of the prairie chicken were generally familiar to humans of the region. Almost inevitably, any habitual resort came to be called an "old stamping ground." That name continues to be used even when males who congregate there do not stamp their feet in order to advertise their wants to spring chickens.

On Cloud Nine

BEFORE the advent of adding machines and calculators, even simple arithmetic was difficult. Persons forced to wrestle with multiplication and division developed special admiration for nine, believed to be the most powerful single-digit number.

This view may have been a byproduct of reverence for the Holy Trinity, since nine is three times three. As late as the Victorian Age, a person sporting the finest possible outfit was often described as being "dressed to the nines." Tradition having asserted that clouds exist in a series of successively higher layers, it was logical to label the ultimate height as *cloud nine*.

A victorious contestant or a person suddenly made exuberant

seems literally to be soaring in the clouds. Naturally, therefore, someone who hits the ultimate in joy is still likely to say "I'm on cloud nine!"

On the Skids

UNTIL modern machines were developed, movement of goods for even short distances could be a major chore. To save time and cut down on labor, Americans constructed ramps and platforms made of heavy timber, or skids. Often slanted sharply, these devices were ideal for rolling logs or barrels. With practice, it was easy to slide many other things down such an inclined framework—especially if it was greased.

Once a barrel or a bale was placed in position and given a push, it was on the skids and headed downward out of control. This strongly suggests that when a person's career or character is seen by others to be on the skids, then he or she is headed for a downfall.

Out on a Limb

A PERSON who finds himself or herself "out on a limb" is in a precarious position, with no sure or easy way to get out of the predicament.

That is precisely the situation of a possum or raccoon who takes to a tree and misjudges the distance to another. Having moved far out on a limb in order to jump to safety, such an animal suddenly realizes that there is no escape from its pursuer. It is too far to jump, and dogs are already under the tree, barking to bring hunters for the kill.

Though barely a century old in literary use, the hunting term born on the American frontier may have been used orally as early as Colonial times.

Pester

SINCE it is possible for someone to pester you at home, on the job, or anywhere else, this doesn't appear to be an outdoor term. Yet for centuries, the activity it names never took place indoors.

Few everyday tasks of long ago were more vexatious than that of trying to tie a horse to graze. Crude gear was likely either to trip and injure the animal, or to come loose and release him. Eventually many persons resorted to use of a drag tied to the foot between hoof and fetlock.

Such a hobble, known as a *pastern,* was adopted in many regions. Slightly modified, the ancient horse term entered modern speech to express the idea of annoying or impeding a person as well as an animal.

Play Hookey

ISAAK Walton, one of the most widely read early writers about fishing, stressed the importance of getting the hook fixed firmly in the mouth of a fighting fish. His followers, conscious that this required a sudden jerk of the line, began to use *hook* as a verb of action. A person who decamped hastily was said to "hook it;" Charles Dickens used the phrase in this sense.

Compulsory education gave some youngsters an incentive to hook it in a new way. When a teacher's back was turned, a truant would bolt off. If this ruse was successful, a student was likely to hide out the next day and fail to appear for roll call.

Adolescents and children being what they are, it became taken for granted that nearly every student would skip school at least once. But even when performed as deftly as a fisherman's master stroke, the jerk of defiance doesn't always work. Parents and teachers know all the ropes—having learned them in their own days of playing hookey.

Play Possum

IMAGINE that you are a member of a group whose leader asks for volunteers. You aren't interested in the project, or don't have time to get involved. What is the best course of action? Sneak hurriedly out of the room? Suddenly become involved in conversation with a friend? Or sit very still, act as though you didn't hear, and "play possum"?

Any veteran woodsman will advise the last alternative. That is because pioneers discovered 300 years ago that a native American animal has traits like few others. White men called the creature opossum, in an attempt to imitate the speech of native Americans. Only purists used that name, though; most persons clipped it to possum.

Captured, a possum shows great skill in pretending to be dead. Even stroking or shaking seldom causes it to open its eyes. So when a person does a good job of playing possum, he or she is— for the moment—dead to challenges or suggestions.

Redneck

SOME of our colorful expressions are all but self-explanatory. When that is true, someone is sure to hunt for and claim to discover an explanation.

That is what a language specialist did a few years ago. Explaining why almost anyone from the rural South may be called a *redneck,* an analyst said it is because anger makes the neck turn red.

However, the simple truth is that most who work in the fields wear clothing that provides a loose and open neck. Day after day, rays of the sun reach exposed skin. A broad-brimmed straw hat provides only intermittent protection. After spending twenty-five years planting and cultivating and harvesting, a fellow's neck is likely to get dark brownish red and stay that way.

Because the American South has been, and is, more agricultural than the industrial North, the term *redneck* has come to be associated exclusively with southerners.

Ride Herd

IN the days of fenceless ranching, some cattle were driven only 300 miles or so to market. Other drives were four times as long.

Cooks and wagon drivers were the lucky ones, comparatively. Their work day extended only from first light to an hour after sundown. Not so the trail riders. To head off stampedes and to round up stragglers was a twenty-four-hour-a-day job.

Cattle usually obeyed, though sometimes they balked before yielding. Today, you don't have to climb into the saddle in order to ride herd. Just concentrate upon keeping everyone moving along at home or on the job.

Ride Shotgun

SHOULD you ever be asked to ride shotgun on a fund-raising campaign or some other enterprise, you will be expected to keep your eyes peeled for trouble.

That is precisely what the shotgun-toting guard did in the Old West. Usually assigned a seat beside the driver, the fellow who rode shotgun paid little or no attention to passengers or to horses. He stayed busy looking for signs of outlaws like Jesse James or for Indians, and kept his weapon at the ready in case it had to be used.

The shotgun rider continues to be a vital member of a team which may face unexpected problems on the way to a goal.

Skid Row

IT is a paradox of modern American life that there is a skid row in every city of a nation famous for its mind-boggling innovations. An unsavory district of an urban area owes its name to the invention of a fast way to get timber to market.

Forestry began in earnest soon after the Civil War. As part of every big logging operation, a track of logs or heavy boards was built from the site of cutting to the nearest road. Often greased with lard, this made it easy to skid or to drag logs.

In a village near a lumber camp, a street lined with shacks was compared with the chute for dragging and was given its name. By the time large-scale logging began to decline, skid roads of hamlets caused any run-down and disreputable street or section of any city to be known as *skid row*.

Skunk

WHEN you skunk an opponent in a game or a rival in business, your victory is decisive and maybe absolute.

That is because our ancestors long ago noticed that the size of a skunk is not a measure of its prowess. When one of these little striped animals sprays its perfume, other creatures—including humans—beat a hasty retreat.

Victory of a skunk is generally total, rather than partial. As early as 1850, its name was being used as a verb to label actions leading to utter defeat.

Smelling Like a Rose

BARNYARD humor was probably born a few days after animals were first herded into a pen. Still going strong, this special brand of humor has been a favorite of many famous folk—including Abraham Lincoln.

Every rustic likes to pretend that no city slicker has sense enough to identify horse or cow dung. Wandering into a barnyard, a fellow who looks down his nose at rubes is likely to fall flat on his face in the manure pile. That outcome is central to many a barnyard story.

But perhaps for the sake of variety, an occasional spinner of tall tales will use a different ending. In such a yarn a person falls into a manure pile as usual—but emerges from it without a trace of foul odor.

That outcome is always described as a result of extraordinary good luck, not skill or wisdom. So it isn't necessary to remember the one about a son of a president who was up to his neck in a savings and loan scandal to realize that once in a while someone in a scrape really does come up "smelling like a rose."

Snow Job

WHEN a person sets out to do a snow job on you, the temperature does not matter. It can happen in a season when falling white stuff wouldn't last thirty seconds after hitting the ground.

But the verbal metaphor really is based on winter weather. That is when snow can pile up deeply before anyone has a chance to clear a path.

A persuasive flow of words aims at overwhelming by sheer mass. So be wary when you face a verbal deluge that is too smooth and allows you no time to think about dealing with it. There is a good chance someone is trying to blanket you two feet deep before you can find the old snow shovel.

String Along

ALMOST from the time men first put halters and bridles on animals, strings of them were formed for some operations. Caravan drivers tied as many as fifty camels together in single file, then handled them with only two or three men. Long strings of donkeys were linked in pack trains, and smaller groups of horses were driven in the same fashion.

A person who is strung along is being led, sometimes by an increasingly long string, and sometimes with an increasingly distant goal.

Sucker

EARLY settlers in the New World discovered an odd fish. A specimen can often be seen swimming near the bottom in order to suck up bit of debris as food. The shape of its mouth and lips led it to be called the *sucker*.

Soon the name was applied to mullet, chub, barbel, and other fish, whose lips suggest they might feed by suction. With so many species bearing the same common name, it was natural that a sucker of some kind could be caught almost every time a hook was thrown into the water.

Ease of landing a sucker led sportsmen to disparage it as an easy mark. As a result, anyone who bites on bait dangled by a swindler, a confidence man, or a skirt-swishing gold digger is known as a *sucker*.

Talk Turkey

HALF a dozen anecdotes seek to explain this expression for speaking plainly. Most of them recount a conversation between an American Indian and one or more white settlers. Discussing the division of game bagged in a joint hunt, the native insists that his comrades talk turkey and hand over to him the biggest bird shot during the day.

These entertaining frontier stories bypass a skill that was long familiar—and important—to veteran woodsmen.

Many a fellow reared in the woods became an expert turkey caller. That is, he so skillfully imitated sounds made by the big wild birds that some who heard at a distance came within gun range. It was this bona fide turkey talk, not banter at the end of a day's hunt, that spawned our American expression for speaking in a clear and forthright manner.

Through the Grapevine

IF you receive a message through the grapevine, it is likely to be gossip. That is because the new-fangled system of communication invented by Samuel F. B. Morse used wires that looked for all the world like vines strung between poles.

Especially during the Civil War, telegraph lines transmitted many wild rumors. Some of them spread so rapidly that soldiers and civilians alike agreed that there must be a grapevine telegraph at work in remote regions.

Most battlefield dispatches were true, but some were unfounded. Enough bogus or suspect messages were transmitted that any person-to-person network came to be labeled a *grapevine telegraph* whose news shouldn't be accepted without question.

Thunderstruck

AS late as the 17th century, few common folk knew that thunder is the noise that follows a lightning flash. Many people caught outdoors in a violent storm feared thunderbolts almost as much as lightning.

Fear and trembling were so common during storms that these atmospheric disturbances were linked with any state of acute terror. A 17th-century poet described a love-shaken youth as being so "thunder-stroken" that he was "void of sense."

Since the time of Benjamin Franklin, we have known that thunder is never dangerous. But earlier notions about it are firmly embedded in language. As a result, a person who seems speechless from surprise or fear is likely to be described as being thunderstruck.

Tuxedo

WHEN you wear a tuxedo, or see someone else sporting this outfit, chances are that you will associate it with a gala evening event rather than the great outdoors. That linkage conceals the background of the garment's name.

Among some American Indians, the concept of a round foot such as that of a wolf was expressed by sounds that whites rendered as tuxedo. That, in turn, named a lake not far from New York City.

When the family of tobacco magnate Pierre Lorillard acquired the region near the lake, it became an exclusive residential area. At a famous Tuxedo Lake party, males wore a newfangled dress outfit. Almost inevitably, it took the name of the resort that bore the name of a wolf's foot.

Up a Creek

MOST rivers of England and Europe are fairly small. Even before the advent of modern highways the rivulets, or creeks, of these regions posed few obstacles to travelers.

Settlers in the New World found a different situation. Rivers such as the Ohio, the Mississippi, and the Missouri were so mighty that even large streams seemed to be creeks by comparison.

A hunter or explorer sometimes tried to cross at an untried spot. If he misjudged speed or depth of water, he might be trapped up the creek until rescued.

Modern bridges have eliminated most hazards posed by flowing water. Yet a person whose feet are not wet may suddenly be caught "up a creek"—stuck in a dilemma from which it is hard to escape without help.

Upshot

VILLAGERS of medieval Britain took archery seriously. Big matches were gala affairs that affected the social standing of participants. Many were conducted like modern sporting events; the winner of a given round moved up to the next.

Competitors were often so closely matched that the last shot of a round determined its outcome. In such circumstances a single arrow caused one man to drop out, another to move up toward a new opponent.

A shot that propelled an archer upward in competition came to be known as an *upshot*. Use of the sporting word by Shakespeare and Milton caused it to enter general speech. We employ it to name any type of result or conclusion, no matter how remote from activities on the village green.

CHAPTER *11*

MAKING FUN OF OTHERS

"On the day of resurrection, those who have indulged in ridicule will be called to the door of Paradise and have it shut in their faces."

—*The Koran*

I f Mohammed, the prophet of the Koran, is right, lots of us won't make it through the pearly gates. For everyday speech includes barbed humor not always easily recognized.

Human nature being what it is, those who first learned to babble in single-syllable words probably used some of them to poke fun at others. We use many inherited verbal jibes—and are constantly inventing new ones.

ASLEEP AT THE SWITCH
BACK NUMBER
COLD-BLOODED
CRAWFISH
DARK HORSE
DRIVER'S SEAT
FIFTH WHEEL
FRENCH LEAVE
FUNNY BONE
HENPECK
KNOW BEANS
LEFT HOLDING THE
  BAG, TO BE

LOWBROW
MOSSBACK
MUG
NOT WORTH A HILL
  OF BEANS
POPPYCOCK
PULL THE WOOL
  OVER ONE'S EYES
PUTTING ON THE DOG
SEEDY
STUFFED SHIRT
WHOLE HOG

SEE ALSO: Boner, Bronx Cheer, Bunk, Dead as a Doornail, Half-baked, Indian Giver, Josh, Lay an Egg, Muff, Poo-Bah, Silhouette, Welch

Asleep at the Switch

A PERSON sitting behind a desk, shuffling papers with eyes wide open, may be asleep at the switch. That is, he or she acts like an old time railroader who failed to execute commands.

Electronic signals now govern the switching of boxcars or entire trains. Until recent times, though, the task of getting the track ready for a switch to be made was performed by a man's muscles. Even when traffic was fairly heavy, the switchman's job was dull and routine. At some spots, it meant undiluted boredom.

Small wonder, therefore, that many a switchman was lulled into slumber. Literal cases of being asleep at the switch spawned today's figurative use of the expression.

Back Number

MANY early American periodicals were issued at irregular intervals, sometimes without dates. Only regular readers knew from a glance whether or not a particular number was fresh off the press.

Printed matter was so scarce on the frontier that settlers prized old newspapers and pamphlets. More sophisticated folk, mostly urban, turned up their noses at this attitude.

Sneering at publications that had been lying around for a while led any outdated person or fashion to be labeled a *back number*.

Cold-blooded

LONG before the rise of scientific medicine, everyday experience showed that there are strong links between emotions and blood. During anger or after activity, sensations in the face and neck hint that the vital fluid has become warmer. Feelings that accompany acute fear can be interpreted to mean that temperature of blood has suddenly dropped.

Medieval scholars found it striking that temperaments vary

widely. Some persons easily become enraged—so furious that their blood seems to be at the boiling point. Others seldom lose their tranquility, so may be derided as passionless or cold-blooded.

Modern science has exploded the myth of wide variations in blood temperature among humans. But influence of the past and the association of cold-blooded reptiles with evil made a lasting impression upon speech.

Practically everyone now knows that a thermometer would show a healthy person's blood to be at 98.6 degrees or there-abouts. In spite of that, we still describe anyone considered cruel or vindictive as being cold-blooded.

Crawfish

As late as the era of Andrew Jackson, crawfish abounded in rivers and creeks. Some settlers ate them when food was scarce and many more used them as bait.

Every child who watched his or her first crawfish in action noticed that the queer creature swims backward. That trait was just right for use in frontier humor. To back out of a promise caused a person to *crawfish*—or act like the odd critter that scientists called the *crayfish*.

Dark Horse

From the beginning of the democratic experiment, election of public officials has been seen as being a lot like a horse race. No one knows who will win until the votes are counted, but almost everyone has a favorite. So no disparagement is intended when a public figure compares a candidate with a spirited horse.

Legend has it that Sam Flynn of Tennessee picked up an easy living by racing a coal-black stallion named Dusky Pete. Flynn usually rode Pete into a strange town as though he were an ordinary saddle horse. Not knowing they faced a champion, local men cheerfully set up races—and lost. As a result, Flynn's dark horse became more than regionally noted.

Formation of a new political term was probably helped by the fact that anything dark is foreboding and unlikely. At any rate, lingo of the track entered smoke-filled convention halls. As a result, professionals often joke that an unknown who shows a chance of winning is a dark horse in the campaign.

Driver's Seat

DRIVERS of buggies and coaches made fun of persons who ventured to try self-propelled vehicles. "Get a horse!" was often shouted to the driver of a stalled car.

By 1912, opinion was changing rapidly. It was clear that anyone behind the steering wheel of a car was in a seat of awesome power. Never before had anyone had fingertip control of power greater than that of a forty-mule team.

In a new and important sense, the fate of a fast vehicle and its occupants rested with one person. Many kinds of drivers had occupied a great variety of seats for thousands of years. Yet it was the driver's seat of an automobile or truck that caused the position to name a person in charge of any enterprise.

Fifth Wheel

EVERY few years, you see a story about an inventor who has come up with a way to turn tap water into gasoline. So far, no chemical or gadget has made a dent in the revenue of OPEC countries.

Long before gasoline became a necessity of life, sharpers took advantage of persons always on the go. All sorts of contrivances were touted as adding efficiency or comfort to surreys and broughams and carriages.

One widely-sold device was a horizontal wheel for attachment to the front axle of a vehicle. Sometimes it provided a little support and stability during sharp turns. On good roads, however, this fifth wheel was a useless addition.

Except for the benefit of tourists, fifth wheels of this sort—and vehicles that sport them—are long gone. Their influence was great enough, though, to form a jocular label for a person who rolls along partner-less with a group.

French Leave

DURING the 18th century, the French had a custom of leaving a party or gathering without saying goodbye to the host or hostess. While this action was not considered rude by the French, other nationalities took offense.

French soldiers were often invited to parties at Colonial merchants' and plantation owners' homes during the American Revolution. Whenever a Frenchman departed without so much as an "adieu," the hosts believed it was because the French thought too highly of themselves.

In time, anyone who departed without paying due respects to the host and hostess was contemptuously described as having taken "French leave."

Spawned long ago in ballrooms of Philadelphia and Charleston and New York, the derogatory saying was in World War I applied to a soldier who deserted from his unit and thereby "left like a Frenchman." Once firmly fixed in speech, *French leave* expanded to name unceremonious and maybe secretive departure from any situation.

Funny Bone

HUMAN anatomy was largely a mystery until comparatively recent times. Because skeletons were abundant, bones were the first body parts to be the subject of scientific study. Terms were chosen from Latin as it was the universal language of scholarship.

There is no record of who first gave serious attention to the relatively big bone that runs from the shoulder to the elbow, but it is technically known as the *humerus* (which is Latin for "upper arm").

Some jokester framed a pun and called the tip of the humerus the funny bone. Bumping this bone is not humorous even to persons unacquainted with classical languages. Yet it yields a distinctively unusual—or funny—sensation when struck against a hard surface.

Henpeck

BIOLOGIST W. C. Allee gained fame by discovering the pecking order among hens. But a fowl's practice of using her beak as a weapon was noticed long before it came under the scrutiny of a scientist.

Aggressive wives were compared with fowls and said to "henpeck" their mates. Beginning late in the 17th century, writers began joking about male submissiveness. Even Lord Byron quipped that great ladies had "hen-peck'd" the nation's lords. Actually, henpecking of this type is limited to humans. Females of the barnyard peck one another with fervor, but let the lord of the barnyard alone.

Accurate or not, the metaphor is firmly established in speech. It is used to describe a female's verbal attacks upon a male— despite the fact that few if any roosters ever undergo henpecking.

Know Beans

MORE than a century ago, rural humor included a brief query: a person was asked to say how many blue beans it took to make seven white beans.

A person who gave up in bewilderment didn't know beans, of course, for the answer was simple: Seven blue beans, peeled, make seven white ones.

Anyone dull enough not to know beans may also be derided as knowing diddly-squat.

Left Holding the Bag, to be

RURAL America of the 19th century had no fraternities or sororities, but hazing was a common ritual. Often it involved taking an adolescent to hunt an imaginary bird, the snipe. Told that the snipe would dash into a heavy-duty bag that is properly held, the victim was made bag holder. Pranksters said they'd beat the bushes and drive the snipe into the bag—then slipped away, stifling their laughter.

When and where snipe hunting was invented, no one knows. But this rural method of poking fun at a gullible youngster was common. As a result, even in big cities where no one would wait for the imaginary snipe, a person who is tricked or swindled is said to be "left holding the bag."

Lowbrow

PEOPLE who poke fun at someone by calling him or her a "lowbrow" usually think of themselves as "highbrows." But they may not be aware that these labels perpetuate findings of a one-time science that has been completely discredited.

Seeking explanations for variations in intelligence, a group of 19th-century experimenters developed what they called *phrenology,* or the study of bumps and shapes of the skull.

Phrenologists swore that they could find out a lot from a map of a person's head, with brows thought to be especially revealing. A person with high brows was judged to be especially intelligent, capable of doing almost anything. But anyone whose brows sat low on the forehead was a hopeless slob—doomed to ignorance by birth.

Phrenology went by the boards a long time ago, but left its tracks behind. We now know that the height of a person's brow is meaningless except as a detail of appearance. Yet speech retains *lowbrow* to label anyone thought to lack refinement and incapable of acquiring it.

Mossback

A FIRST-TIME visitor to South Carolina's low country or to coastal Georgia is likely to be overwhelmed by the Spanish moss hanging from trees. Verbal descriptions, even by great poets, fail fully to convey initial impressions felt in such settings.

Early travelers, awed by the moss, were less than favorably impressed by persons living there. Genuinely isolated, many natives of such regions were not abreast of what was happening in the rest of the world.

Poking fun at a resident who had never ventured outside live oak country, self-styled sophisticates from other areas took to comparing a swamp dweller with a heavily festooned tree. From this derisive usage, *mossback* entered mainstream speech. Now it labels anyone judged to be behind the times.

Mug

WHEN you speak of a friend's face as his or her "mug," you make use of a relatively new word.

Beer mugs of the late 18th century were often shaped to represent human heads. Some depicted famous persons, others were caricatures of ordinary heads.

A person not especially noted for classical beauty often bore a more than superficial resemblance to a face on a mug. That inevitably led to joshing from friends and associates. As an aftermath of humor in the pottery shop, every face came to be called a *mug*.

Not Worth a Hill of Beans

OFFERED "a stand-out bargain" at a flea market, you may decline by silently or orally dismissing merchandise as being "not worth a hill of beans."

These days, you would be hard put to find a literal hill of beans. In the era when many households grew their own food, everyone had plenty of them.

A cluster of seeds covered with a mound of earth constituted a hill. Long rows in the garden included so many hills that no one bothered to count them. For practical purposes this meant that a single hill of beans was so nearly worthless that its value couldn't be estimated.

Poppycock

AT the age of twenty-four, Charles F. Brown adopted the pen name of Artemis Ward. His yarns became immensely popular soon after they began appearing in the Cleveland *Plain Dealer* in 1858.

Since his real name was concealed, Ward ignored convention. In lieu of stilted prose, he used language that prim readers condemned as coarse or incomprehensible.

Taking a dig at political oratory, he adapted a Dutch barnyard term for soft dung. The hot air spouted by the aspirants for office, said the humorist, was "nothing more than pure poppycock."

Sensing that Ward's new word was earthy, his fans applied it to congressional debates without knowing its meaning. Soon any kind of worthless talk or nonsense came to be called poppycock.

Pull the Wool Over One's Eyes

ONLY a few centuries ago, most men of importance wore large wigs. Since judges were especially dignified, they adopted appropriately prominent wigs.

Regardless of how skillful its maker, a woolen transformation for the head was likely to be clumsy. Many of them slipped in use, temporarily blocking vision.

A typical lawyer who succeeded in tricking a judge bragged and laughed simultaneously at having "pulled the wool over his eyes." Use in legal circles was so common that the expression came to stand for any ruse leading to deception.

Putting on the Dog

HUGE profits were made during the Civil War by contractors who provided goods to the army. At the cessation of hostilities, fortunes were won from land speculation and railroad building.

Members of the newly rich had plenty of money, but usually lacked culture. Seeking to win social acceptance, persons such as Diamond Jim Brady made a vulgar display of opulence.

Lap dogs were all the rage among wives of the wealthy. They spent large sums on pets, and each tried to top the excesses of others. Pampered poodles became linked with the desire for show, so a person making any sort of flashy display was ridiculed as "putting on the dog."

Seedy

OWNERS of large tracts of land seldom did any work until modern times. Sharecroppers and day laborers got dirty and sweaty in the fields while their employers dressed as gentlemen and lived the life of Riley.

During the seasons when rye, barley, oats, and other grains were being planted, a fellow who spent his days in the fields was likely to be covered with seeds. Derided as being *seedy,* such a rustic was linked with work-worn clothing.

Once the derisive title entered common usage, it came to mean anything run-down—from shacks to individuals.

Stuffed Shirt

FARMERS have been making scarecrows for centuries. They were designed, of course, to frighten away small animals and other birds in addition to pesky crows.

In order to make a male figure, an old pair of trousers and a shirt were stuffed full of straw. A figure topped by a battered hat would be kept erect by means of a broomstick or a pole. Apparently standing in the field, it just might keep varmints away.

Some persons, even in positions of authority, show few signs of action. Male or female, a human stuffed shirt is about as vital— and as commanding in the eyes of colleagues—as a weather beaten scarecrow guarding a corn patch.

Whole Hog

A PERSON who sets no limit upon planned action is likely to be described as willing to go "whole hog."

For decades, waves of Crusaders poured into the Holy Land in an effort to recapture the region from the Moslems. Many ridiculed followers of Mohammed because of the dietary laws that forbade the eating of pork.

Members of some Moslem sects reputedly made brushes from bristles of swine and prized skins for use as water containers. Back in England or Europe, many a Crusader argued that if skin and bristles were valued, Moslems might as well go "whole hog" and use swine as food. As a result, the expression came to indicate readiness to stop at nothing.

CHAPTER 12

SOME THINGS ARE NOT WHAT THEY SEEM

"Clothes do not make a monk, and wearing of gilt spurs does not make a knight."
—Thomas Usk, *Testament of Love*, 1387 A.D.

Compared with our language, clothing is almost childishly simple. A word or a phrase can have a contemporary connotation quite different from that of the past.

Once you develop a pattern of looking beneath the surface of written and spoken words, you will discover that a few pages of a book or a few minutes of conversation will almost always involve usages that have undergone radical change.

APPLE PIE ORDER
BARGE IN
BITTER END
BLACK LIST
BRIBE
BUNK
CHEW THE RAG
DOUBLE-CROSS
EASY STREET
FACE THE MUSIC
GRAVEYARD SHIFT
INDIAN GIVER
LEFT-HANDED
  COMPLIMENT

LOCK HORNS
MANUFACTURED OUT
  OF WHOLE CLOTH
MARK TIME
MORON
NAG
NOT TO BE SNEEZED
  AT
PATIENT
SCUTTLEBUTT
SECRETARY
SHODDY
SHOOT THE BULL/
  BULL SESSION

SEE ALSO: Ax to Grind, Blue Jeans, Bullpen, Carry a Torch, Clean as a Whistle, Crackpot, Dive, Drug on the Market, Fly-by-Night, Freelance, Get the Sack, Get One's Goat, Go by the Board, Gravy Train, Great Scott!, Haymaker, Kick the Bucket, Leadpipe Cinch, Let the Cat Out of the Bag, Mickey Mouse, No Bones, Paint the Town Red, Pork Barrel, Powwow, Putting on the Dog, Red Letter Day, Short Shrift, Sleazy, Tomboy

Apple Pie Order

DID you ever examine a freshly baked apple pie whose surface was crisscrossed with precisely laid strips of pastry? If so, it probably seems logical to you to say that anything truly neat is in "apple pie order."

Logical though it seems, the expression has nothing to do with apple pies baked in wood-burning ovens of New England or anywhere else. Much older than the earliest English settlements in America, it comes from a corrupted form of a French label for neatly folded linen.

After all, a precisely folded dinner napkin has one thing in common with one of grandma's apple pies—both are pleasing to the eye.

Barge In

IF you barge into a conference room and take a seat, your actions will not remotely resemble those of a clumsy cargo vessel. Yet movements of such a ship gave rise to our expression.

It was brought back to Europe by Crusaders who were impressed with a small sailing vessel they saw on the Nile river. Adapting the Egyptian name, similar ships built in Britain were called *barges*.

Especially designed for use in shallow water, the barge proved useful in canals as well as in rivers. Eventually steam replaced sails on these flat-bottom craft that were sturdy but clumsy. Accidents were frequent, for once a barge got under way it was difficult to stop it or to change course rapidly.

By 1800, shippers were comparing hasty action of any sort with the heavy rushing of a cargo boat. As a result, we continue to say that a person bursting into any situation is barging into it.

Bitter End

MANY early English ships were equipped with a bitt, or heavy log mounted on an axle. With one end of a cable attached to the bitt, the other was tied to an anchor. Should anything happen to the bitt, a ship was in trouble—for there was no way to drop anchor in order to resist winds and tides.

In some waters, even a very long cable was not adequate. Played out until no more was wrapped around the bitt, it still didn't permit the anchor to touch bottom.

Such a situation was always alarming and often dangerous. As a result any unpleasant final result came to be called a bitter end— now often regarded as meaning an unpleasant taste in the mouth.

Black List

DEANS of noted British colleges and universities often had to deal with misconduct. Many kept ledgers in which they recorded the names and misdeeds of students who broke rules.

A dean's register of offenses was typically bound in black, so the records it held made up his "black list."

Owners of business firms were less precise about notebooks used in order to jot names of customers who didn't pay promptly. A record of people who should be denied credit took the campus label, in spite of the fact that a merchant's black list might be kept in a blue or brown book.

From these specialized usages, the black list expanded in meaning. Today it names any kind of records that identify persons who should be denied membership or watched carefully.

Bribe

FRENCH householders of the 13th century commonly called a piece of bread broken from a loaf a *bribe*. That is what was likely to be given to an itinerant holy man who asked for food. In return for the bribe, the recipient often volunteered to remember the donor in his prayers. So sometimes a person would give a bribe for the sake of prayers, rather than out of generosity.

During the 16th century the meaning of the word shifted and was used to label corrupt financial transactions. Judges and officials seemed to have exacted bribes in return for light sentences.

Since then, *bribe* has come into general use to name any illicit exchange of money for favors or help from an official or ordinary citizen.

Bunk

MANY individuals have been responsible for specialized words that are seldom used. Revolutionary general Felix Walker contributed to everyday speech—though he didn't intend to do so.

Buncombe County, North Carolina, sent him to Congress where he often took the floor to speak at length. Always, he explained to bored lawmakers that he was not attempting to speak for the nation—he had been elected in order to speak for Buncombe.

"Speaking for Buncombe" caused the county's name to be used as a label for foolish chatter. Abbreviated to *bunk,* Americans use it to name any burst of hot air as meaningless as an old soldier's oratory on the floor of Congress.

Chew the Rag

EARLY explorers of North America noticed that some natives liked to chew dried leaves, while others smoked them in pipes. Sailors sampled tobacco, liked it, and introduced it in Europe. Many landsmen took up smoking, but in wooden vessels tobacco users were restricted to chewing. Soon the quid in cheek was almost as familiar a trademark of the sea as were tarred pigtails.

On long voyages, tobacco supplies became exhausted. That led sailors to turn to whatever substitutes they could find—pork rinds, soft leather, and rags. Rag-chewing sessions in the forecastle were often linked with animated conversation. Consequently, modern-day people who chew the rag are likely to be off-duty idlers who like to indulge in talk.

Double-cross

IN frontier America, a person unable to write was often required to sign a document. Under such circumstances, in lieu of a name it was legal to sign with an "X" on the form. Abraham Lincoln's mother followed this usage, along with multitudes of her contemporaries.

Often, a party to a contract agreed to it under pressure and didn't want to observe its terms. Oral lore insisted that when crosses were doubled, one being placed over the other, the first was cancelled or made null. Primitive as it sounds in the computer age, this double-cross was common enough to give its name to any act of deception or betrayal.

Easy Street

ANY time you find that a new acquaintance is living quite comfortably, you may think to yourself that he or she is living on "Easy Street."

This expression sounds as though it might have come from Bunyan, Dickens, or Thackeray. It is not difficult to picture a broad avenue bearing this name, perhaps located not far from London's famous Grub Street.

Oddly, though, the designation originated in the New World. It seems to have first appeared in print in a 1902 novel, one of whose more than prosperous characters "could walk up and down Easy Street."

It seems logical to describe a person in comfortable circumstances as having an address that summarizes his or her life style. Catching the expression from the story entitled "It's Up to You," *Easy Street* was soon widely familiar.

Face the Music

IF you are known to be ready to face the music, take it as a compliment—of sorts. Chances are that when facing an unpleasant or difficult situation, you grit your teeth and wade into it.

That is exactly what an old-time soldier who was being dismissed had to do. In his case, there was no choice. After having been handed his walking papers, many a deserter or slacker was made to march slowly between ranks of former comrades. Drums and other instruments marked time for this "rogue's march." Even though the situation offered no choice, it meant meeting the unpleasant head-on.

Today, a person who decides to face the music may be innocent of wrongdoing—but ready to act as bravely as a fellow who knew he was likely never to see comrades again.

Graveyard Shift

EVERY industry that operates around the clock has a graveyard shift. Some persons who punch a clock at odd hours think their time of work has some sort of connection with burial places. But the true origin is not quite so obvious.

Any thick liquid was called gravy for a long, long time. Only special kinds of gravy went on the table. "Humour running from the eyes" caused some people to be called "gravy-eyed."

In addition to disease, late vigils in bed led to bleary eyes. Sailors who had the watch that started at midnight were often gravy-eyed before they went off duty. That led them to speak of the middle watch as the "gravey-eyed shift."

Landlubbers who heard the expression didn't fully understand it. Aided by superstitions about cemeteries, the sea-born label became the graveyard shift in industry.

Indian Giver

BECAUSE Columbus thought he had discovered a new passage to India, native Americans came to be called Indians. Many were peaceful, but some were not. Women, bounty hunters, and many woodsmen were constantly alert to the danger of attack by Indians.

Frontiersmen coined dozens of phrases that included the name of their foes. Anything substandard, undesirable, or troublesome was called "Indian." That is why a person who made a gift with conditions under which it could be reclaimed was ridiculed as an "Indian giver."

In recent decades, admiration for whites who pillaged a continent and habitually broke treaties has diminished. At the same time, respect for the native Americans has mounted. Yet a person who holds an option for reclaiming a gift is still an Indian giver.

Left-handed Compliment

A REFERENCE to a left-handed compliment appears, on the surface, to refer to something laudatory said by a southpaw. But our everyday words and phrases often invite a look beneath the surface. In this case, such a peek takes us to medieval Germany.

Trying to discourage romances between noblemen and commoners, legal barriers were created. If a man of blue blood married beneath his class, a special ceremony was used for the wedding. In such a rite, the groom was required to give the bride his left hand rather than the customary right hand.

To a visitor from abroad, the special ceremony seemed quite ordinary. But a left-handed marriage hardly deserved the name. Neither the man's wife nor their children could gain his rank or property. This state of affairs led anything whose surface appearance was deceiving to be called "left-handed."

After the 16th century, the left-handed wedding ceremony was seldom performed. But it made so lasting an impression that you get a left-handed compliment when offered an insult that masquerades as praise.

Lock Horns

WHEN you comment that a pair of antagonists "lock horns," the expression may evoke an image of two angry steers going at one another head-to-head.

While such contests do take place in cattle pens, domestic animals did not give rise to the expression. It comes from the wilds of North America, where an old bull moose may boast antlers that weigh as much as sixty pounds.

Males are shy and unapproachable during most of the year, but become aggressive as the autumn mating season approaches. Nature affords few spectacles more dramatic than that of a pair of giant swains with their spreading sets of horns locked in battle.

In frontier speech, angry humans were often compared with battling moose. As a result, we say that people who clash have "locked horns."

Manufactured out of Whole Cloth

AN unbelievable story is likely to be described as having been "manufactured out of whole cloth."

Whole bolts of cloth are the raw materials fed into modern clothing factories. Until the rise of automated industry, garments were handmade. As a first step, a tailor or seamstress used patterns to guide scissors in cutting numerous segments of cloth. Unless the pieces were properly cut, sewing them together was out of the question.

Anyone who pretended to sew without first having cut was an obvious liar; you simply couldn't make a shirt or a chemise out of whole cloth!

Mark Time

WHEN we say a person is forced to mark time, we use an expression that seems to be based upon watching a clock. In its earliest usages, it had nothing to do with timepieces of any kind. Instead, the term stems from activities of drill sergeants about 200 years ago who demanded precision in movement.

One new exercise launched by the command "Mark time!" involved repeatedly lifting the feet without moving forward or backward. A soldier engaged in this drill expended a lot of energy, but got nowhere. As a result, the sergeant's command came to designate any futile activity by soldiers or civilians.

Moron

ALMOST everyone has been called a moron at least once. People who toss that label around usually do so without knowing that it is one of a handful of words formally voted into our language.

In 1910, a convention held by the American Association for the Study of the Feeble Minded assembled. Delegates complained that they didn't even have a name for persons with whom they worked. Someone reminded the crowd that a famous play by Moliere had a dull-witted character named Moron who spends a lot of time center stage.

Maybe because the name is properly literary—and French, at that—workers with people we now label handicapped agreed to call every slow-minded individual a moron.

Nag

FOLK tales from the Middle Ages reveal that rats were prevalent in many towns and cities. They not only ate food that humans needed, their gnawing was a constant source of irritation. Householders could do little to get rid of rodents, so they simply had to endure their noise.

An old Scandinavian term for the process of gnawing passed through German into English—and emerged as *nag*. Eventually it was applied to any persistent irritation, not simply the biting on wood and nuts of rats and squirrels. Contrary to logic, therefore, the word has nothing to do with the activities of a worn-out horse.

A common source of annoyance, then and now, centers in persistent scolding by a member of the family, a fellow worker or friend. Hence we still say a person who gnaws at another by constant fault-finding is nothing but a nag.

Not to be Sneezed at

A SNEEZE often confers a sort of mild exhilaration and was long thought to clear the mind.

High society made a complete surrender to the craze for sneezing. Everyone who was anyone carried a box of ground herbs. Snuffed into the nostrils, a pinch of the mixture that included tobacco produced a hearty sneeze.

Largely restricted to the leisure class, the self-induced sneeze became a mark of indolence. After hearing news or gossip, some member of a group was sure to sneeze as a way of indicating boredom. This practice was so common that anything not to be sneezed at isn't precisely as it sounds; because it doesn't evoke a sneeze, it is important!

Patient

SOME persons under medical care are irritable and full of complaints. Yet even a habitually impatient person is called a patient.

The riddle is solved by a look at medieval medical practices when most havens for the sick were operated by the church. New workers soon learned that every group of sufferers includes some who never complain. From an ecclesiastical term for "one who suffers," a person who endured pain calmly was termed a *patient*.

Eventually the label expanded to name anyone receiving medical treatment. Early manuals urged health care professionals to be patient even with the impatient. A 1547 volume stated: "Surgeons ought never be boisterous about their patients, but lovingly comfort them no matter what."

Scuttlebutt

IF you want inside information, forget public relations releases and listen attentively to the scuttlebutt. Much of it is meaningless or erroneous, but by mining this vein of talk you may come up with an occasional gem.

Scuttlebutt is half rumor and half gossip, of course. That is because it was first heard when British sailors gathered around a large butt, or cask, of water. For no known reason, such a container was nearly always placed close to a vessel's scuttle, or hatch with a movable cover.

Crew members who went for a drink of water liked to exchange the latest rumors with their mates, so talk under a scuttle that sheltered a butt became *scuttlebutt*.

Secretary

A LATIN term naming a secret gave rise to the English word *secretary*. Persons who held this title were originally in charge of the secret and confidential affairs of wealthy noblemen.

Many an early secretary soon discovered that correspondence required a great deal of time and energy. As writing of letters became increasingly important, significance of the occupational title gradually shifted. Eventually any man or woman employed to conduct correspondence—with or without secrets—took the old title.

Which means that present connotations of the label do not point to a secretary's earliest functions. Such titles as Secretary of State survive as a reminder that it might be wise for every secretary to keep quiet about business conducted for an employer.

Shoddy

MODERN recycling, aimed at saving our environment, is not new. Scarcity of wool long ago led to the salvaging of rags in order to turn them back into yarn to make new cloth. Arising from the slang of textile workers, such recycling was called *shoddy*.

Shoddy came into its own during the U.S. Civil War. Demand for uniforms was so great that it could not be met by conventional means. Mills began shredding old woolen goods in order to turn out shoddy uniforms. They looked all right at first, but didn't hold up with wear.

So many Union soldiers were forced to wear shoddy that anything of second-rate quality took the name of cloth from recycled wool.

Shoot the Bull/Bull Session

CONFINED in a pen, two or three bulls are likely to devote much of their energy to bellowing back and forth at one another. Experienced handlers know that the sounds produced, though frequent and loud, pose no threat. They are simply one effect of the way this male animal likes to make all in earshot aware of his presence.

Male humans, voluntarily penned in a room, tend to devote a lot of their energy to idle talk. Like noises made in a cattle pen, their sounds may mean very little—but seldom stop.

Inevitably, a fellow talking too much will be called down for his tendency to shoot the bull, while a session in which several talk back and forth constitutes a bull session.

CHAPTER 13

GOING PLACES—
THEN AND NOW

"If you will be a traveler, have always the eyes of a falcon, the ears of an ass, the face of an ape, the mouth of a hog, the shoulder of a camel, the legs of a stag, and see that you never want two bags very full—one of patience and the other of money."

—John Florio, *Second Fruits*, 1591 A.D.

T hough the automobile age has been very brief by comparison with eras of travel on foot and by use of animals, it has enriched language at interstate highway speed. Old or young, expressions created by our proclivity for going places may give no hint of their background until examined closely.

AUTOMOBILE
BLOWOUT
BLUFF
COASTING ALONG
CRANK
FAST LANE
FREE-WHEELER
GIVE THE GUN
GOES WITH THE
   TERRITORY
HAND-OVER-FIST
HIGHBALL
HIGH GEAR
HOLIDAY

JEEP
JERKWATER
LAID-BACK
MIDDLE-OF-THE
   ROAD
MILESTONE
PIT STOP
PLAIN SAILING
RUN A HOTBOX
SMOKEY
STEERING WHEEL
STEP ON IT
THREE SHEETS IN/
   TO THE WIND
TWO-WAY STREET

SEE ALSO: Backseat Driver, Blow Off Steam, Booby Hatch,
   Cadillac, Chuck Hole, Driver's Seat, Fifth Wheel, Hightail,
   On the Beam, Rack and Ruin, Ride Shotgun, Slush Fund

Automobile

LOTS of fellows who got a look at early self-propelled vehicles laughed. "Better stick with the horse," they shouted.

H. H. Kohlsaat, owner of the Chicago *Times-Herald,* paid no attention. As a publicity stunt, he planned a race between contraptions that didn't use harness or reins. To sweeten the pot, he offered $500 for the best name for horseless wagons.

Inventors had already come up with "buggyaut," "autokinet," and "buckmobile." Three who entered the contest suggested "motorcycle," so prize money was split between these winners. From now on, said the rich man from the Windy City, *motorcycle* would name "any kind of wagon driven by a steam plant, storage batteries, or a self-contained motor."

Hardly anybody paid any attention. Borrowing the Greek word *auto* for "self," and the French *mobile* for "moving," consumers began to call the self-moving wagon the *automobile*.

By 1910, the brand-new name that didn't win a prize was in general use among Americans—whose bragging spread it around the world.

Blowout

DAVY Crockett used to say that a fellow who turned red in the face and started hollering was having a "blowout."

Town and city folk picked up the expression coined by tellers of tall tales and used it to mean an outburst of anger. By the time Washington Irving and Sir Walter Scott put it into their novels, everybody knew what it meant.

But a rush of hot air from an early pneumatic tire made a blowout by a riverboat gambler seem tame. Seventy pounds of pressure against thin rubber on unpaved roads made tires almost as explosive as liquid refreshments at a big shindig.

Thicker, tougher tires and asphalt roads cut down on highway blowouts, so our living language turned back upon itself. With frontier emphases revived, you are now a lot more likely to be involved in a blowout in someone's living room or den than on the interstate.

Bluff

HORSEMEN of the 16th century developed a new type of wide blinder that they called a bluff. Used sporadically for generations, it suddenly swept into prominence. Big, closed vehicles called coaches were introduced from Hungary for use of the wealthy. Since such a device required four to six horses, each animal had to be fitted with a bluff in order to reduce nervousness.

By 1640, the stagecoach began to replace the stage wagon in transporting passengers. Scheduled runs made possible by horses fitted with bluffs were figured at five to six miles an hour. Business boomed, and stables expanded.

Every stagecoach rider became familiar with the bluff that made animals easier to handle. From everyday use with them, the name of the device came to convey the notion of restricting vision of persons as well as horses. As a result, any ruse that hoodwinks a person of the automobile age is called a *bluff*.

Coasting Along

CAPTAINS of ocean-going vessels, facing weeks on the water, were early advocates of speed. A windjammer headed across the Atlantic was likely to have all sails spread when the wind was strong.

By contrast with fast ships of this sort, schooners that were involved in the coastal trade seemed to be slow, even leisurely. They traveled short distances, so their masters seldom bothered to use every possible yard of canvas.

Some vessels in coastal waters may have been more hurried than they seemed. Whether that was the case or not, their apparently casual movement became proverbial. As a result, a person far from water who shows no signs of effort or haste is still described as "coasting along."

Crank

A SOLDIER killed in medieval combat, often lying in a contorted position, came to be known as a crank. From the idea of crookedness linked with a twisted corpse, a bent arm or shaft took the military name. Special kinds of cranks were used to turn machines and to start motors.

With the advent of the horseless carriage, the crank became universally familiar—and hated as a common source of broken arms and sprained backs. So many persons cranked cars that the name of the tool came to indicate action started by it.

Hand cranks gave way to floorboard starters. These yielded to ignition switches that turn with a twist of the wrist. But speech remained static while technology changed. Today's driver continues to crank the car despite the fact that he or she might not recognize the old-fashioned kind.

Fast Lane

UNTIL the automobile changed the nature and pace of society, no one talked about life in the "fast lane."

Builders of the New Jersey Turnpike, two lanes wide in both directions, had a revolutionary idea from the start. Traffic would flow much more freely, they suggested, if slow-moving vehicles were required to stay in the right lane.

Experiments showed that the concept was correct, and it soon became standard practice for fast-moving vehicles—initially cars only—to use the left lane. Highway practices spawned talk about life in the fast lane, dangerous for everyone if adopted by slow-pokes behind the wheel or anywhere else.

Free-wheeler

IMMENSE amounts of capital backed the original free-wheeler of the highways. During the 1930s a drawing board wizard outlined plans for a brand-new kind of car. Built with capacity to coast freely without being slowed by the engine, it was touted as capable of putting the competition out of business.

Several versions of the free-wheeler went on the market, and were briefly sensational. Then it was found that there are serious drawbacks to fast movement by the force of gravity alone. So many sets of brakes were burned out and so many cars crashed that automakers returned to the time-honored practice of linking wheels with motors.

Abandoned by Detroit, the free-wheeler survives in language as a tribute, of sorts, to what some engineers consider benighted genius.

Give the Gun

IF you decide to speed up a car or boat or movement, you can give it the gun without the use of a weapon or ammunition.

Combat planes of World War I were slow and clumsy. In attacking an enemy, it became standard practice to climb above and dive in order to gain speed. Giving his engine all the gas it would take, a pilot would open up with his machine gun— causing an increase in speed to be linked with gunning.

Once fixed in the speech of aerial fighters, the expression expanded. Now it names rapid acceleration in everything from souped-up sports cars to sales campaigns.

Goes with the Territory

IF you are offered a new job, it might be a good idea to ask what goes with the territory. Many times, a spot that looks tempting has requirements not immediately apparent that are less than desirable.

Since the first traveling salesmen hit the road, that has been the case with people who choose this way to make a living. Few if any sales territories offer only plums; there is always at least one tough nut to crack and maybe a day or two of nearly impossible schedules.

Already widely recognized, the fact that something unpleasant goes with the territory was embedded in speech through the impact of Arthur Miller's hit play, *Death of a Salesman*.

Hand-over-fist

ROPE ladders leading to main spars of many sailing vessels made it easy to climb into the rigging. When a gale blew up suddenly, a captain might order men aloft at top speed. Once canvas was furled, men needed to get on deck quickly in order to avoid being tossed overboard when the ship lurched. Rope ladders were too clumsy for such descent. It was customary for a man to grab a big rope, then climb down hand over hand.

Speed of such descent caused any rapid progress to be labeled "hand-over-hand." Influenced by popularity of boxing in the 18th century, the expression was modified to "hand-over-fist."

Steamships quickly made the hand-over-fist descent of a rope obsolete, but the expression was firmly fixed in speech. A curious twist of fate led to inversion of its original sense. Today, a person who ascends the business world rapidly is likely to be described as making money hand-over-fist.

Highball

NO matter what the make and model of your car, when you get in a tearing hurry you are in danger of being stopped for "highballing."

That is because radar and radios didn't exist in the era when the iron horse became king of the road. Engineers were frustrated because they had no way to receive information while trains were in motion.

An inventor rigged a metal globe to cross-arms and a system of ropes and pulleys. He advised railroaders that a train should be halted when his ball was lowered. Thus a ball raised to the top of its span was a signal for "full speed ahead."

By the time semaphore signals replaced this crude system, it had made a permanent contribution to everyday speech. Regardless of the mode of transportation used, anyone proceeding at top speed is still said to be *highballing*.

High Gear

ANYTIME others notice that you are in high gear, you are sure to be going at a project or a campaign at top speed.

Until auto gears became automatic, shifting of them took considerable attention and energy. Many sports cars now use the pattern: low gear, second gear, third gear, high gear, and reverse.

A vehicle equipped with four on the floor doesn't take to the road in high. Low gives power to start things rolling. Second offers an increase in speed, but reduces pulling power. When the vehicle moves into fourth gear it is ready for the maximum speed that horsepower and road conditions will permit.

All of which means that when you are in high gear you are moving very quickly and efficiently—that is, until you come upon a steep hill.

Holiday

IN medieval England, a holy day was designed primarily for worship and no ordinary tasks were performed. Enforced leisure made it inevitable that festivals and amusements should begin to flourish at such a time. Now marked by fun and worship, old verbal elements combined and the period of observance came to be known as a *holiday*.

Some religious groups still emphasize a holy day at intervals, and many nations observe legal holidays on which official business is not conducted.

Hold-overs from the past remain influential. Yet the holiday notion is now strongly linked with taking a trip. Persons for whom a holy day once meant freedom from work in order to worship would be hard put to comprehend the modern holiday on wheels or in the air.

Jeep

ELZIE Crisler Segar's name is far from a household word. But comic strip characters he created are known everywhere. Popeye the Sailor, launched about 1930, made a quick and lasting hit.

Eugene the Jeep, an animal friend of Popeye, appeared on March 16, 1936. Slender but very strong, he was widely admired by readers.

Soon after becoming acquainted with Eugene the Jeep, soldiers began working with a new vehicle. Small and drab, the sturdy car had four drive wheels instead of the then-standard two.

Military supply officers initially stenciled the little heavy-duty car G.P.—for "general purpose." Influenced by its initials, G.I.'s compared the new vehicle with Eugene the Jeep. As a result, both the military Jeep and its civilian relatives perpetuate the name of a remarkable animal made famous by a comic strip.

Jerkwater

EVEN a brief stay in a jerkwater town is enough to let you know that the label is not a compliment.

In the golden years of railroading, cities and large towns were watering stations. Trains stopped to discharge passengers or freight, and workmen leisurely filled the water tenders—the first cars behind steam locomotives.

Villages didn't warrant a regular stop, but when watering stations were far apart a locomotive could get very dry. To solve this dilemma, rural water towers were fitted with big pipes that could be lowered by a rope.

Impatient at having to stop at a crossroads, a train's fireman was likely to jerk the water pipe into place so that gravity would cause the tender to fill in seconds. The jerking of water occurred so frequently that these actions of railroaders formed a label for the hamlets where they took place.

Laid-back

MOST of your friends would say they were paying a compliment if they described you as being "laid-back." In an era of tension it's a rare person, indeed, who deserves such a label.

It sounds as though it may have been inspired by envy of someone sprawled on a sofa, going nowhere and caring little. But in the world of language, logic seldom prevails. Couches and divans and beds did not give rise to the saying.

The design of many motorcycles is such that the rider seems almost to be reclining—a position quite unlike stiff and upright posture. Consequently, their laid-back posture came to symbolize a relaxed and easygoing manner in business as well as in pleasure.

Middle-of-the-road

UNTIL a generation after the Civil War, few great roads were built in America. Even those that linked major cities were likely to be narrow and poorly tended. Wheels of wagons and carriages kept the edges of many roads cut well below the level of the middle. That meant a person who walked along one in wet weather had to stay clear of the edges in order to keep feet dry.

Late in the century, cautious members of the Populist Party opposed union with Democrats. They wished to take a safe middle ground between extremes supported by political opponents. Someone mockingly referred to the cautious ones as Middle-of-the-roaders.

This label stuck and continues to signify avoidance of extremes, long after the Populist Party died.

Milestone

KEENLY interested in human development, observers of the modern scene tend to call any significant event or change a "milestone" of life. Suggestive though it is, this usage is miles away from that of the Romans who often went places and wanted to know how much distance was covered.

The Latin word for one thousand (*mille*) gave birth to the ancestor of the modern mile. Among the Caesars, this unit represented one thousand paces of five feet each. In order to make it easy to mark distances from the center of Rome, trained pacers placed stones along imperial roads at the end of every unit.

Scholars who translated classical documents reported systematic use of milestones at 1,000-pace intervals. Adopted into English, the ancient term broadened to designate a turning point in a person's career or an important event in life.

Pit Stop

THE advent of the automobile created a need for a special kind of pit, or hole in the ground. Heavy-duty hydraulic jacks with which to lift cars had not come into vogue. In order to make repairs or give a grease job, a mechanic could wriggle about on his back—or crawl into a pit.

At the Indianapolis raceway, the place where mechanics worked had little in common with the corner service station but the familiar name stuck to it. To a driver needing fuel or new tires, a pit stop was essential even though it meant the loss of precious seconds.

Importance of the pit stop at the Indy 500 and later races added color and variety to everyday speech. As a result, an interstate highway traveler in desperate need of a toilet or a cup of coffee is likely to make a pit stop at a place which has no pit.

Plain Sailing

LONG after use of round globes was adopted, many seamen preferred to stick to familiar maps. These and other guides for navigation were drawn or printed on flat paper, or plain sheets. As a result, such a set of directions was called a plain chart and the course mapped by it was known as plain sailing.

Though a plain chart might include major errors, it seemed easier to use than a spherical one. As a result, any task regarded as simple and uncomplicated came to be called "plain sailing."

Run a Hotbox

WHEN agitation or irritation becomes visible, a person is likely to be warned: "Cool off—otherwise you'll soon be running a hotbox."

Overheated axles were common in pioneer days of railroading before someone perfected a sprinkler that doused hot bearings with water. The system remained in use until about 1850.

Improvements in the chemistry of grease and the development of new mechanical devices reduced but did not eliminate the hotbox problem. For decades, a train spotted at night might be conspicuous as flames spurted from an overheated journal.

Even when standing dead still, a person who is overheated in personal relations may "run a hotbox."

Smokey

ANYTIME you drive into a state where radar detectors are outlawed, you had better keep your eyes peeled for a "Smokey." These days, he can come at you out of nowhere in an unmarked car.

Don't blame Smokey the Bear if you pick up a ticket. It all started during the decades when the U.S. Forest Service was going all-out for prevention of forest fires. Smokey the Bear became so familiar that he was almost like a member of the family.

Rangers displaying the Smokey symbol wore broad-brimmed hats of a style sported by few civilians. But many a state highway patrol system adopted a hat like that as part of the uniform. A really alert driver doesn't have to watch for a blue light on top of a car. All he or she has to do is to spot one of those distinctive hats in order to know that a Smokey is on the prowl.

Steering Wheel

HENRY Ford's hand-built car of 1896 wasn't easily guided. Any sailor could see that its cumbersome steering device, or tiller, was modeled after those used on ships.

For his #999, the first racing car driven by Barney Oldfield, Ford scrapped the tiller in favor of a cranking device. It proved so clumsy that in 1903 he offered steering by means of a wheel.

Rival makers adopted the steering wheel about the same time as Ford. Prospective buyers to whom it was shown were assured that abandonment of the tiller severed all ties between ships and autos.

So they thought! Many veteran tars remembered that steering wheels were used on ships as early as 1750. An engineering manual described such a device as the "wheel that guides a ship, giving motion to the rudder by means of a tiller rope."

Which means that anyone behind the steering wheel during rush-hour traffic may still find himself or herself all at sea.

Step on it

ENGINEERING changes enabled motorists to pick up speed rapidly before World War I. Some models still used hand throttles to regulate the flow of fuel, but most employed the relatively new "foot feed" not yet commonly called the accelerator.

Known by whatever name, the foot-controlled mechanism freed both hands for steering. That meant a driver could keep a car in the road even when moving from ten to forty miles per hour in seconds. Reporting such an exploit, an autoist was likely to talk about having stepped on the gas.

Regardless of whether or not you drive a car with a foot feed, when planning to speed up action of any sort it is customary to announce intentions to "step on it."

Three Sheets in/to the Wind

ESPECIALLY on New Year's Eve and other festive occasions, you need to keep a close eye on any driver who seems to be "three sheets in the wind." Whether legally intoxicated or not, anyone who weaves across the road and frequently changes speed is a source of danger.

Sailors in danger of losing their lives created the phrase. Many old-time vessels performed best when rigging was symmetrical. Outfitted with four masts and four sets of sails, a craft was expected to use all of them under most circumstances. Sometimes, though, the fourth and final sets of canvas were not spread. A four-master with only three masts in action was in big trouble when hit by a sudden gale.

The rolling and pitching of a poorly rigged ship was much like the actions of a human who has downed too many drinks. A comparison was appropriate and inevitable; as a result, a thoroughly tanked human barely able to get under way is described as lacking an essential set of canvas sails.

Two-way Street

INTRODUCTION of automobiles created a demand for new and better rural roads. At the same time, the new vehicles posed fresh problems in many cities—especially those of Europe. A cobblestone boulevard wide enough to permit vehicles to pass one another and hence to move in either direction is still a rarity in Toledo, Spain, and other old cities.

In land-rich America, wide streets are commonplace. Since traffic moves simultaneously in both directions on such a thoroughfare, we speak of any situation or relationship that can be approached from opposite directions as a "two-way street."

CHAPTER *14*

ONE PERSON'S FOOD . . .

"What is food to one man may be fierce poison to others."
—Lucretius, *Nature*, about 45 B.C.

N ot only is one person's food another's poison, the language of food in one era may be something altogether different in succeeding ones. Some expressions that seem to point directly to food have little or nothing to do with the table. Others that are deeply rooted in food have taken on new meanings so distinct and familiar that association with eating can be seen only dimly and after careful scrutiny.

ADAM'S APPLE
BOARDER
CHEW THE FAT
CHICKEN À LA KING
COOK ONE'S GOOSE
DEVILED
EGGS BENEDICT
FAT IS IN
  THE FIRE
FREELOADER
FULL OF BEANS
GARBLED
GO TO POT
GRAVY TRAIN
GROGGY
HALF-BAKED
HIGH ON THE HOG,
  TO LIVE/EAT

HOT DOG
HOT POTATO
HUMBLE PIE
LAMPOON
NO BONES
PORK BARREL
POTLUCK
POT SHOT
PUNCH
REHASH
SANDWICH
THRESHOLD
TOADY
TOM AND JERRY
UPSET THE APPLE
  CART

SEE ALSO: Apple Pie Order, Bean Pole, Booze, Bribe, Bring
    Home the Bacon, Chow, Cocktail, Lazy Susan, Melba
    Toast, Pig in a Poke, Seedy, Sirloin, Whole Hog

Adam's Apple

MANY a man, such as Abraham Lincoln, has had a prominent Adam's apple. Male chauvinism is responsible for the centuries-old name.

Pioneer English anatomists were puzzled by the section of cartilage that refused to stay in one spot. Folktales explained that Adam should not have taken that apple from Eve in the Garden of Eden. When he yielded to her temptation, a piece of fruit stuck on the way down. Ever since, it has moved when men eat or talk in order to warn: "Beware of the temptress!"

In truth, the growth of the visible knot is stimulated by male hormones. Because women have a small amount of this hormone, they also have a small version of the Adam's apple.

Boarder

MANY an early table consisted of a single hand-hewn board laid across a trestle. Early inns gave no service with their meals. Landlords simply piled food on the board and let every person pitch in. Charges were simple; a guest paid a flat fee for a place at the board. By the 15th century, it had become customary to sell board space by the week. This practice led to use of the label *boarder* for any person eating regularly in an establishment.

Boarding houses, once found in nearly every American town and city, are commemorated in the novels of Thomas Wolfe and other great writers. But a detailed description of many present-day communities would reveal that there is not a single boarder in town.

Chew the Fat

SALT pork was basic to the diet of seamen in the great age of sailing. As none was wasted, pieces of skin were saved for emergencies. When supplies ran low, each member of the crew might receive a chunk of it in lieu of a slice of meat.

A rind, or skin, was tough and unpalatable. But the layer of fat attached to it was better than nothing. Sailors to whom rinds were doled out chewed off the fat, then often held skins between their teeth for an hour or two.

Casual talk was a natural accompaniment of chewing on rinds. Shipboard sessions with rancid pork were so common that the sailors' expression was adopted by landlubbers to label indulgence in idle talk.

Chicken à la King

REGARDLESS of whether or not you have a taste for chicken à la king, listing of it seems to give a touch of class to a menu. That is appropriate, since it seems to have been first prepared in a world-famous hotel.

For generations Claridge's of London has been favored by both natives and tourists who could afford it. Several times, a notable event has inspired a chef to concoct a brand-new dish.

That was the case in 1881, when a horse owned by J. R. Keene won the Grand Prix. To celebrate this victory, the kitchen crew came up with chicken à la Keene—a name just sufficiently French to imply elegance.

By the time the new dish spread from Claridge's into general use, few remembered the temporary fame of a racetrack winner. But nearly everyone who borrowed or adapted the hotel recipe agreed that this kind of chicken was good enough for royalty. Transformed in speech from *chicken à la Keene* to *chicken à la king,* it is in worldwide use a century after it was created.

Cook One's Goose

A FAMILIAR old story centers on a marvelous goose that laid a golden egg every day. Greedy owners killed the bird for the sake of eggs still in the pouch of the goose. For downright stupidity, few actions rank with the notion of killing the goose that laid the golden egg. That fable may have led some persons hoping to defeat another to threaten to "cook his goose."

A more commonplace explanation makes more sense, however. For centuries, geese rather than chickens dominated the barnyard and were prized at Christmas and other times of feasting. When a householder was down to a single bird, he would be out of luck when that one was gone. A rival threatening total defeat might express his intention by saying: "Old fellow, you've had it—I'm going to cook your goose!"

Deviled

EXPLORERS brought to Europe red pods of a South American shrub and offered them as Cayenne pepper. Tested in kitchens, it added zest to chopped dishes.

A taste of the New World pepper made persons feel as though they were on fire, so a connection with hell was common.

Chopped lamb, chicken, or veal that included the new condiment was described as *deviled,* or bewitched by Satan. Soon the name of the devil's pepper became linked with any dish resembling those that frequently used the South American pod.

Whether or not tiny particles of the devil's fiery coals are included, if the texture is right anything from eggs to crabs is enjoyed as deviled.

Eggs Benedict

LEGEND suggests that Saint Benedict is responsible for the combination of foods that seem to bear his name. Oral tradition long current in greater New York City credits the term to wealthy Samuel Benedict, about whom little is known.

Many scholars say that neither the saint nor the New Yorker

had anything to do with creating and naming the perennially popular dish.

Instead, they say, it stems directly from the culinary interests of banker-yachtsman E. C. Benedict. He inherited a Connecticut fortune and reached the zenith of his power in commercial circles about the turn of the century. Benedict then began spending more and more time on the water.

It was on his yacht, says an account that stems from about 1902, that the man whom friends called "Commodore" insisted that hollandaise sauce be added to the long-standard poached eggs on toast with ham. When guests tried the new delicacy, they took to it like ducks to water. As a result, we still use the water-loving banker's name to designate the dish that is high on the list of favorite foods.

Fat Is in the Fire

WHEN a project suddenly goes awry, news of the turn of events can be conveyed: "The fat is in the fire!" Probably old when Columbus first sailed for the New World, the expression was long used literally.

It was customary to roast big cuts of meat on a spit that turned slowly over an open fire. Sometimes the attendant turned aside for a few minutes. That is when a big chunk of heated fat was likely to separate from the roast and drop into the flames. Once the fat was in the fire, nothing could be done to remedy the situation.

Smoke and flames from the minor catastrophe in the kitchen came to name any sudden disruption of plans or blunder that cannot be corrected.

Freeloader

AT every old-fashioned picnic sponsored by a church or a lodge or a community, a few zealous people did more than their share of the work. When the food was spread, such a gathering was sure to attract at least one person who brought along nothing but a tremendous appetite.

A man, woman, or half-grown child who loaded his or her stomach with free food was usually tolerated, but was not urged to come back the following year. Invited or not, such a person was likely to show up again, even more hungry than last time.

Soon the freeloader became a stock character, always present where there was something to eat. Spawned at the picnic table, the title transferred to any sponger or moocher who is a conspicuous consumer but doesn't contribute to expenses.

Full of Beans

BY 1850, practically every Englishman knew that any person "full of beans" was bursting with energy.

Without solid evidence to back the belief, every veteran horseman was sure that beans constituted a unique kind of food. An animal regularly fed on them, said tradition, was noticeably frisky and energetic.

Small wonder that any lively two-legged creature seeming to have boundless energy was compared with a horse that was full of pep. Regardless of actual diet, any unusually zestful person was described as being "full of beans."

Garbled

EMPIRES have been built upon the spice trade, and battles have been fought over additives to foods; both now flow freely in today's international commerce.

During eras when spices were scarce and costly, English lawmakers tried to make sure that they would be pure when they reached consumers. In London and other major English port cities, a special official tested shipments for impurities. From an ancient name for sifting through canvas, this person was known as a *garbler*.

In garbling spices, trash and filler material was removed. But persons vaguely familiar with the operation focused upon the act of removal rather than the targets of this procedure. As a result, when pertinent material is removed from a written or photographed report, we say that the distorted residue represents a garbled version of the original.

Go to Pot

A PERSON, a business, or a community can "go to pot" very rapidly. No person or enterprise is immune from danger of taking a downward course named from household customs of long ago.

English squires of the 15th century ate much more meat than do most modern people. Beef was favored, but mutton and pork were also consumed in large quantities. After the best pieces were cut off a roasted joint, the remnant was likely to be used in making stew. This meant that it went into a pot along with potatoes, onions, and other vegetables.

Degeneration of all sorts came to be designated as "going to pot"—the description of the downward journey of a once splendid roast.

Gravy Train

IF you go in for meat, you probably enjoy gravy. From pot roast to country ham, any cut can yield this by-product that may be more tasty than the meat itself.

Gravy is an "extra," or bonus from cooking. So the name of the tongue-pleasing liquid is applied to anything gained without effort or cost. In the era when home-cooked gravy was most abundant, a favorite way to travel was by train. Many railroad workers began using *gravy train* to name a well-paid run that required little work. During the financial boom of the 1920s, railroad lingo moved into financial circles to designate a non-demanding position that paid a big salary.

Today, we call any easy job or activity that pays more than it seems to be worth a *gravy train*—non-edible and involving little or no movement.

Groggy

ANY time you get up in the morning, feeling a bit groggy, take pity on 18th-century British seamen.

Admiral Edward Vernon was a fine-looking figure standing on the poop deck of a vessel wearing a luxurious coat. Many of the men under his command despised him and as a gesture of contempt, they used "Old Grog" to name the man identified by his grogram coat.

At the height of his career, the admiral issued an order that was brand-new to Her Majesty's navy. Henceforth and hereafter, he stipulated, every cask of rum must be diluted with water before any drinks were served. Furious sailors gave the watered-down beverage the name of the man who had invented it.

Even though it wasn't as potent as rum, grog could make a fellow dizzy in short order. Hence, anyone inclined to wobble while walking came to be described as being *groggy*.

Half-baked

EACH type of bread and pastry not only has its special recipe of ingredients—it also must be baked at the proper temperature for the right length of time.

A person learning to bake is often afraid of burning his or her product. As a result, a beginner is likely to take bread out of the oven too soon. Once cooled and cut, it cannot be put back for additional baking.

Anyone or anything raw or incomplete or foolish is likely to be called *half-baked*—about as desirable as under-cooked products of the oven.

High on the Hog, To Live/Eat

EVEN if you are dining on seafood, when you are enjoying the best that is available you'll be said to eat "high on the hog." That colorful expression doesn't have a complicated history.

When small farms dotted the countryside, every household raised a pig or two. No part of the animal was thrown away; even the intestines were savored as chitterlings.

Present-day purchasers of country cured hams often saw off hocks and use them to season soup. Small slices that include whorls of fat can be cut from the lower part of the ham. But for a real feast, slices must come from high on the hog—above the center of the animal's leg.

Hot Dog

NO one knows who was first to put links of mild sausage into long buns and serve them hot. Requiring no implements in order to be eaten, the new delicacy proved a hit when vendors began selling it on the streets of cities.

At first, the German word for this special food was *frankfurter,* and later its kin *wienerwurst* appeared. Both were soon clipped to *franks* and *wieners.*

But the abbreviated labels seemed tame and non-descriptive. Vendors and devotees decided that the long and lean sausage resembled the body of a prized pet. That is why the slender and low-slung dachshund caused wienerwurst in a soft bun to take the name that is now universal: *hot dog.*

Hot Potato

A HARDY plant that yielded big red tubers was discovered by early explorers of North America. It was taken to England quite early, but attracted little attention except among botanists. Regarded as a curiosity, it had only one known use: when dried and powdered, a tuber provided an abundant supply of what was thought to be an aphrodisiac.

While English gentry dropped powder into their drinks, frontiersmen began experimenting with the plant. They found the tuber to be wholesome and appetizing and began to call it a *sweet potato*.

As the sweet potato was easily baked, it gradually became a staple of farm life. Impatient boys and girls seemed never to learn that a potato hot from the ashes must be left to cool.

Erupting from speech of rural households, *hot potato* came to stand for any problem too hot to handle.

Humble Pie

THOUGH we do not use the expression as frequently as in the past, it is not uncommon to hear someone refer to eating "humble pie."

For centuries, dainty pies were made of the umbles or intestines of sheep. Just as chitterlings from intestines of swine are regarded as delicacies in many quarters today, umble pie was considered a mouth-watering confection in medieval England.

Differences in pronunciation led people to add an initial letter that transformed the meaning of the ancient term. Seldom available from the kitchen of a manor house these days, humble pie has come to be regarded as linked with humiliation rather than feasting.

Lampoon

THE *Harvard Lampoon* is high on the list of our nation's oldest humor magazines. Everyone who has read it, and many who have not, recognize that the title suggests a generous use of biting satire.

But in one of its earliest senses, a lampoon was not a verbal or pictorial caricature. Instead, it was a drinking song that took its name from an old French expression meaning "Let us drink!"

In France, as well as across the English channel, students often gathered in public houses for sessions of drinking. Such gatherings were marked by singing of many bawdy songs about school officials, public officials, and authorities in general. Rollicking verses permitted the use of almost any name singers might select.

Eventually the broad humor associated with group sessions at the tavern overshadowed the French expression for drinking. As a result, overt mockery—not necessarily linked in any way with a tavern—came to be called a *lampoon*.

No Bones

ESPECIALLY when made with fish, stew or soup is likely to include a few bones. Large fragments seldom cause trouble, but tiny slivers may bring discomfort or worse.

When a cook points to the pot and assures family members or guests that there are no bones, that is a signal to dig in. No need to pause in order to check for the presence of a tooth-jarring or gum-pricking bone.

Sometimes a person talks with no more hesitancy than a hungry diner shows before a dish of boneless stew. Especially when frankness is deliberate and premeditated, the speaker is said to make "no bones" about telling it exactly as it is.

Pork Barrel

SALTED pork, packed in barrels, was once basic to the diet of seamen. Sailing vessels often ran out of every other staple food. Generally known to include more fat than a comparable quantity of mutton or beef, a slab of pork near the bottom of a barrel was likely to be found floating in lard.

Abundance of fat near the butt of a sailors' pork barrel led keen-witted American politicians of the 19th century to adopt the container's name. At Tammany Hall and other centers of power, men used it disparagingly to name an appropriation made by opponents—but never applied it to the fat-filled bills they sponsored.

Everyday speech borrowed from political talk, with the result that *pork barrel* came to label any enterprise in which funds or jobs are dispensed without accountability.

Potluck

MEDIEVAL gentry usually had plenty of rich food, frequently serving four or five kinds of meat at a meal. But families in the lower economic classes had no such abundance. Often a struggle was required to get enough food to prevent hunger.

In order to stretch her food, the wife of a commoner would keep an iron pot on an open fire. She threw all her leftovers into it each day, and kept it simmering much of the time. If a relative arrived unexpectedly, he was likely to have to eat from the pot without having any idea of what odds and ends had gone into it.

This early and literal form of taking "potluck" came to name the act of eating any meal for which the host or hostess has made no special preparation.

Pot Shot

MEDIEVAL sportsmen developed elaborate rules that governed hunting. By the time chivalry began to decline, such regulations had become well-entrenched customs. There were seasons for various game animals and birds, and restrictions designed to give quarry a sporting chance.

A householder who simply wanted something to put in his pot tended to ignore the rules of good sportsmanship. Such a fellow seldom hesitated to shoot a young animal, or one out of season. Sometimes fields were baited so that birds could be slaughtered from ambush.

All rules were thrown aside when a person was shooting for the pot. Hence we call a less than sporting attack upon a two-legged target a *pot shot*.

Punch

LONG before writer Rudyard Kipling helped the English-speaking world become acquainted with India, Britain mastered the land and lived in almost royal style during their early decades of domination.

In some northern districts, newcomers found a native drink so pleasing that they swore it surpassed anything available at the court of their queen. Inquiry revealed that its base was alcohol made from rice. Tea, lemon, and sugar combined to flavor it and water was added to dilute the potent native alcohol, *arrack*.

From a Hindi word for the number five, the British used *punch* to designate the beverage compounded of five ingredients. Long after the original recipe for it was abandoned and then forgotten, the name survives. These days it may designate a refreshing bowl that includes as many as eight or ten components—or as few as three or four.

Rehash

ENGLISH squires, long famous for their hearty appetites, were depicted with ridicule in the classic novel *Tom Jones* by Henry Fielding. Many of these folks wasted as much meat as they ate, but artisans and craftsmen and others tried never to throw away food.

At a middle-class inn where guests expected meat on the table, the landlord couldn't afford to toss away a shoulder after the choice slices were cut from it. So cooks often made hash from leftovers and guests usually complained. If they pushed hash aside, they were likely to get it the following day in the form of meat loaf.

Such a warmed-over dish, scornfully dubbed a *rehash*, was served frequently. So many persons ate it, willingly or reluctantly, that we've expanded the meaning of its name. Now we use it, not just to label leftover food, but to designate a debate or speech in which old arguments are trotted out, thinly disguised by new words.

Sandwich

ANYTIME you eat a sandwich, you help to perpetuate the memory of an English nobleman in the 18th century.

John Montagu, fourth Earl of Sandwich, became first lord of the admiralty in 1748. Any time he could slip away from his offices for an hour or two, he indulged his passion for gambling. Since his time was usually limited, he often directed a servant to bring him roast beef between slices of bread so he could eat at the gambling table.

He may not have been the first to enjoy this concoction, but he was clearly the only world leader who did so frequently in public. As a result, his royal title attached to this early form of fast food and *sandwich* soon became familiar throughout the world.

Threshold

WHEAT, oats, rye, and barley were once harvested by hand. Once the grain was gathered, bundles were placed on a hard surface. Then the stalks were threshed, or beaten with flails to separate seeds from straw.

Threshing took place in the room with the hardest and flattest floor. Often it was the only room in a hut that was equipped with a plank under the door to keep out vermin.

In Old English, *hold* was widely used to name what we now call *wood*. Consequently, the beam or plank leading to the threshing floor came to be known as the threshold.

Today's point of entrance may have metal or stone underfoot, instead of a doorway plank. When you enter a house, regardless of its construction, a walk across the threshold is a reminder that grain is essential to survival of the human race.

Toady

NEARLY every group of people includes a toady who is ready to brown-nose a person in authority whenever others voice criticism. Such an apple-polisher bears the name of an ancient aide to a swindler.

In 17th century, toads were regarded as poisonous. Taking advantage of this attitude, itinerant quack doctors had their assistants pretend to swallow one of the ugly creatures. Every such "toad-eater" soon turned red in the face and began gagging. That is when a bunco artist would administer a secret potion, then claim a rescue from death and peddle his nostrum.

Slightly abbreviated, the name of the toad-eater survives long after his function became obsolete. No longer linked with faked life-and-death situations, the modern toady tends to concentrate upon servile flattery.

Tom and Jerry

THOUGH every distinctive beverage has its own name, only a few bear the names of persons. A blend of spiced and sweetened rum, beaten with eggs, milk, and spices, is in a class all by itself.

Tom and Jerry were fictional characters in the novel *Life in London,* published in 1821. A book about the nightlife in London, author Pierce Egan wrote of the exploits of Corinthian Tom and Jerry Hawthorne, Esq.

Enormous popularity of Egan's book caused the popular drink to be quaffed "in honor of Tom and Jerry." This tavern ritual took place so frequently that the names of Egan's fictional men-about-town attached to the beverage.

Upset the Apple Cart

VENDORS of fruit, baked goods, and smoked eels are still common on the streets of some English cities. Most of them display such food in sidewalk stands or booths.

Americans selling apples on the streets began using carts, so that they could move where their potential customers were most abundant. This change in technique boosted sales, but created a new hazard. When a vendor of apples struck a rut or cobblestone too hard, he upset the apple cart—causing fruit to roll in every direction.

Though never frequent, this special kind of accident occurred often enough to give its name to any unexpected incident that halts the execution of a set of plans.

CHAPTER 15

BORROWED FROM THE BRITISH

"It is beginning to be hinted that we are a nation of amateurs."

—Lord Rosebery, *Rectoral Address,* Glasgow, 1900

Regardless of Lord Rosebery's views, for centuries the British have been the primary developers of English. Some of their distinctive expressions have not been adopted, but many have become popular in the United States. Though Americans have picked up phrases from all shores, those coming from the island kingdom have been the most abundant.

BONFIRE
BUMPED OFF
CONDOM
DERRICK
DIVE
FORK OVER
GADGET
GIBBERISH
GO OFF HALF-
  COCKED
HIDEBOUND
KEEP A STIFF
  UPPER LIP
MASTERPIECE
MUFF
ON THE HOUSE
ORDEAL
PAGE

POLL
POOPED
PUT THE SCREWS TO
PUT THROUGH THE
  MILL
RACK AND RUIN
RIGHT DOWN ONE'S
  ALLEY
RIGMAROLE
SIDEKICK
SKELETON IN THE
  CLOSET
SMOKE OUT
STIGMATIZE
STOOL PIGEON
TOE THE MARK/
  LINE, TO
WITCH'S BREW

SEE ALSO: Derby, Fanny, Feather One's Nest, Full of Beans, Get the Sack, Go to Pot, Hanky-panky, Horsepower, On the Nose, Pandemonium, Pig in a Poke, Play Hookey, Plush, Posh, Read the Riot Act, Sirloin, True Blue, Welch

Bonfire

THERE is nothing quite like the combination of festivity and food at an evening picnic that includes a bonfire.

This source of fun and frolic is particularly American, but we borrowed the word *bonfire* from our English ancestors. It once referred to a bone-fire, which was a primitive form of cremation. After the practice was abandoned by ordinary folk, it was observed with bodies of saints. Ashes from the burning of a saint's bones were potent good luck charms.

When roaring blazes ceased to be used to consume bones, the spelling of *bone-fire* changed and any hearty outdoor fire came to be known as a *bonfire*.

Bumped Off

DURING races on the Thames and other rivers of England, boats were launched one at a time. When a crew caught up with a rival and bumped its shell, the latter was disqualified. Popular meets meant heavy gambling, so many a spectator groaned or cheered when a boat was "bumped out" of the race.

London's underworld borrowed from the sporting world and began to say that a person coming to a violent end had been "bumped off." Famous mystery writer Edgar Wallace picked up the expression and used it in some of his thrillers.

During the Prohibition era, gangsters bumped off so many rivals that the boating term from England became fixed in American speech.

Condom

UNTIL the rise of AIDS prompted a surgeon-general of the United States to talk bluntly, polite conversation seldom acknowledged existence of the condom. Originally fashioned from lamb skins, it was around a long time before anyone spoke of it except in a whisper.

A trio of famous—or infamous—English members of the fox hunting set may have been first to break the silence barrier. In 1667, lords Rochester, Roscommon, and Dorset put their name upon a pamphlet that lauded the virtues of the device then called *condum*. Along with many others, they credited its invention to Col. Condum of the Royal Guards.

Condum lived in the swashbuckling era of Charles II, and may have been first to discover what kinds of oil will make dried intestines soft and pliable. Another candidate for the honor of having perfected the sheath is 18th-century English physician Charles Condom.

Regardless of which man deserves lasting tribute for inventive genius, the name of Condum—or of Condom—became permanently attached to the now-lauded gadget rarely mentioned in public until modern times.

Derrick

THESE days you are likely to see at least one derrick any time you drive around a growing city or town. In states like Texas you would see a number of oil well derricks. Both kinds are large frameworks for handling heavy equipment.

Before the advent of industry as we know it, *derrick* meant "gallows." At the end of the 16th century in Tyburn, England, there was a famous hangman named Thomas Derick. His name first became synonymous with hangmen in general before being applied to the gallows.

Thousands of condemned persons were lifted to death at Derick's direction, if not by his own hand. Eventually the original association was lost, however, and by the 18th century *derrick* simply meant any hoisting apparatus.

Dive

MANY a nightclub and dance hall is so cheap and shoddy that there's only one thing to call it: *dive*. We owe the birth of this title to everchanging fads in the world of furniture.

Late in the 19th century, Londoners became enamored with divans—or lounges—that were modeled after Turkish originals. Any owner of a public place who could afford such opulence was proud to say that it was equipped with them.

Many a smoking and gambling haunt was a financial loser. Managers let these places become rundown and disreputable, but the once-fashionable divans often remained in them. Worn and soiled furniture in the Turkish mode caused any place that included it to become more or less notorious as a *dive*.

This usage might have dropped from speech had it not been strengthened by the fact that a drinking den—legal or illegal—was often situated below ground level. This arrangement required a patron to "dive into the bar," swiftly disappearing from the sight of passersby.

Fork Over

NOBLEMEN owned most of Britain's good farmland until modern times. Peasants who wanted to rent were required to promise to pay in silver.

At harvest time, landlords sent collection agents for the annual rent—often before crops could be sold. A tenant without silver had to make payment in kind with his produce.

Shrewd agents often allowed less than market value for grain or other staples accepted in lieu of silver. So a farmer forced to deliver his rent with a pitchfork cursed under his breath while making his payment.

Today, substitutions for money are rarely, if ever, accepted. Also, a person is more likely to be forking over greenbacks to a creditor or a bookie than to a landlord of noble birth.

Gadget

NO kitchen or tool shed is complete without assorted gizmos that look impressive but aren't very useful. When you need help in reaching one of them and cannot remember what to call it, you are likely to request: "Please hand me that gadget from the shelf."

Sailors in Britain's vast merchant marine gave us this indispensable term, which they adapted from French. Impressed with small mechanical parts of new-style rifles made across the British Channel, 19th-century seamen stumbled over the French word *gâchette*. Already used in France to label any small mechanism—from guns to locks—the English sailors adopted *gadget* for the same purpose.

Responding to what they claim is consumer demand, manufacturers now load cars, stereos, and other devices with conspicuous gadgets that may be more costly than helpful. As every aficionado knows, any widget or dingus of this sort is at least distantly related to some earlier gadget.

Gibberish

EARLY in the 16th century, villagers of England noticed that many swarthy foreigners were afoot. Since these queer folk had black hair and tawny skins, it was assumed that they came from Egypt. For a time known as Egyptians, common folk soon shortened their title to Gypsies. Always keeping their distance from others, close-knit bands of Gypsies perpetuated ancient customs.

Even their language was distinctive—the speech of a typical Gypsy sounded much as though the dark-skinned person was jabbering pure nonsense. The English coined a special word, *gibberish*, to name such talk. Half a century after the title entered speech, it became associated with sound-imitating words such as *gibber* and *jabber*.

Firmly established in everyday speech, the title expanded and we now use it to label any incoherent jumble of sounds.

Go Off Half-cocked

As late as the time of the American Revolution, the sportsmen of England shot game with heavy and clumsy muskets. Their weapons had to be loaded slowly by hand, for they wouldn't fire until cocked.

As a safety measure, many a musket was made so that it could be half-cocked. From that position, it took a less complex set of movements to get the weapon ready to fire.

Veteran hunters were careful to cock their muskets as soon as they came close to game. Beginners who hadn't learned to do this were likely to develop "buck fever" at the sight of a deer. While trying to fire from the half-cocked position, a fellow might see a coveted trophy scoot out of sight, unharmed.

Like an amateur hunter, a person failing to make final preparations before trying to launch an enterprise may be stymied as a result of having "gone off half-cocked."

Hidebound

The production of feed for domestic animals is now big business. But until modern times, farmers knew little about bone meal and molasses—or vitamins and antibiotics.

As recently as the reign of King George III, many of the cattle in the empire were in a sorry state by late winter. The skin of emaciated animals was stiff and clung to their backs and ribs. Since the skin was so tight and dry, it lost all flexibility.

More than 400 years ago, a hidebound animal was often compared with a human whose mental activities seemed cramped and restricted. As a result, the farm-born word borrowed from the English refers to anyone whose ideas are as stiff as an ill-fed cow's skin.

Keep a Stiff Upper Lip

FOR at least a dozen centuries, men of England alternated between shaving and growing whiskers. Razors were used every day during most of the reign of Queen Anne. To make up for what the razor took, many a sporting fellow donned a wig. When wigs were abandoned by most people except barristers, facial hair made a comeback.

Soldiers may have been first to give up beards in favor of mustaches. But military men who grew them discovered a serious drawback. Hair on the upper lip, no matter how carefully clipped and waxed, moves at the slightest twitch of a muscle.

Many a stern old officer, himself slow to adopt the newfangled mustache, roared and pitched. If a young fellow insisted upon growing hair under his nose, he would have to learn to keep a stiff upper lip. Movements of a mustache when standing rigidly at attention might even be considered a breach of discipline.

Spreading from barracks room talk of men hoping to become known as officers and gentlemen, the phrase came to label self-control in any difficult situation.

Masterpiece

TRADE guilds of past eras required an apprentice to learn by working under a veteran for nearly nothing, perhaps for years. The guilds stipulated that a person wishing to own his own shop had to be recognized as a master. After working for years as an apprentice, and later as a journeyman, a man could make a piece in his craft that would be considered that of a master's.

Once a man's master piece was approved, he was allowed to start his own business and hire an apprentice. For the rest of his life, he might look back upon his master piece as the finest example of his skill and ingenuity.

Passing from trade and industry of England to the fine arts, the term *masterpiece* came to label the finest individual piece of work or any product of an artist's most creative years.

Muff

MANY times, a person given a rare opportunity will "muff"
it. That is often because a high-level challenge causes adrenalin to
flow, and too much adrenalin can make you clumsy.

Clumsiness came to be expected of English gentry who
brought to the island a garment long familiar to the Dutch.
Cylindrical and open at both ends, a muff made of fur was ideal to
keep hands warm in the brisk British climate. But a person whose
fingers were toasty from being inside a muff wasn't in the best of
shape to grab a hat blown off by the wind.

Comfortable though the muff-wearer was likely to be, use of
the gear was often a source of awkward and delayed action.
Hence we continue to say that anyone who drops the ball has
muffed what may have been the chance of a lifetime.

On the House

ANYTHING distributed free of charge, courtesy of the management, is "on the house."

Originally, the house involved was an English pub or tavern.
Owners often invited newcomers to sample their stock by offering
a free drink. This small taste often whetted the appetite for more,
and the barkeep could expect the sale of several more drinks.

Some U.S. states prohibit a barkeeper from offering freebies;
in other regions, rising costs have made the custom obsolete.
Despite this, we say that gifts to a consumer from a business
owner are "on the house."

Ordeal

WHEN you undergo an ordeal at work or on a shopping
expedition, you've had an exhausting and probably painful time.
Pain was the essential element in medieval rituals that concerned
the judging of others.

In the eras before accused Englishmen were brought before judges and juries, innocence or guilt was frequently determined by an *ordeal*. Authorities sometimes heated a bar of iron and offered it to a person suspected of crime. If grasped without burning the flesh, their deity was considered to have rendered a verdict of innocent. Numerous other ordeals were used with accused persons; in all of them a person was pronounced guilty if he or she showed signs of suffering.

Expanding from kangaroo courts into everyday life, the name of the physical test came to indicate a relatively low-level experience that is only trying or vexatious.

Page

FRENCH-SPEAKING Normans who invaded England in the 11th century called a stripling boy a *page*. Since youngsters performed many menial tasks, the term came to designate a male servant of any age. Kitchen pages, scullery pages, and stable pages could be found in many big establishments.

It was only proper for bewigged lords and beribboned ladies to send a page to deliver a message. Hence a person was said to be *paged* when a search was made for him or her in a public place.

Although today we use electronic speaker systems instead of uniformed pages hurrying about with messages on a silver tray, the term *paged* retains its old meaning.

Poll

HARDLY a week goes by without the announcement of results from a Harris poll, a Gallup poll, or a poll by a news magazine or television network. Techniques that users consider to be scientific have made poll results newsworthy, regardless of the topic.

This modern activity, which may have impact upon public opinion, is rooted in practices of ancient Britain. There the early census-takers didn't ask a bundle of questions. They simply counted heads, or *polls,* in order to learn how many people lived in a town or borough.

This means that even when conducted by telephone and tabulated by computer, in its literal sense a poll is simply a count of heads.

Pooped

LOTS of people find themselves pooped at the end of a hard week. Some manage to function when feeling this way most or all of the time. Don't go searching in the bathroom or barnyard for the background of this term. We use it today because our ancestors took to the sea for most of their long-distance journeys.

Englishmen headed toward the New World found that violent waves did most damage when they crashed against the stern, or poop, of a vessel. Strong winds and turbulent water could last for weeks. Any ship that lurched out of a long bout with nature was sure to be badly "pooped"—lucky to be afloat after days of pounding.

Sailors who described the splintered stern of a ship to buddies in the tavern or to family at home frequently confessed that they felt as pooped as their vessel looked. Landsmen who heard the sea-going expression borrowed it and put it to use. As a result, we still turn to it in order to describe our feelings in times of total fatigue.

Put the Screws To

IN today's high-pressure world, it is common to see a corporation "put the screws" to a competitor. Reasons for doing so range from plans of a takeover to forcing a rival into bankruptcy. Whatever the motive behind the action, and regardless of how it is done, the phrase describing it comes from an era in which torture was common practice.

No jailer was worth his salary until he learned how to use thumbscrews. Fastened upon a captive whose hands were strapped to his sides, these instruments of torture were tightened slowly.

A sudden and abrupt turn of a screw might make a person pass out from pain and thus be unable to confess or tell where loot was hidden.

Today, actual thumbscrews are seen only in museums. Yet it is still an everyday practice for a wheeler-dealer of some sort to put the screws to a business or industry in order to try to get something from it.

Put Through the Mill

THE British were using grinding wheels for cereal grasses as early as the fifth century. Made of native stone, such a wheel was operated by water power or was turned by oxen. When it became customary to erect a special house for grinding, the builders called it a *mill*—derived from a Saxon word.

Machinery remained simple for centuries. But farm boys of medieval times saw few wonders. It was a real adventure to visit a mill and see wheat go under a stone and come out as flour.

Wheat and other cereals were so quickly pulverized by stones that any person getting rough treatment came to be described as being "put through the mill."

Rack and Ruin

IT hurts to see a beautiful lawn or a thriving enterprise go to rack and ruin, but you've no doubt seen it happen. At first look, *rack* may seem to come from an early form of torture, but the truth is less complicated.

One of the original Old English forms of *wreck* was *wrack*. While the second spelling ceased to be used long ago, its pronunciation was retained in the old phrase *rack and ruin*.

Wrecks were most commonly associated with ships on a dangerous sea. If a merchant's ship was wrecked with a full load of goods, he could be ruined financially.

A shipping accident need not happen today for someone or something to go to rack and ruin.

Right Down One's Alley

MOST English cities and towns of long ago had many more narrow alleys than broad streets; most of them still retain that pattern. Except for members of the wealthy gentry, people were more likely to live on an alley than not.

Asked to make a delivery or purchase close to home, it was natural to respond, "That's right down my alley!"

This very British expression for "it's close to home" seemed to early Americans just right as a way of indicating "that is something I'm just the person to do!"

Rigmarole

ALTHOUGH origin of the title is obscure, *ragman* was the designation applied to a feudal official by a statute instituted by Edward I of England. When he invaded Scotland in 1296, his aides forced all nobles and gentry to sign a ragman's roll as a token of allegiance. Once they finally complied, the king sent couriers all over the country reading these lists. He hoped that announcing the submisson of leaders would bring resistance of the ordinary folk to an end.

Whether from weariness or carelessness, Edward's messengers reeled off the names so quickly that they were difficult to understand. Hence any jumble of words was compared with a flow of names and called a *ragman's roll*.

Streamlined from frequent use, the old term for the loyalty list is now familiar as *rigmarole*—a label for a nearly incoherent jumble of fast flowing words.

Sidekick

PICKPOCKETS abounded in London and other English cities during the time of Victorian author Charles Dickens. They anticipated modern youth gangs by forming close-knit organizations. A recruit had to go through an apprenticeship, much as though he were in training for an honorable craft.

Pickpockets developed their own slang vocabulary. In their speech a *pratt* was a hip pocket, while a *pit* was a breast pocket. They used *jerve* to name a vest pocket and *kick* to designate a side pocket in a pair of breeches.

Even a veteran of this special kind of crime was likely to have trouble with a kick. It lay close to a potential victim's leg, and was in constant motion. Worldy-wise London merchants learned that money placed there was safer than that in any other pocket.

It became proverbial that a fellow who didn't want to lose his bundle should stash it in his sidekick. As a result, any faithful partner always at one's side took the name of the trousers pocket that is most resistant to pickpockets.

Skeleton in the Closet

ENGLISH physicians eager to learn more about the human body were long under severe restrictions. Only the body of an executed criminal could be dissected until a controversial Anatomy Act was passed in 1832.

Many an early doctor dissected only one cadaver during his career. Naturally, he prized the skeleton highly and didn't want to dispose of it. Yet public opinion warned against keeping it where it might be seen. So the prudent anatomist hung his prize in a dark corner where visitors were not likely to discover it.

Patients weren't complete numbskulls, however. Most knew or suspected that their physician had a skeleton in his closet. From this literal sense, the phrase expanded to indicate hidden evidence of any kind.

Smoke Out

KING Edward III of England personally led armies that invaded and plundered France. But when he and his victorious warriors returned home, they brought the Black Death with them. Plague broke out in 1348 and soon swept through the kingdom.

Doctors didn't understand the nature of the disease and had no cure. Many agreed with common folk that demons spread the fearful malady.

Everybody knew that there was just one sure way to drive evil spirits out of a house: fill the place with dense smoke. Since demons who brought the plague might linger after victims died, any house visited by the Black Death was likely to be fumigated. Even bed linens and clothing of the dead were carefully smoked.

This practice caused people to say that anyone seeking concealed information is trying to smoke out a secret. Such a quest may be as important as purifying a house after the Black Death, but few who follow it nowadays burn sulphur and herbs.

Stigmatize

A NEIGHBOR or fellow worker who is stigmatized in some way may be considered dishonest or immoral, but you can't discover this by looking. That was not the case when the expression came into use.

Borrowing from ancient Greek, British officials called a branding iron a *stigma*. Widely employed both to punish and to identify culprits, any person displaying a visible legal brand was likely to be avoided by law-abiding citizens. An iron displaying the letter "A" was used in cases of adultery, "T" indicated a convicted thief, and other letters of the alphabet symbolized other crimes.

Abandoned three centuries ago by most English courts, stigmatization retains its vitality because verbal labeling and identifying can still cause a person to feel disgraced.

Stool Pigeon

BOTH in England and on the American frontier, pigeons were an important source of meat for generations. Many were captured by trappers. Others were shot down by hunters, but damaged meat was considered less tasty.

Trappers learned how to use a tame bird, or decoy, in order to lure wild ones into snares. Many a fellow spent much of the day waiting for game to come, while his decoy was tied to a stool so it couldn't escape.

Such stool pigeons were common for many years. Since each of them functioned to entice others into a trap, the name was adopted to designate anyone who betrays colleagues or comrades.

Toe the Mark/Line, to

UNLIKE their American cousins, entrants in a properly British foot race of the last century were not required to come up to scratch. Instead, the official solemnly intoned: "Gentlemen, toe your marks!"

Naturally, every contestant wanted to be as far forward as possible at the moment a race began. But an entrant who pushed toes a trifle past the starting mark was thrown out of the contest, with no second chance.

It took both practice and careful attention to toe the mark without going past it. Hence the English sporting term came to be used on both sides of the Atlantic to mean meeting a standard or abiding by a rule.

Witch's Brew

NEITHER witches nor their male counterparts, warlocks, commonly pretended to be in league with the devil. Most were herbalists and midwives, while others charged fees for peering into the future or the secrets of nature.

Popular thought credited a witch with supernatural power even if she didn't claim it. To ordinary folk, such a woman seemed to be forever boiling some mysterious brew in a cauldron—often a homemade cold remedy. When ready for use, this potent stuff was believed capable of influencing the fate of individuals and nations. Shakespeare immortalized the concept when in Macbeth he described "dreadful charms" simmering in a big iron pot.

Despite modern health concerns for natural ingredients, few today bend over pots in order to concoct a witch's brew. But the name of the mysterious stuff lives in speech to designate any potent compound prepared with unknown motives.

CHAPTER 16

STORIES TO BE TAKEN WITH A GRAIN OF SALT

"His imagination resembled the wings of an ostrich. It enabled him to run, though not to soar."
—Macaulay, *Essays: John Dryden*

Sleuths seeking the origins of words, better known as etymologists, often confess failure. Evidence may be lacking or confused, causing scholars to note that there is no plausible explanation for the particular usage of a word or a phrase.

Since nature abhors a vacuum, imagination often rushes in where scholarship fails. Numerous widely circulated accounts of the way in which an expression was formed are products of folk etymology. That is, ordinary folk make up explanations that are transmitted orally before breaking into print. Because of their intrinsic interest, such accounts are not to be dismissed out of hand. Rather, they are to be savored as what they are—verbal flights on wings of ostriches.

BABY
BIGOT
BOOZE
CHARLEY HORSE
CHIP ON ONE'S SHOULDER,
  TO HAVE A
COCKTAIL
CROCODILE TEARS
DUN
ELBOWROOM
GAGA
GRIN LIKE A CHESHIRE
  CAT
HARLOT
HOGWASH
HOODLUM
HOOKER

KNOCK ON WOOD
LAZY SUSAN
LIMERICK
MONKEY WRENCH
ON THE NOSE
PAY THROUGH THE
  NOSE
PETER OUT
POSH
PULL UP STAKES
PUSSYFOOT
RATFINK
SEE RED
SIRLOIN
TELL IT TO THE
  MARINES!
TOMBOY

SEE ALSO: Achilles' Heel, Dogwood, Don Juan, Eager Beaver, Grain of Salt, Green-eyed Monster, Lick into Shape, Lowbrow, Pooh-Bah.

Baby

MOST people like an occasional moment as the center of attention such as that showered on a baby. According to a story that some scholars take seriously, to "baby" a lover, spouse, or aging parent is to behave as though diamonds were being sifted.

An American inventor is credited with having developed a device capable of shaking soil in order to sift diamonds from it. From his name, Babe, his machine is supposed to have been known as a *baby*. Rocking motions of Babe's baby was much like the rhythmic soothing of an infant. Hence anyone who gets over-zealous attention is said to be *babied*.

It would be easier to swallow that explanation if a patent by Ralph or Lawrence or Adolph Babe could be found. Lacking such evidence, it seems that someone has gone to a lot of trouble inventing a yarn that isn't needed. After all, what is more logical than to say that others baby a person by simply giving him or her the same solicitous care given to an infant?

Bigot

YOUR circle of acquaintances is unusual if it doesn't include at least one outspoken bigot. Racial, religious, and political intolerances continue to flourish all over the world.

A legend has it that the word *bigot* was born of a dramatic incident at the court of King Charles III of France, known as Charles the Simple. As the story goes, he demanded absolute obedience and required noblemen to kneel in order to kiss his foot.

One stout fellow, Rollo of Normandy, was led before the king for the customary ceremony. At the last minute he decided not to conform. So instead of kneeling, the story goes, he held himself erect and blurted: "Ne se, bi got!" (No, by God!). Charles scolded him severely, and as a result any person who doesn't accept conventional standards came to be known as a *bigot*.

That colorful tale may have been invented as a result of the fact that "Bi got!" really was a commonly used oath among Germanic peoples. It was bestowed on Norman invaders of England as a mocking nickname. Possibly this helped to form the label we apply to stubbornly opinionated people.

Booze

LITTLE or nothing is known about Philadelphia merchant E. G. Booze, says tradition, except that he is commemorated in everyday speech. According to a common story, he bought moonshine whiskey anywhere he could get it. A bottle shaped like a log cabin was his standard container, but it lacked the customary maker's label.

Customers who liked his prices didn't quibble over brand names, and applied the merchant's name to a bottle of his stuff. Since Philadelphia was a major city, its term for unlabeled whiskey spread from that center into every town and village.

That story about E. G. Booze seems to have taken shape because there is no solid evidence about the origin of the word that is now universally familiar. Possibly rooted in an old Dutch term meaning "to drink to excess," it disappeared from use for generations. Revived perhaps four centuries ago, it began to be spelled as it sounds, producing our universally familiar but mystery-shrouded *booze*.

Charley Horse

MANY an attendant at a gym or trainer of athletes can tell you why you call a muscular spasm a *charley horse*.

The story is that at the old Chicago White Sox ballpark, there was an old horse named Charley. All during the 1890s, he was used to pull a roller across the infield. His work was repetitive, so his leg muscles got so stiff he could hardly walk. Players and spectators who suddenly caught a cramp thought of the old fellow, and called it a *charley horse*.

Though that explanation doesn't hold up under scrutiny, it

survives because there is no solid alternative. Before veterinary science was widely known, jockeys and trainers used *horse ail* to name any obscure ailment of a racer. In the same era, a night watchman was a *charlie*—whose pounding of the cobblestones probably produced many an aching muscle. Foot or leg cramps experienced by a charlie could have been compared with ailments of a lame animal in order to produce the term *charley horse*. Both are more probable than the Chicago-based story of the ballpark horse.

Chip on One's Shoulder, to Have a

A WIDESPREAD tale insists it was once common for a rural bully to threaten, "Knock this chip off my shoulder, if you dare!"

Even exaggerated tales do not report the use of wood chips in this fashion. Popular speech isn't restricted to reality, however. Making fun of hotheads, it was said that some didn't know dried buffalo dung when they saw it.

This special kind of earthy chip was once abundant. Imagination said a tenderfoot was likely to place it on his shoulder—constituting a challenge likely to evoke laughter instead of fear. Any fellow who walked around with a buffalo chip on his shoulder was constantly belligerent but not worth fighting.

Cocktail

IF you drop in on cocktail parties, sooner or later someone is sure to challenge you: "Why do we call a mixed drink a cocktail?" In truth, there are several possible stories to relate.

One is the tale of the beautiful Aztec princess, Octel. She got tired of eating from golden dishes, so she scrounged around and found a drinking vessel made of glass. Beverages poured into her glass varied in color, and she mixed the ingredients to watch the swirling of liquid in the glass. That is why Octel gave her name to the cocktail.

Swallow your drink—not the yarn!

Mixed drinks may be as old as mankind, but our title for them is modern. It is odd that at least fifty explanations for it have been offered. One of the best is from England, where the docked tail of a fast horse was called a cock-tail. Many a nag with a cock-tail got off to a roaring start. So do some persons who down two or three mixed drinks in succession.

According to this account, racetrack influence caused *cocktail* to name a mixed beverage that confers such a jolt the user is ready to challenge the field.

Crocodile Tears

GREEK and Roman explorers who first encountered the awesome crocodile came home with a bundle of tall tales. According to them, the creature with a huge mouthful of teeth moaned like a woman in distress in order to lure victims within snapping distance.

Once a person went down the crocodile's path, the animal sobbed out of pity for its most recent meal. At least, that was the story circulated centuries ago and used by writers as late as the time of Shakespeare.

The tall tale was repeated orally for generation after generation. As a result, stories about crocodile tears caused any bogus show of contrition to take that name.

Dun

ANY time circumstances force you to dun someone who owes you money, you may wonder how this pursuit got its name.

An old wives' tale says that Joe Dun was a bailiff in London during the reign of King Henry VII. Because he was particularly hard-nosed and persistent, the act of dogging the heels of a debtor took his name.

The truth is that many bill collectors went around town beating drums while shouting the names of their quarries. A noisy fellow of this sort made a great *din*—a word that long ago was once spelled *dun*.

Elbowroom

MANY British soldiers and Hessian mercenaries who fought under Gen. John Burgoyne had one thing in common: they despised the aristocratic commander whose peers knew him as Gentleman Johnny.

According to a story dating from the time of the American Revolution, Burgoyne was much better at bragging than at fighting. Arriving in the vast region he was sent to subdue, he boasted that he would have plenty of elbowroom in which to operate. His remark, says legend, caused *elbowroom* to become a label for a maximum of space. That makes a story good enough to appear in more than one reputable source. But it is hard to believe that a single casual remark could have lasting impact.

What could be more natural than to say that an area adequate for work or leisure gives a person room to move the elbows? As a term for a minimum of space, elbowroom was in use two centuries before Burgoyne's birth. That makes it highly improbable that Gentleman Johnny had anything to do with the fact that we continue to use this expression today.

Gaga

NEXT time you are going "gaga" over a singer, entertainer, or brand-new fashion, someone may suggest that you have suddenly gone wild about the work of French artist Paul Gauguin.

An old tale has it that early admirers of the painter had difficulty pronouncing his name. Struggling with it, they settled for repetition of the first syllable. People who were absolutely mad about Gauguin's work were derided as being "Ga-Ga."

The only part of that story that is true is that the word is of

French origin. Meaning "fool" or "old fool," the French used the word as an echo of the fool's mindless sounds.

Grin Like a Cheshire Cat

CHESHIRE County, England, was an independent political unit for centuries. Justices of the peace named by the king had no jurisdiction, and Delamere Forest became notorious as a refuge for highwaymen.

During the reign of King Richard III, a new forest warden was selected. Mr. Caterling put a stop to poaching and captured dozens of felons, more than 100 of whom were hanged.

Caterling took great pride in his record and, grinning broadly, he presided over every execution. His unpleasant leer became so familiar that anyone smiling broadly was described as "grinning like the Cheshire Caterling."

In parts of Cheshire, natives still swear that the fellow who cleaned up the region causes us to say a person who smiles broadly is grinning like a Cheshire cat. Whatever the origin, the expression has been in frequent use since the late 1700s, and writers like Lewis Carroll made it even more popular.

Harlot

NO one ever mentioned a harlot in polite talk of yesteryear, but the term that long preceded hooker could be found in racy novels. Some readers of naughty literature swallowed a harlot story, hook, line, and sinker.

According to it, the ancient label for a prostitute can be traced to early Normandy. Robert le Diable reputedly came upon Arlette, the daughter of a tanner, bathing in the nude. He is supposed to have pulled his horse up short, jumped from the saddle, and sired William the Conqueror on the spot. This caused Arlette's name to become a label of shame that was soon modified to *harlot*.

William probably was born out of wedlock, for his devilish father tried to take every ravishing woman he saw. But linguistic sleuths say that *harlot* was an old French word meaning any rogue or vagabond. Eventually it referred only to rogue, or wild, women, giving us a euphemism for *prostitute*.

Hogwash

IN Old England, male swine were often castrated so that their meat would remain tender and juicy. The castrated males were called *hogs*. This practice was followed by a ceremonial washing, after which the water was thrown out as worthless. This, according to oral tradition, gave rise to the expression *hogwash*.

That makes a good story, but *hogwash* involved neither castration nor cleansing. For generations this was the common name of swill fed to swine. Since the watery stuff might include no nourishment except table scraps and a little flour, it hardly rated as genuine food.

Exaggerated claims and tall tales are verbal hogwash, or talk that is not substantial.

Hoodlum

ACCORDING to oral tradition, one of the most notorious ruffians of the Barbary Coast was known only as Muldoon. As leader of a large gang, he commanded so much muscle that authorities were afraid to order his arrest.

During a clean-up campaign led by a San Francisco newspaper, a reporter had a great idea. Instead of referring directly to the underworld boss, he spelled the name backward as Noodlum. Then he changed the initial letter from "N" to "H." Readers weren't long in figuring out who the mysterious Hoodlum was, and talk about his exploits propelled the made-up word into general speech.

That's the story still current in some parts of California, but wordsmiths believe it came from German immigrants. In German, the word *huddellump* means "wretch, miserable fellow" and thus "scoundrel."

Hooker

TRADITION says that the name of hard drinking Gen. Joseph Hooker of Civil War fame is behind the common label for a prostitute.

Orally transmitted stories have it that as military commander of Washington, D.C., Hooker encouraged prostitution "for the sake of the fighting men." Truth is, he never supervised the city's defenses. His longest hitch in D.C. was spent in what was once the insane asylum. When it was turned into a military hotel, he occupied a room briefly.

Another theory links today's label with the Corlear's Hook area of New York City. For many years, says tradition, this region was dotted with brothels patronized by sailors who referred to resident females as *hookers*.

Far less titillating but much more plausible is the theory that the hooker gained her name from one of the most innocent of sports: fishing. Until a prospective "John" takes the bait by looking, there is no need to waste time with him. Once his attention is hooked, there is a good chance that he will be added to a string of catches.

Knock on Wood

IT is a common practice to knock on wood with knuckles in order to try to ward off trouble or to seek good fortune. Almost invariably, this action of the hand is accompanied by a verbal announcement that it is taking place.

Ask a dozen acquaintances how this started, and at least one is likely to say that knocking turns a person's thoughts to the wooden cross on which Christ was crucified.

Knocking on wood as a form of asking for luck may just as easily stem from the play of children.

In many forms of the game of tag, trees afford sanctuary. A boy or girl who tags an oak or a pine is momentarily free from capture. But such knocking on wood doesn't count unless it is accompanied by a shout of triumph. That is, both actions and an announcement are required in order to assure the good luck that comes from safety.

Lazy Susan

IN the antebellum South, some plantation owners were stern taskmasters. Others gave some servants, particularly those who worked in the kitchen, considerable latitude. One bright young woman, variously identified as having lived in Louisiana or in Alabama, decided to reduce the work of taking serving dishes from one person to another. She devised a variation of the rotating dumbwaiter usually used for wine. Since she had no surname, the circular rotating shelf she placed in the center of a dining table was jocularly called "our lazy Susan."

Though the yarn seems credible, it has no foundation. In use maybe a century ago, the name did not identify its inventor. Rather, it stood for any pert housemaid—or Susan—accustomed to working about the table of a rambling old homestead in Massachusetts or Connecticut.

Limerick

MANY people either enjoy limericks hugely or positively hate them.

Enjoyment of the funny little poems is natural, according to one account of the word's origin. Norse conquerors of Ireland built in the south a brand new town of their own about 920 A.D. Borrowing from their own language, they called the place Limerick. When the invaders were driven out, the victorious Irish sang a taunting refrain in which the Norse were asked, "Will you come up to Limerick?"

Detective work by scholar Ernest Weekley turned up a modern essay by a Jesuit priest. In it, Father Russell wrote that a single-stanza poem from Edward Lear's *Book of Nonsense* was not a lyric, but a learic. Stumbling over the invented title, readers confused it with the name of the Irish city and called the special form of verse a limerick.

Monkey Wrench

A FRIEND or associate doesn't have to sport a long tail in order to throw a monkey wrench into plans and disrupt them. If monkeys used tools at all, a hammer would be easier to handle, so imagination long ago got busy trying to explain how their name attached to the tool.

One report has it that London craftsman Charles Moncke invented this special form of wrench and gave it his name. But even today, the British say "adjustable spanner" and not "monkey wrench." Another account would have you believe that the monkey wrench was developed by an American named Monk. No one has ever been able to find evidence that the tool was named for the first person to make it. A more probable explanation is that the people who first saw it may have laughed heartily. After all, a wrench whose lower jaw goes down or up at a twist of the fingers is about as ludicrous as a monkey jawing at onlookers in a zoo.

On the Nose

SOME folks will tell you that *on the nose,* meaning "exactly right," comes from the racetrack. While it may seem logical, the phrase comes from the studio, not the track.

Directors of early radio programs found that they often had to communicate with people in front of live microphones. In order to give directions without making sounds, a special sign language was developed. When a program was running precisely on schedule, the person watching the time put a finger alongside his or her nose.

So a horse who wins by a nose has nothing to do with this familiar expression, which finally appeared in print in the 1930s.

Pay Through the Nose

ANYONE caught in a squeeze that cannot be escaped without meeting an exorbitant demand will have to "pay through the nose." This unpleasant course of action, according to legend, stems from the brutality of warriors who overran Ireland long ago.

According to the story, Norsemen who mastered the land about 1,000 years ago demanded heavy tribute. Anyone who couldn't or wouldn't pay was seized and suffered a slit nose. Those who escaped this brutal punishment told their descendants that, once upon a time, they were forced to pay through the nose.

It makes a great tale—Ireland really did fall to Norse invaders in the 9th century. But there is no record that conquerors offered the option described. Eight hundred years passed before a literary work included a character who was forced to pay through the nose.

Common sense, not backed by proof, suggests a much later and more commonplace origin. When a quarrel erupted over money and one party ended with a bloody nose, the victor surely could have crowed that the loser was made to pay through the nose.

Peter Out

PETER Schmidt, says oral tradition, wandered into the Ohio River valley as a day laborer. He talked a good game and found it easy to get a job. For a day or two, maybe even a week, he would work hard from sun up to sun down. Then his pace would slow down and he would begin cutting his hours. Before the end of a month, he would "Peter out" and be fired.

Explanations like this one, called folk etymology by scholars, don't stand up under scrutiny. Instead of being named after a man who burned hot and then rapidly cooled, miners coined the phrase we use to mean dwindling to an end.

Forty-niners used a mixture of charcoal and saltpeter—the active ingredient—to make explosive charges. With its name clipped to *peter*, the stuff made short work of stones. But liberal use of peter could exhaust a seam quickly.

A mine seen to be yielding less and less dust was recognized by veterans as about to "peter out." Fixed in speech during the gold rush, the effect of using explosives is applied to any business or enterprise that is obviously dwindling.

Posh

UNTIL recent times, elegant and fashionable clothing and surroundings were never called *posh*.

This great-sounding title, say widely printed accounts, is an acronym. That is, it is made up of the initial letters of a memorable phrase: Port, Out; Starboard, Home.

Port-side staterooms were said to be preferred by British travelers heading out to India during the colonial era. According to the same tale, starboard quarters commanded a premium when a vessel was headed home. Supposedly, these quarters were out of the heat of the sun and thus preferable. The earliest printed use of the nautical acronym was in a 1952 issue of the *New Yorker* magazine.

Some scholars spend their lives stalking clues about the origin of words and phrases. There is no evidence to support the acronym story, but other educated guesses are just as insubstantial. The origin of *posh* remains a mystery.

Pull Up Stakes

A PERSON restless at work and not happy with the climate or job opportunities may be ready to pull up stakes and go elsewhere.

This expression, from a commonly told tale, owes its existence to Phineas T. Barnum's great American circus. Seldom spending more than two or three nights in one location, the circus was performed in tents whose ropes were secured by stakes driven into the ground. When the circus moved, pulling the stakes up came to be synonymous with moving.

Though it sounds great, that explanation is a long way off the target. When public land in the West was grabbed by a homesteader, he was expected to stay within survey lines marked by stakes. But many a greedy fellow went out after dark, pulled up the stakes and relocated them to suit himself.

Legality of such action was rarely challenged. Today, a person who wouldn't know a boundary marker if he met it in the middle of the street is said to "pull up stakes" when an old location is abandoned in favor of a new one.

Pussyfoot

AN old and almost plausible tale says we use *pussyfoot* to express the notion of care and hesitancy because of a law enforcement officer.

There seems actually to have been a marshall named Johnson who operated in Oklahoma's Indian Territory for years. He gained a wide reputation for skill in sneaking up on lawbreakers, especially those who ignored statutes governing the use of whiskey. Johnson's movements, almost feline in nature, caused friends and foes alike to call him Pussyfoot. His activities, according to legend, put his nickname in general speech.

Truth is, many decades before W. E. Johnson earned his nickname, lovers of cats wrote poems praising the stealth of these agile animals. It took only a smidgen of imagination to compare an evasive or extra-cautious person with a stealthy cat and say that any hesitant person is likely to pussyfoot around an issue.

Ratfink

MOST of us want nothing to do with a dirty ratfink who spills things told in confidence. Anyone branded with that label should be avoided.

That was precisely the case, according to southern tradition, with German-born Albert Fink. As the head of detectives who worked for the Louisville and Nashville Railroad, he is supposed to have sent men to infiltrate unions when strikes were in the air. Fink's man—naturally called a *Fink*—sat still, listened quietly, then ratted on fellow workers. Workers wanted nothing to do with such a fellow or his supervisor. Hence ratfink came to designate any squealer, scab, or breaker of confidences.

That would be believable—if only the L&N had records of having employed Albert or some other Fink as chief detective. Lacking verification, the story smells like an attempt to explain how a *Pink* who worked for pioneer private eye Allan Pinkerton was transformed into *Fink*.

See Red

IF you "see red" once in a while, you're normal—occasional anger is an ingredient in the mix we call living. But do not rebuke yourself for a brief incident that makes you seem like a bull who is being taunted by picadors.

That was the story circulated to explain why a show of temper is linked with red rather than with, say, purple or yellow. Tradition says that red banners or clothing are used by bullfighters in order to infuriate animals.

There is no truth to the story though it has circulated for many years. Scientific tests have shown that bulls pay no more attention to red than to other colors. It is the waving of fabric or movement of a matador that catches an animal's eye and induces him to charge.

At least one investigator says that the waving of a white cloth will enrage a bull even more quickly than movements of a red cloth. Even if that is gospel truth, it won't affect our everyday speech. For generations to come, our descendants will still be saying that a person who indulges in a visible burst of temper is seeing red.

Sirloin

ONCE upon a time, according to a widespread story, King Henry VIII—or maybe it was Charles I or James I—came upon a little inn. He was served beef not quite like any he had eaten before, and found it the best ever. Beginning to be a bit tipsy, he pulled out his sword and knighted the cut of meat. That is supposedly why you can order a "Sir Loin" in many a fine eating place these days.

That story may be interesting, but the origin of *sirloin* is not a mystery to etymologists. The word comes directly from the French *surlonge,* meaning "beef just above the loin."

Tell It to the Marines!

HAVE you ever had a friend try to fool you with some tall tale that you are too smart to fall for? If so, you may have said: "Go tell it to the Marines!"

Some people say this retort stems from the Union blockade of southern ports during the Civil War. With few ships plying the coastal waters, ingenious Confederates used convoys of wagons to move heavy goods. The drivers who served in this impromptu "horse marine" were easily fooled by anything an old salt said.

A much more likely version rests on the fact that British sailors in the early 1800s regarded the marines as greenhorns. When told some preposterous story, the career sailors would suggest that the yarn be told to the Marines—who were so gullible as to swallow it, hook, line, and sinker.

Tomboy

A TOMBOY, says oral tradition, gets her name from the fact that she is a changeling, or a female who has been given the appearance of a male. Though the idea is plausible enough, it isn't true; it has been manufactured out of whole cloth.

Tom and Jerry cartoons are modern, but the characters that give them their name are not. During the reign of England's King George IV, his subjects became enamored with an 1821 volume about *Life in London*. It featured the antics of Tom and Jerry—who were as zany as today's cartoon characters.

Popular talk about goings-on of the fellows who were credited with making London life lively was enhanced by using "Tom" to denote maleness, as in *tom cat*. As a result, any long-ago predecessor of Bart Simpson came to be called a *tomboy*. With its origins forgotten, the label attached to a young female whose looks are as deceptive as were actions of early Toms—real or imaginary.

CHAPTER *17*

COMPARISONS THAT
FROZE IN SPEECH

"To liken them to your auld-warld squad, I must say that comparisons are odd."

—Robert Burns, *The Brigs of Ayr*

A ny activity or event can attract enough interest and attention to cause a comparison to be made. Once a new term fashioned in this way becomes widely used, it may remain vital for decades or for centuries. In many instances, a word or a phrase does not immediately reveal the comparison that brought it into being.

ASSEMBLY LINE
BALK
BATTLE-AX
BEAN POLE
BEEF
BIG SHOT
BOLSTERED
BOW AND SCRAPE
BULLDOZER
CHIME IN
CLEAN AS A WHISTLE
COME TO A HEAD
COTTON UP TO
CUT AND DRIED
DEAD AS A DOORNAIL
FIRESTORM
FISHY
FIT AS A FIDDLE
FLAK
FRAME UP
HARP

HARROWING
HECTIC
HORSEPOWER
HOUND
JUMPING-OFF PLACE
MELTDOWN
NARROW-MINDED
NIP IN THE BUD
PULL IN ONE'S HORNS
RAKE-OFF
SLEAZY
SOFT PEDAL
STEAMROLLERED
STRAIT-LACED
TACKLE
TAPER OFF
TEASE
UNCLE TOM
WITHIN AN ACE
YARN

SEE ALSO: Bikini, Blowout, Bombshell, Bumped Off, Cheese-cake, Crackpot, Crank, Fallout, Fork Over, Graveyard Shift, Hamstrung, Limelight, Live Wire, Loose Cannon, Wet Behind the Ears, Pecking Order, Put the Screws To, Read You Loud and Clear, Rub the Wrong Way, Smoke Out, Stand Pat, Stem-winder, Sweetheart, Tee, Threshold

Assembly Line

MASS production of cars was late in starting. Henry Ford got the idea from watching an overhead trolley in a Chicago packing plant. In order to build automobiles in large quantity, he had Model-T flywheel magnetos move slowly past workers who performed only one or two operations each.

Production soared 400 percent, so he moved from magnetos to engines and transmissions and then to complete cars. Model-T's in the making, conveyed at six feet per minute past workers who used standardized parts, were sold at prices not imagined when cars were handmade luxuries. Ford launched modern mass production, yet the workers soon complained that their jobs were monotonous.

Even when performed at the keyboard of a computer instead of beside a conveyor belt, any highly repetitive work is likely to be criticized as an assembly line job.

Balk

THROUGHOUT much of northern Europe, early farmers used unplowed strips as dividers between fields. Ridges of this sort served to separate the crops of one man from those of his neighbors. From a word linked with the idea of missing or avoiding, the ribbon of earth avoided by the plow was known as a *balk*.

Naturally, having a balk was of considerable importance and even gained loose legal significance. One man could not cross another man's balk without permission—when plowing his own field he had to stop at the balk. So the word became associated with other kinds of avoidance and refusal, such as the jerk made by a horse in turning away from an outstretched bridle. By the 16th century, a person who protested an order was said to balk at instructions.

Battle-ax

BY the 11th century, the battle-ax was a regular part of the equipment issued to British warriors. Often fastened to the wrist by means of a chain, such a weapon was fearful, indeed. On June 23, 1314, the day before the famous battle of Bannockburn, Robert the Bruce felled Sir Henry Bohrn with a single blow of his battle-ax.

The invention of firearms soon made other weapons obsolete and the battle-ax became a favorite among collectors. Specimens are prominently displayed in the Tower of London and numerous other museums.

A first glimpse of this brutal and intimidating old weapon almost always evokes awe. As a result, comedians began to compare it with a quarrelsome and irritable person. Since performers were male, the butt of humor was invariably female. This usage, sexually biased though it is, leads many a modern male to mix jest with affection and refer to his wife as a *battle-ax*.

Bean Pole

BEANS have been cultivated for a long, long time. Early ones served mostly to provide feed and litter for animals. So when a climbing variety turned out to bear seeds that humans liked, it became a garden favorite.

Named for the color of its flower, the scarlet runner was recognized as a real curiosity—it twined in a direction opposite to the apparent motion of the sun. In the story of "Jack and the Beanstalk," this queer vine played a central role.

Stakes or poles are essential to growing scarlet runners. Six feet or more in length, poles are saved for reuse season after season. These special pieces of gardening gear are often compared with tall, lean persons. Abraham Lincoln thought little of it when he was called a "bean pole of a country lawyer."

For many years this old garden term has been used as a label for a slender person above average height.

Beef

IN order to get them from their ranges to railroads, herds of beef cattle were once forced to trot for day after day in all kinds of weather.

According to cowboy lore, something was wrong if the steers weren't bellowing continuously by the third day of a drive. Noise level mounted as time passed, so that a herd near the trail's end could be as ear-splitting as modern heavy-duty machinery.

Residents of railhead cow towns didn't need to be told when a rancher and his cowpokes were getting close—noise made by the "beef" could be heard for miles.

Cattle drives are long gone, but a person who is loud in finding fault is still said to *beef*—or bellow like a tired and thirsty steer.

Big Shot

LARGELY self-taught, John A. B. Dahlgren designed some of the largest guns used in the Civil War. A cannon that took his name, immense at the breech and tapering toward the muzzle, played decisive roles in numerous battles.

A sailor or soldier who saw an eleven-inch Dahlgren for the first time was often speechless. This big gun made earlier ones seem tiny and powerless. Fighting men compared an admiral or a general with the huge weapon and called the man in command a *big gun*.

Since Dahlgren's big guns spewed big shot at the enemy, any person of great importance was also known as a *big shot*.

Bolstered

EVEN in the households of nobles and princes, bedtime hasn't always meant easy slumber. There were many centuries in which the nearest approach to a headrest was a type of hard cushion that extended across the bed. From an early word describing anything that was swelled, such an enlarged bag was called a *bolster.*

People who first adopted use of the device lacked soft or springy material with which to fill it, so the early bolster was far from comfortable. About the best that could be said for it was that it elevated a sleeper's head.

When individual pillows came into use the bolster was generally abandoned, but left its mark on language. A person's ego is "bolstered" by anything that pushes up self-esteem—much as a stuffed bag once pushed up the head of a sleeper.

Bow and Scrape

MEASURED by any standard, most peasants of the Middle Ages were rough and uncouth. Even noblemen were often illiterate and nearly always unwashed. Many tried to make up for such deficiencies by using elaborate social rituals.

Ceremonies were particularly frequent and intricate at court. There, every gesture had to be made in accordance with custom. A person presented to a king had a difficult time of it. The subject had to make a deep bow while twisting one foot backward in a prescribed fashion. This required considerable skill, for an awkward move might throw a person forward, face down. Anyone going to court for the first time often practiced until at ease while executing the maneuver of "bowing and scraping."

Actions dictated by protocol made some observers think of people who were habitually obsequious. At least since 1650, perhaps longer, the English-speaking world has used the court-born phrase figuratively to name engagement in servile acts of fawning.

Bulldozer

IN the aftermath of the Civil War, many Louisiana vigilantes called themselves *bulldozers.* The punishment overseers had traditionally exacted upon slaves was likened to doses of punishment fit for a bull. Post-war bulldozers carried a black-snake whip and at least one big pistol. When such a fellow moved into action, people got out of his way in a hurry.

Long dormant, the terrorist name was revived prior to World War II. It seemed an appropriate word to designate a powerful earth-moving machine that easily pushed opposition aside.

After being widely used in military operations, the mechanical bulldozer became standard equipment in construction work.

Chime In

WELL before the 14th century, an unknown musician discovered that bells can be rung by striking them. Music produced in such fashion came to be known as *chimes,* usually involving a simple melody repeated many times. After the first chord is struck, other bells simply echo it.

Conversations often resemble the chimes from a cathedral tower. A person of importance will give an opinion, and those who hear it will mumble agreement.

Resemblance between harmony from a bell tower and speech by anyone who echoes another's opinion causes us to say that such a person does little except "chime in."

Clean as a Whistle

SHOULD you ever be a member of a team that has to investigate finances or conduct of an official, here's hoping you will be able to report: "Clean as a whistle!"

"Clean as a sheet just out of the washing machine!" would seem to be a more appropriate phrase. But speech often ignores logic and retains time-honored comparisons.

As every old-timer can tell you, a good whistle made from a reed or a piece of wood emits a clear tone—but is easily damaged. Even small particles of debris, or a few drops of moisture, will change the sound of a handmade instrument. In order to emit the pure notes intended by its maker, a whistle has to be absolutely clean. Anything or anyone as clean as a brand-new whistle or as clear as its sound is bound to be good.

All of which means that an organization or person called as "clean as a whistle" has been judged to be guiltless or flawless.

Come to a Head

HALF a century before Columbus's first voyage, English farmers began cultivating an odd plant. So long as it remained young, with loosely packed leaves, it was called *colewort*—a name preserved in coleslaw. When it formed a hard loaf in July or August, the mature vegetable was known as *cabbage*.

Even in this period, many townsfolk preferred to buy vegetables rather than grow them. In dry years they became impatient when cabbages did not come on the market as usual.

Explanations by growers centered in the fact that purchasers would simply have to be patient and wait until the plants "came to a head." Maturing of any plan or enterprise was compared with cabbage, and the concept of "coming to a head" passed from the vegetable garden into general use.

Cotton Up To

COTTON was grown and spun in ancient Egypt and China, but was rare and exotic until more recent times. Some of the great voyages of exploration had as one of their goals the discovery of a place where cotton was abundant.

Weavers who produced a piece of cotton cloth by hand knew it would bring a fancy price. To enhance its value, it was customary to rub newly woven fabric until it produced a visible down, or nap. This operation yielded quantities of fluff. Bits of it clung to hair and clothing of workers, who had difficulty picking it off.

A swain clinging closely to the lass of his choice or a person tenaciously seeking a favor was compared with particles of the fiber and was said to "cotton up to" his target.

Cut and Dried

HERBAL medicine, now undergoing a revival, was almost universally practiced until modern times. Shops stocked camomile, senna, and a variety of other native or imported leaves.

Practitioners wanted their medications to be compounded with precision. So it was commonplace for a herb doctor to ask for leaves that had been cut and dried, rather than those just plucked.

Soon anything ready-made was compared with leaves that had been stored in jars. Jonathan Swift applied this concept to hackneyed literary styles, and ideas or plans lacking freshness and potential for change were challenged as being "cut and dried."

Dead as a Doornail

ANYTHING from a withered house plant to a failed project that is beyond resurrection is likely to be described as being "dead as a doornail."

Both mechanical and electric doorbells are of recent invention. In earlier centuries, a visitor's arrival was announced by pounding with a knocker upon a metal plate nailed to the door.

Sometimes it took several heavy blows to attract attention. That meant nails holding the knocking plate suffered a lot of punishment. Repeatedly hit on its head, such a nail had the life pounded out of it so effectively that nothing could be deader.

Firestorm

A SINGLE sentence, less than carefully delivered, can unleash a firestorm of criticism in the aftermath of a presidential press conference. So can a decision by an executive or a member of the family, for that matter.

In such instances, reaction is quick and furious. Even though only words may be involved, destruction can be awesome. Which is why the term that took shape during war is appropriate for use in many civilian situations.

Wave after wave of planes dropped incendiary bombs on enemy cities before Allied forces achieved victory during World War II. Triggered by aerial bombing and spreading so rapidly that there was no way on earth to stop it, a firestorm could wreak havoc comparable to that caused by an atomic bomb.

These highly specialized missiles once used in great quantities have been made all but obsolete by more sophisticated weapons. But the firestorm set off by tons of incendiaries lives in speech as a memorial, of sorts, to the raging destruction it symbolizes.

Fishy

BENJAMIN Disraeli, first earl of Beaconsfield, is famous as having been a prime minister of England, making his way up the political ladder against great opposition. Had it not been for his brilliant wit and colorful use of language, he might have remained a small-time politician.

Disraeli wrote the novel *Coningsby* in order to influence public opinion. As he had done in earlier novels, the statesman tried to write as people talk and made many comparisons. As a result of this style, a famous piece of description includes a comment about the "most fishy thing I ever saw." The odor of fish made him think of doubtful political deals, Disraeli observed, noting also that both fish and politicians may be slippery.

Brought into speech by the writer-statesman, the new expression came into general use to label any situation that includes suspicious elements.

Fit as a Fiddle

IN one form or another, the stringed fiddle was popular in England nearly a thousand years ago. Sizes and shapes varied, as did the number and length of strings.

All early fiddles were hand made, and most were used in rural settings. Listeners as well as players knew when the tension of the strings was not right or when an instrument was warped. Only an undamaged one that was properly adjusted was in top shape, or fit to use with an audience.

Hundreds of years later, a person in vigorous good health is still said to be as "fit as a fiddle"—undamaged, and well-tuned, that is.

Flak

ANY time you rise a little above the crowd, by virtue of achievement or election, you had better be prepared to take some flak. Criticism and blame go with the territory.

Aviators learned the original meaning of *flak* during World War I. German engineering and technology were combined to produce a new kind of gun. Specifically designed to bring down aircraft, the German name for it was *Fliegerabwehrkanone*.

Allies who had considered the skies safe soon learned better. It didn't take some of them long to find out where those high-flying bullets were coming from. Few tried to master the humongous name of the German gun, they simply abbreviated its name and applied it to high-altitude shots. Always dangerous and frequently lethal, by definition *flak* is assumed to be discharged from enemy territory.

Frame Up

IF you wake up some morning and suddenly realize you've been the innocent victim of a frame up, don't think of yourself as the Lone Ranger. It happens every day, sometimes in the best of circles.

In an era when prefabs were not even in the dream stage, construction workers followed a long-standing formula. With a foundation in place, it was customary to frame up—or erect the supporting frame—as the next stage. Even a novice could look at a frame and see what shape the building would eventually take.

Persons who put confidence games together were less forthright than were carpenters and builders. Some of them learned to outline a scheme in such a fashion that it looked as though an elegant finish was in sight. A product of artifice rather than honest skill, this frame up gave its name to any scheme using false evidence in order to make an innocent person seem guilty.

Harp

HARPS were widely used in medieval Europe. When singing lays and ballads, a minstrel frequently accompanied himself with this instrument. It was rather easily made and played, but had one major drawback. Even when stroked by a master, it produced only a few notes. In the hands of a beginner, all the tones sounded alike.

Music from many a harp was almost as monotonous as talk by a crank obsessed with a single idea. So it became customary to poke fun at a bore by saying that he or she "harped" on some favorite subject.

Many improvements were later made in manufacture, as well as in techniques for playing the harp. Additional strings equipped with pedals make the modern harp of forty-six strings extremely versatile. Despite these changes, we continue to use its name to disparage tedious talk that revolves about a narrow range of topics.

Harrowing

LONG before Columbus discovered America, European farmers were using a heavy wooden frame equipped with many sharp teeth. Dragged over plowed ground, a harrow uprooted weeds while pulverizing the soil.

A city dweller was likely to be startled, even awed, at his first sight of a harrow in action. Comparing a time of trouble with ground subjected to the toothed implement, a painful experience was described as *harrowing*.

Sir Walter Scott used the earthy expression in his *Lady of the Lake*, thus making the term popular in standard speech.

Hectic

LONG before the nature of tuberculosis was understood, it was recognized as likely to be fatal. From a Greek term meaning "habitual," the fever that stayed with a sufferer was called *hectic*.

Hot, dry skin and flushed cheeks of a victim were often compared with a state of feverish excitement. Rudyard Kipling didn't contract the illness, but his notebook for 1904 includes a reference to a hectic day.

Modern medicine has conquered the habitual fever, but the name given to it continues to label any condition of restless activity.

Horsepower

A STEAM engine invented by James Watt worked well, but was criticized because there was no way to rate its power. Watt responded by measuring the pulling ability of a pair of big draft horses. One such animal, he calculated, could haul 33,000 pounds one foot in one minute. So he named that unit of work the *horsepower*.

Soon afterward, in 1806, mechnical engineers said Watt had made a serious error. "Measurement of engines by horsepowers is wrong," they said, "because a typical horse can barely raise 20,000 pounds one foot in one minute."

Debate continued for a century, during which the unit devised by Watt was called "shockingly unscientific." And yet engines powered by gasoline and electricity, as well as by steam, came to be universally rated in terms of their horsepower as measured by Watt.

From the Volkswagen to the Rolls-Royce, cars would be rated differently had Watt based his unit on the pulling power of ordinary nags instead of the heavy dray animals he actually used.

Hound

BEFORE the Norman conquest of England, French hunters bred a keen-nosed dog that they called the St. Hubert. One of their rulers, William, took a pack to England and hunted deer—following dogs on foot.

Saxons had never before seen a dog fierce enough to seize its prey, so they named William's animals *hunts*, meaning "seizure." Altered over time to *hound*, it was long applied to all hunting dogs. Then the meaning narrowed to stand for breeds that follow their quarry by scent.

Many medieval noblemen kept large kennels that included deer hounds, boar hounds, and hare hounds. Though they varied in size and appearance, all hounds were noted for their tenacity. A pack would follow a scent for miles. If the trail was lost, dogs would often double back and find it again. The animals were admired for the way they pursued game with such singular determination.

A human who engages in relentless pursuit of a goal or plan, dogging the footsteps of someone else, is still compared with a hunting dog and is said to "hound" his or her quarry.

Jumping-off Place

DURING the era in which the frontier was flowing westward, trading posts represented civilization's last fringe. Traders who ran their prices sky-high were likely to have as neighbors only a few criminals and adventurers.

Many people preferred open country to spots infested with two-legged skunks. But a fellow planning to jump into the wilderness had to go to a trading post for supplies. Almost every spoken and written reference to such a jumping-off place was disparaging. Adopted by many persons who have never been outside a city, the frontier term is now used to label any remote area or the spot for beginning a journey.

Meltdown

MAYBE you caught a news story about a group of Canadian financiers in deep trouble. According to *Toronto Life,* these notables expected to face a credibility meltdown.

Can there really be a meltdown in credibility?

Not in the sense of the colossal tragedy at Chernobyl in 1986. But the advent of nuclear energy brought with it the potential for unmitigated disaster. Long applied to less dramatic processes, *meltdown* attached to nuclear accidents and gained global usage.

We are continually making new verbal comparisons, but often the majority don't last. Not so this one. It is firmly embedded in speech and has no exact counterpart. So the label made memorable in Russia is likely to be alive and well long after hoped for safety innovations reduce the danger of a nuclear meltdown.

Narrow-minded

THOUGH he never held the title, Ben Jonson is widely considered to have been England's first poet laureate. After producing a smash hit in 1598 he became the chief literary lion of his era.

His last great work, *The Staple of the News,* was finished in 1625. By then, anything he wrote was sure to be widely read and quoted. So when he used a vivid title for a prejudiced person, it became popular in language. Writing of a man whose "thoughts be dwell All in a Lane," Johnson described him as being "narrow-minded."

Launched in this fashion, the expression was quickly adopted by sophisticates of the era. Many used Johnson's term jokingly at first, but it proved so expressive that we still turn to it when we wish to label a person as having a restricted outlook or being provincial.

Nip in the Bud

CRUDE beginnings in scientific horticulture were made many centuries ago. At least as early as the 14th century, gardeners knew that many plants produce an excessive number of blossoms. So it became customary to pinch off the majority in order that those which were left might produce large fruit.

This practice improved the quality of garden produce—but was devastating to individual buds. It became proverbial that when a bud was nipped off, no fruit would be produced at that point. Comparing the gardening practice with human activities, a person who calls an early halt to a plan or enterprise "nips it in the bud."

Pull in One's Horns

SHOULD anyone ever suggest that you would be wise to "pull in your horns," that will be a diplomatic way of urging: "Back off! Take it easy, now!"

Logic suggests that this phrase grew out of activities in the Old West. But when you think about it a bit, you realize that there is no way that a steer can retract its horns.

Tracks left in literature indicate that the expression was very old when the American West was still young. It has been found in letters and other documents dating from the 16th century—where the context clarifies the meaning. As a matter of fact, it is the snail that actually pulls in its "horns" when it is ready to retreat into its shell—or back away from action.

So it is this common outdoor crawler, not the snorting bull, whose actions gave rise to an expression that is still alive and kicking after more than 400 years.

Rake-off

ANY time a person manages to pocket a nice rake-off, there is a gambling hall comparison that people involved in a deal may not notice.

In every casino, as well as in the place Miss Kitty operates in "Gunsmoke," one job of the croupier is to see that the house gets its share of every pot. Using a rake, cash or chips must be cut from the center of the table before the final showdown.

Laws now limit the percent that a house can take. But in the roaring decades of unlicensed gambling places, rake-off by the house sometimes reached one-third of the money wagered. Society tends to look suspiciously upon casino owners using "rake-off" for a perfectly legitimate rebate or commission judged by some to be a trifle on the shady side.

Sleazy

A ROW of cheap condominiums is likely to be recognized as "sleazy" within a few months after having been finished. A tabloid newspaper may get this name before it rolls from the press.

Decades ago, it took a while for potential consumers to be sure that cloth from Germany would not hold up well. A special kind of linen, called *Sleasie* because it came from the Silesian district, served as a come-on for London merchants. Having bought a wagon load of the stuff for nearly nothing, a vendor could offer it at a low price and still make a killing from it.

By the time consumers learned to distinguish Sleasie by quick examination, lots of the substandard linen had been sold. Consequently, the cloth name attached to anything shoddy or grungy or obviously inferior in quality.

Soft Pedal

ANYTIME you try to soft pedal claims of a political party or aspirant for office, your technique is borrowed from music.

When the pianoforte first came on the market, it was regarded as a marvel. The musical instrument's original name, now clipped in half, proclaimed that it produced both soft *(piano)* and loud *(forte)* sounds.

It was the radical new soft pedal that made the instrument really distinctive. By use of it, a player could soften notes by a touch of a toe.

There is no such handy device with which to deemphasize claims of an organization or party in which you believe. But a little practice will help you learn how to soft pedal emphases that you judge to be so loud that they are abrasive.

Steamrollered

STEAM provided energy for pumps in England's coal mines for decades before the modern steam engine was developed. After efficient models were devised, they were reserved for heavy-duty use.

Road builders modified an early type of locomotive in order to produce a machine that replaced horse-drawn rollers. Equipped with wide wheels and used for packing roadways and crushing stones, a steamroller was as powerful as many animals. Especially in the United States, but also in Paris and other Old World cities, a glimpse of the road building machine provided fodder for animated conversation.

Now obsolete, the mechanical monster was one of the most powerful devices of its era. People who saw it in action were so impressed with its relentless advance that we still say a person or movement crushed by overwhelming force has been *steamrollered*.

Strait-laced

SHOULD someone describe you as "strait-laced," your views will determine whether to regard this as complimentary or disparaging. For the old garment term may be interpreted either way.

Rather elaborate corsets were sometimes worn in classical times. But the garment didn't become widely popular until a few centuries ago. In the gilded era that followed discovery of the New World, many great ladies went wild about clothes. For the sake of fashion, a grand dame might pull her bodice so tight that her waist seemed to shrink. Since anything tight and narrow was called strait, a woman strapped into a whale-bone corset was literally "laced strait," or strait-laced.

It was inevitable that comparisons should be made. As early as 1526 a person of strict convictions was given the name of a woman laced into a corset so tightly that she could hardly breathe.

Tackle

WHEN you tackle a problem, you use language that compares your action with work of ancient fishing gear. More than 600 years ago, a sportsman wrote that "the fish comes oftener to newe tackle that is set for him, than to olde." Though that verdict is debatable, in all eras some sportsmen have taken it seriously.

New or old, gear designed to snare fish was used by many people who gained fame through other pursuits. Samuel Johnson once made a trip into a region where he was surprised to find that fish abounded. Ruefully surveying a lost opportunity, the great man of letters told his faithful Boswell, "I indeed now could fish, give me English tackle!"

Many kinds of tackle were developed before we entered the age of plastics and fiberglass. Use of prized gear was so widespread that its name causes crowds to cheer when a football player is tackled. What's more, the fisherman's equipment names action from grappling with a new job to volunteering for an assignment.

Taper Off

FIRE has been associated with worship since prehistoric times, a practice that led to use of candles, or tapers, as symbols of purity and devotion.

Early candles were crude, but worshippers gradually learned how to make long, graceful ones that would burn for hours. Beeswax was and still is employed for many of the finest. Hand-dipped, such a taper is distinctive in shape. Gradually growing smaller, it comes to a definite point at the top.

From the shape of a fine candle, a colorful comparison entered general speech. Anything that diminishes gradually, whether it gives off light or not, is said to "taper off."

Tease

WHETHER made by hand or by machinery, cloth requires many operations. As late as the Middle Ages, one of the most irksome jobs was the initial straightening of raw materials in preparation for spinning.

Such work was compared with tearing or pulling things to pieces, so an old expression for that chore was adopted. Crude wooden combs were used to "tease" fibers apart so that they could be spun into thread.

Frequently one member of the family picked at another almost as persistently as though teasing tangles from wool or flax. Consequently the household task gave its name to any person who wages a deliberate and continued campaign of annoyance.

Uncle Tom

ANGRY at continued tolerance of slavery in the United States, Harriet Beecher Stowe wrote a novel that depicted the system at its worst. When it appeared in book form in 1852, it created a national sensation.

One of her major characters didn't want trouble and was inclined to seek peace at any price. Even when he was sold by his owner, Uncle Tom made no outcry—he simply resigned himself to the hand of Providence.

Few novels have affected life so greatly as did *Uncle Tom's Cabin*. Few characters have aroused more controversy than the slave who accepted his fate without questioning. Today, an *Uncle Tom* is a black man who behaves deferentially to whites. The term, of course, is in the highest order of insults.

Within an Ace

GAMBLERS whose language was old French used a special term for the lowest throw of the dice. Since that consisted of two single dots, such a marking came to be called an *ace*.

Transferred to playing cards, instead of being nearly impotent the card with a single dot packed plenty of power. A player often held a losing hand that an ace would have made into a winner.

Like a player whose luck would be changed by a single card, anyone who falls barely short of an objective comes "within an ace" of reaching it.

Yarn

ROPE was among the major commodities of 16th-century Europe, as enormous quantities were used on ships. Each rope consisted of several strands, all of which were made up of numerous small segments, or *yarns*. Special wheels, different from those used in making thread, were employed in making the stuff. Most of it was produced by males, who worked in groups of three to ten.

After a man became accustomed to the work, little concentration was necessary. Spinning hour after hour, day after day, was about as monotonous as anything a fellow could do. Small wonder, therefore, that the yarn loft became famous as a spot where workmen entertained one another by inventing stories.

By association with the work of spinning yarn, the telling of tales took that designation, and the tall tale itself came to be known as a *yarn*.

CHAPTER *18*

ACTION IS THE NAME OF THE GAME!

"Action may not always bring happiness; but there is no happiness without action."

—Benjamin Disraeli, *Lothar*

Britain's famous prime minister and well-known author was primarily a man of action. Perhaps he realized that many of our familiar expressions are based upon actions of the past, and that action of one sort or another is indicated by many words and phrases that appear to be static. Here's hoping your happiness index will rise as you become more familiar with terms of action.

ALL OVER BUT THE
  SHOUTING
BACK-SEAT DRIVER
BANDWAGON
BLOW OFF STEAM
BRING HOME THE BACON
BRONX CHEER
CALLED ON THE CARPET
FLY OFF THE HANDLE
FRAZZLED
GIMMICK
GRANDSTAND PLAY
HOCUS-POCUS
LAND-OFFICE BUSINESS
LIKE A HOUSE ON FIRE
LIVE WIRE

NIP AND TUCK
OFF THE DEEP END
PANIC BUTTON
PARK
PULL THE PLUG
RAILROAD
SELF-STARTER
SHINDIG
SIREN
SPARK PLUG
TAILSPIN
TAKE THE BULL BY
  THE HORNS
TESTIMONY
WHISTLE BLOWER
WISDOM TEETH

SEE ALSO: Shot in the Arm, Automboile, Barnstormer, Coasting Along, Dukes, Face-off, Fast Lane, Feisty, Flak, Freewheeler, Galvanized, Game Plan, Get a Rise, Gravy Train, Hightail, High Gear, Jaywalker, Make the Grade, Maverick, Peter Out, Plug Away, Pull Strings, Pull Up Stakes, Pussyfoot, Ride Shotgun, Ride Herd, Ride Roughshod, Roll with the Punches, Screwball, Start the Ball Rolling, Step on It, Talk a Blue Streak, Two-way Street

All Over But the Shouting

UNTIL modern times, adult white males who paid taxes or could prove military service were the only voters. Election day was set aside for talking, drinking, and carousing after having voted.

Ballots were hand counted, so results were not announced until long after the polls had closed. Especially in a tight election, announcement of the count was likely to trigger a roar from supporters of the winning candidate.

In a one-sided contest, everybody knew the winner long before the last ballot was counted. This meant that when the polls closed, the outcome was unofficial but decided—it was "all over but the shouting" of victory.

Back-seat Driver

BARNEY Oldfield's Ford #999 held only the driver. Single seats of some early cars held two or three people. Rear seats weren't added until the auto age was beyond its infancy. A back seat held additional riders, but these found it difficult to talk to the driver.

In 1912, things began to change. The four-cylinder Essex coach was offered with a box-like body that was comfortably enclosed. Other makers soon copied the idea.

Passengers immediately took advantage of their chance to be heard. Calling for action or telling the person at the wheel where to turn or stop, the back-seat driver caused his name to label any person who volunteers advice to the one in charge.

Bandwagon

AMERICA'S first great showman, Phineas T. Barnum, didn't wait for the public to come to him. Instead, he took his attractions to the people. Arriving in a city for an engagement, he would hire a high wagon of the sort used by local bands of musicians for outdoor performances.

Parading through streets with odd-looking men and women aboard wagons, "Barnum's Great Scientific and Musical Theater" was a sensation. Onlookers were encouraged to hop on the bandwagons in order to ride with the performers and add to the excitement.

Many political clubs built bandwagons of their own, then gave rolling concerts to publicize candidates. The impact of Barnum and elections on speech proved lasting. Any person who agrees to become a part of a movement, campaign, or simply joins the crowd is described as climbing on the bandwagon.

Blow Off Steam

IT took years for trainmen to learn how to handle locomotives. Hot fires were required in order to keep up enough steam to move. But when an engine halted, steam pressure could rise quickly. There were no safety valves; at intervals, the engineer had to pull a lever and blow off the steam to prevent an explosion.

In the 1830s, a locomotive was a thing of awe when quiet and still. A person who for the first time saw the iron monster blow off steam never forgot the incident.

Observers compared such an explosive incident with a sudden display of temper. Soon adopted into the speech of merchants and travelers, anyone indulging in a colorful outburst was said to "blow off steam."

Bring Home the Bacon

COUNTY fairs ranked high among entertainment events of rural America in the past. Along the midway, games of chance or skill offered prizes that had lots of glitter but were worthless.

When the time came for chasing the greased pig, it was a

different matter. A lucky entrant who managed to catch and hold the slippery animal won cash put up by the merchants.

"The bacon" was already in use as a label for a prize of any sort. With a pig as the target, the animal's catcher was able to "bring home the bacon" in a special sense.

County and state fairs are different than they used to be. But the term of victory born from chasing an elusive porker rooted its way into speech to signify success in any enterprise.

Bronx Cheer

BABIES discover very early that the range of sounds they can produce is almost infinite. A perennial favorite is made by placing the tongue between the lips and blowing vigorously. Ensuing vibrations, commonly known as *raspberries,* produce sounds familiar to nearly every parent.

Large numbers of adults didn't often make that sound simultaneously in the relatively sedate era that ended with World War I. But in Yankee Stadium, fans sitting shoulder-to-shoulder were anything but sedate in the 1920s.

Few games passed without a bad call by an official or an awkward play by one of Babe Ruth's teammates. Anything that drew the ire of the masses came to evoke a chorus of raspberries. This unique chorus of sounds was heard so often in the Bronx stadium that the vibrating noise enjoyed by infants came to be known everywhere as a *Bronx cheer.*

Called on the Carpet

UNTIL modern machinery made mass production possible, carpets were expensive and relatively rare. A business or industry was likely to boast only one carpeted room—the head office. Many a worker entered such an office only when summoned there to receive a reprimand.

Even in a home with no bare floors, a spouse or offspring may be called on the carpet in order to stand meekly while taking a scolding.

Fly Off the Handle

IF you've ever seen a person "fly off the handle," you may have been impressed at the energy and speed involved with that eruption of anger.

Frontiersmen found it hard to control their tempers when tools suddenly failed them. A common cause of such a turn of events was the shrinkage of wood—universally used for tool handles.

After having hung in a shed for months, the handle of a hoe or a rake was likely to come off after a few strokes. In the case of an ax, badly worn or shrunken wood is positively dangerous because the head of the tool can come loose at the first lick.

When the blade of an ax flies off the handle, it endangers the user and everyone standing nearby. That makes it almost as great a source of danger as a violent explosion of temper.

Frazzled

ANYTIME you confess to being frazzled, you compare yourself with the frayed end of a rope.

At least as early as the era in which Britain was busy establishing colonies in North America, sailors had special words for kinds and conditions of their all-important ropes.

A length of hemp that had seen considerable use, but could be repaired, was *frayed*. In many cases, damage went so far that a section had to be cut off before the shortened rope could be used again. Such a piece of disheveled hemp was so much like the body and mind of an absolutely exhausted person that both came to be called *frazzled*.

Gimmick

TRAVELING carnivals were a major source of entertainment for decades. Lights, sounds, and odors of the midway formed a pattern unlike anything else a person ordinarily encountered. Confidence men, or grifters, vied with one another in attracting customers and spoke a language known only to themselves.

A nickel or a dime was good for a spin of a wheel that offered showy but valueless prizes known to carneys as *gimcracks*. Every gimcrack peddler kept his hand on his *gimmick*—a little brake-like control that enabled him to stop the wheel of fortune at any point he wished.

So many gimmicks governed the dispensing of so many gimcracks that the name of the pitchman's device was bestowed on any small gadget, and was used to name the cheating or hooking of someone.

Grandstand Play

IF a colleague or fellow citizen makes a *grandstand play,* it may bring publicity without affecting the outcome of an issue.

Long before baseball offered million-dollar contracts, players were popular heroes. Maybe because most accolades went to pitchers and batters, some fielders developed a way of attracting the attention of spectators. With a little practice, a fellow could learn to make an easy fielding play look as though it required a lot of skill and effort.

Such a maneuver had no effect on the final score. But it could be the talk of the town among fans who were thrilled by it. Enough dramatic stunts were pulled that *grandstand play* was adopted into general speech.

Hocus-pocus

IF you've ever played around with rhyming words, you are among company. This form of verbal recreation has been practiced for centuries in all cultures.

Early jugglers altered a Latin phrase used in the service of Holy Communion—a ritual in which ordinary bread is transformed. Magicians took the word *hocus* from classical terms for "Here is the body . . ."

Once that term had been coined for use in sleight-of-hand tricks, it was easy to form a rhyming partner. The result was *hocus-pocus,* which means you had better pay close attention, or you will be badly fooled by what happens next.

Land-office Business

WHEN the vast American West was opened to settlers, offices were set up for the registration of homesteads. Once established, a land office often served as a place to handle mining claims as well.

When a rich new territory was opened, the land office would have an enormous rush of applicants. No other establishments of the period, not even the saloon, attracted such hordes of patrons.

Settlers and tradesmen who went back to the East told tall tales about awesome land-office doings. The frontier term came to name any commercial enterprise that draws exceptional response from customers, thus having a land-office business.

Like a House on Fire

UNLIKE householders of Old World cities, early settlers in North America seldom used stone when building. It seemed absurd to them to think of spending months in a quarry when there were plenty of splendid trees available for the cutting.

Logs as well as boards from a sawmill had one serious drawback: most structures built of these materials relied on a creek or a well for water. If a place caught fire, dry wood often burned so rapidly that it was impossible to salvage a single piece of furniture.

So many houses and cabins went up in smoke that it became common to say that a fast horse could go "like a house on fire." Washington Irving popularized this expression for extreme rapidity in his 1809 *History of New York*.

Live Wire

IN the early days of household electricity, ordinary folks hardly knew anything about the newfangled way to control and use energy. Staring at a maze of wires, it was difficult or impossible for most people to fathom them.

Yet two things became common knowledge very early. Some wires carried no current and felt no different from anything else casually touched. But another wire in the same cluster would often yield a first-class jolt—or worse—when touched.

A wire of the latter kind was considered "live" because of the strong current in it. Some people are so full of energy that their blood seems to flow like an electrical current. Hence anyone who is always vibrant and ready to serve as the life of the party is known as a "live wire."

Nip and Tuck

MANY common words and phrases were brought westward across the Atlantic Ocean from England. Once the Colonies were flourishing, the stream of language began to flow eastward to the mother country. That was the case with an expression now linked with a neck-and-neck finish of a contest of any sort.

Since cloth was scarce and expensive, Colonial tailors followed their patterns very closely. This skimpiness could pose problems when a segment was being fitted into a garment.

Skilled workers learned how to nip a problem piece here and there with scissors, then tuck it into place. This procedure might produce a tight fit, but it saved a lot of cloth, and cloth was money.

Originating in the speech of Colonial tailors, *nip and tuck* was borrowed by the English—who, like us, use it to describe a contest so close as to leave the outcome in doubt.

Off the Deep End

FRIENDS are likely to say that a person ready to take an unnecessary risk is about to go "off the deep end." Sometimes the same expression is applied to one in danger of flipping his or her lid or overreacting.

Indoor swimming pools proliferated about the time of World War I. In many YMCAs or other recreational buildings, there were no lines showing the depth of the water. Swimmers familiar with the place knew which end was deep, while newcomers who hit the water at its deepest point were sometimes in trouble.

It was these swimmers—rash to take on more than they could handle—that inspired the expression.

Panic Button

SHOULD circumstances ever cause you to hit the panic button, that would be a signal for others to act quickly in order to forestall disaster.

The original panic button could be found on a U.S. bombing plane—a B-24, or a B-17. When that button was pushed by the pilot, it activated a bell that functioned even when the intercom system was shot full of holes. Numerous crew members were at a distance from the cockpit, unable to know when flak damage called for ditching the plane. At the first signal from the panic button, they dropped what they were doing and prepared to get out. A second signal constituted an imperative command: "Jump! Jump now!"

Transferred to civilian life, the airman's signal for quick action to avert catastrophe led us to say that a person who issues an imperative warning—orally or in writing—has hit the panic button.

Park

IT is usually simple and easy to park an automobile. But the operation takes its name from a complex series of developments.

Noblemen of ancient Gaul used an Old German word for an enclosure holding game animals. When they invaded England they found the island thickly wooded and well stocked with game. Many deer parks were developed, with animals being held inside them by thick hedges or stone walls.

Military leaders adopted the practice of forming a square of wagons at the end of a day's march. Horses and cows were put inside and turned loose to graze, causing such a camp also to be known as a park.

Wagons and artillery wheeled into place to form a military park were described as being *parked*. Eventually the act of putting a vehicle in place, whether around the rim of a military park or by the side of a street, was designated by the name of an enclosure.

Pull the Plug

IF financiers or authorities "pull the plug" on a project, there is a good chance it will go down the drain. Still, this way of expressing the idea of bringing something to an end is not indebted to round rubber plugs used in old-fashioned bathtubs.

Rather, it was the pulling of an electrical plug from an outlet that gave rise to the phrase. Borrowing from everyday experience, early in the electrical age it became common to express the idea of termination by using the phrase spawned by bringing early appliances and machines to a halt.

Railroad

ONCE the steam locomotive was found to be powerful and effective, the United States launched a binge of building. Hundreds of miles of track became thousands of miles in a short period.

Builders learned to push across rivers, through forests, and over mountains in an awesome fashion. It became an unspoken watchword that the railroad had to be built in a hurry, regardless of obstacles.

Pell-mell overriding of difficulties spawned a phrase that has long outlasted the era in which it was first used. A person or group pushing an idea or an enterprise without regard for opposition is described as "railroading" it.

Self-starter

BYRON T. Carter of Cartercar fame stopped one day in 1910 to help a lady in distress. Trying to crank her car, he broke his jaw and eventually died from the injury. Largely because of that incident, Cadillac builder Henry Leland gave Charles Kettering an order for 4,000 electric starters.

Most engineers said that an electric self-starter for autos couldn't be made. They calculated that a five-horsepower motor would be needed for it; with batteries, a car would be too heavy to move under its own weight.

Kettering adapted an electric motor used on cash registers. With generator, clutch, and storage battery added, his self-starter was used on the 1912 Cadillac. Now anyone could crank the car by pushing a button with the toe of her shoe.

So much wonder was evoked by the self-starter that it came to indicate any person capable of getting things rolling at the push of a mental button.

Shindig

ANYONE who has ever attended a wild and wooly hoedown in Maggie Valley, North Carolina, knows that it is the square dance capital of the world. Almost any night during the tourist season, you can find a shindig in progress at the Ole Stompin' Ground.

If you have ever participated in a rural dance that included a few beginners, you know that a swinging foot can dig into a partner's shin mighty easily. Any veteran square dance caller will tell you that bruised shins show up every Saturday night. Naturally, a carouse that leaves tell-tale marks on lower legs of the participants is a *shindig,* no matter what else it may be. What better name could possibly be given to such an affair?

Siren

FRENCH scientist Cagnard de la Tour experimented with sound for many years. In 1819 he invented a device designed to produce musical notes and measure their vibrations. Immersed in water, his gadget yielded a "singularly sweet and sonorous sound." At some speeds in the air it sounded almost like a human voice.

The name for this device was taken from Greek mythology. One of three sea nymphs, the Siren's songs lured sailors to destruction. Since his soundmaker sang under water, de la Tour borrowed from mythology and called it a *siren.*

Within fifty years the acoustical instrument found an unexpected use. Built to a larger scale, it served—not to lure persons to destruction—but to warn them. Steam-powered sirens sitting on tall buildings signaled "Fire!" long before smaller ones mounted on ambulances and fire engines screamed "Get out of the way!"

Spark Plug

GOTTLIEB Daimler's 1885 auto was equipped with a tiny platinum tube mounted in its single cylinder. Heated by a benzene-fed Bunsen burner, the hot tube fired gasoline vapor mixed with air.

Seeking more exact control over ignition, inventors developed an electrical gadget. Having a gap of 1/16th inch, it screwed into a cylinder and yielded sparks with conducting current. About the size and shape of a plug used to stopper a barrel, it was natural to call it a *spark plug*.

For years, some drivers and mechanics stuck to hot tube ignition. However, the spark plug eventually became the standard device for firing fuel in a cylinder.

It worked so well that people who prodded things into action were compared with it. Expanded in meaning, *spark plug* now names anyone good at getting an organization or business fired up and ready to move.

Tailspin

EARLY planes sometimes tipped sharply downward, then went into a combination roll and yaw—or turn about the vertical axis. Engineers who studied the complex action called it *auto-rotation*. Airmen rejected that big word in favor of *tailspin,* even though it was the entire plane and not just the tail that spun.

Until 1916, no pilot came out of a tailspin without a crash. Caught in one that year, the great Eddie Stinson decided he might as well die quickly—so pushed the stick forward. To his amazement, the rate of spinning slowed and he regained control. After that, barnstormers often performed tailspins to thrill crowds.

Risk of an involuntary downward spiral has been all but eliminated from aircraft. Yet the hazard faced by aviation pioneers left a legacy in language. Whether arguing at a cocktail party or asking for a raise, a person threatened with a loss of self-control is still said to go into a tailspin.

Take the Bull by the Horns

MANY a cowboy was as tough as those depicted in movies and television. No sport was considered very worthy unless it involved some danger. Yet some grizzled horsemen hesitated when challenged to wrestle steers.

It was useless to grab the legs or neck of a fiesty young male, attested the veterans of these contests. In order to win, the human challenger had to seize an animal's horns. Gripping them firmly, with skill and luck a fellow could throw his four-legged opponent to the ground before being gored.

Cow camp recreation enriched general speech. Anyone who wades head on into an opponent or a problem is said to "take the bull by the horns."

Testimony

CASTRATION of human males was widely practiced until modern times. Consequently, it was not unusual for a man to be called upon to prove that he was not a eunuch. There was only one way to do so: he had to exhibit his testicles.

Both words have their root in the Latin *testis,* which comes from an ancient word meaning "three." The idea of an objective third party led *testis* to mean "witness."

Oral tradition says that a man giving evidence in a medieval trial was likely to place one hand on the "seat of his manhood" while taking the oath. Since testicles proved that a fellow was what he seemed, evidence he gave came to be called *testimony.*

Whistle Blower

A WHISTLE blower who is interviewed for the television shows "60 Minutes" or "20/20" is likely to get results. Nuclear plants, suppliers of military hardware, and manufacturers of chemicals are prime targets.

The whistles of police are still heard in some cities. Their impact may have had a little influence in the formation of the modern title for an informer. However, action on the basketball court has been much more significant. Watch a game in the NCAA finals and count the number of times an official blows a whistle.

Most of the time, the sound of an official's whistle means "Stop instantly!"—which is the goal of the industrial or environmental whistle blower as well. The main object of whistle blowers is to stop illegal action and infringement on the rules of the game.

Wisdom Teeth

PRACTICALLY all primitive societies develop rituals through which young people become adults. Usually such ceremonies are conducted when initiates are in their teens.

Among the ancient Greeks, it became proverbial that no youth would cut his third molars until inducted into manhood. Because adults made the rules, they considered themselves wiser than boys and girls. Since third molars marked the transition into adulthood, they automatically meant increased wisdom.

Formal rites of passage were abandoned long ago, and most persons in the modern western world know there is no connection between sagacity and teeth. But the ancient Greek title for "tooth of knowledge," remains in universal use. That is why molars that seldom appear before adolescence are still called *wisdom teeth*.

CHAPTER *19*

SAY, DID YOU KNOW?

"What is all our knowledge? We do not even know what weather it will be tomorrow."
—Berthold Auerbach, *On the Heights*

M uch of what we know about the origins of what we say and write can be found in the twenty volumes of the *Oxford English Dictionary*. A cursory glance at a few of its pages helps us to see how little we do know.

Nearly every word and phrase treated in this volume can be a conversation starter. Some that especially lend themselves to "Say, did you know . . . ?" are included in this section.

ALCOHOL
ALL QUIET ON THE
  POTOMAC
BAND-AID
BLESS OUT
BOOBY HATCH
BURY THE HATCHET
CRACKED UP
DICKER
DUD
FEEL ONE'S OATS
GO BANANAS
GO TO THE WALL
HACKER
HAVE SOMEONE'S NUMBER,
  TO
HEART IN THE RIGHT
  PLACE
HELL ON WHEELS

HYPE
INSIDE TRACK
KNOW THE ROPES
LOOSE CANNON
MEXICAN STANDOFF
NIT-PICKER
OVER A BARREL
PIPE DOWN
PLUG-UGLY
POWWOW
SECURITY BLANKET
SMALL FRY
STONEWALL
SWAT TEAM
SWEETHEART
TRUE BLUE
WRONG SIDE OF
  THE BED

SEE ALSO: Amp, Beef, Big Shot, Blue Jeans, Blurb, Cash on
    the Barrel Head, Chew the Fat, Clip Joint, Cotton To,
    Decibel, Diesel, Donnybrook, Face the Music, Goon,
    Gung-ho, Haymaker, Hep/Hip, High Muckety-muck, Hog-
    wash, Hotbed, Jerry-built, Know Beans, Lead-pipe Cinch,
    Let the Cat Out of the Bag, Lowbrow, Lynching, Make the
    Grade, Mossback, O.K., Pipe Dream, Poinsettia, Red-letter
    Day, Roger, Run a Hot Box, Screaming Meemies, Scut-
    tlebutt, Shoot the Bull, Short Shrift, Skid Row, Stem-
    winder, Talk Turkey, Whammy

Alcohol

ANTIMONY is a mineral common in Egypt and the Middle East. Arabs made a fine black powder with the antimony and called it *kohl*. Daubed on the eyelids, the stain was one of the earliest cosmetics.

Queens and women of wealth spent fortunes on the finest variety of eye shadow, which they called *al-kohl*—literally "the powder." Queen Shub-ad of Ur kept her al-kohl in a silver box 5,500 years ago.

By the early 17th century, western travelers used *alcohol* for "fine powder that stains." Eventually it referred to any substance obtained from an essence—and particularly distillation. Thus *alcohol of wine* meant the "essence of wine." Soon it became simply *alcohol*, causing today's liquid refreshments to bear the name of eye shadow used by beauties of ancient Egypt.

All Quiet on the Potomac

GEORGE Washington's favorite river became a dividing line during the Civil War. Confederates talked freely of crossing the river in order to capture Washington.

That was no idle threat; for in the early days of the conflict the nearly defenseless capital was in constant fear of invasion. Not until militia units arrived from the northeast and fortifications were built did Abraham Lincoln and his advisors begin to breathe easily.

When a show of Confederate strength on the Virginia side of the river ceased to be a source of dread, Washington's defenders were glad to report: "All quiet on the Potomac."

War-born, the American expression came to label a period of relaxed quiet during any situation in which high-level stress is a possibility.

Band-Aid

IN one report by the *Wall Street Journal,* experts were asked to cure a fiscal ill, and they spent a lot of time trying to make a diagnosis. Since they couldn't agree about the cause of the sickness, "all they did was to put a Band-Aid on it."

Even the head honcho of a big pharmaceutical company didn't anticipate that its ready-made bandage would make such a hit. Little bandages in a box solved minor household problems galore, but were useless in a major emergency. The popularity of Johnson & Johnson's Band-Aid caused its name to be associated with any small adhesive bandage, and eventually with patching up a large problem as well as a small injury.

Bless Out

DURING the Dark Ages, Europeans lived in fear of demons and evil spirits. They could take possession of a person, animal, tree, piece of furniture, or even an article of clothing.

Once a person or thing became the dwelling place of a demon, there was only one sure cure. A priest had to drive out the evil spirit by making the sign of the cross, accompanied by a suitable blessing in Latin.

Many who watched a man of God "bless out" a demon didn't understand a word that was said. But they knew the evil spirit was getting the worst of it. By the 17th century, anyone who administered a tongue-lashing was compared with a priest attacking a demon and said to *bless out* the person on the receiving end.

Booby Hatch

MANY sailing ships had deck openings, or hatchways, that led to sections below. As a safety measure, every hatchway was supposed to be covered with a trapdoor or grating. In time, the movable covers took the name of the holes they protected.

On long voyages, sailors often became delirious. Such "boobies" had to be kept below for their own safety. Naturally, a hatch that prevented a booby from coming on deck came to be known as a *booby hatch*.

Cartoonist Milt Gross picked up the old seafaring expression and used it in World War II newspaper strips. That is why we use *booby hatch* as a label for a mental institution.

Bury the Hatchet

TRAPPERS and soldiers in contact with American Indians on the frontier knew little about native customs. In addition, most of them didn't care to learn.

White men mistakenly believed that the stone tomahawk had no use except in battle. Among some tribes, ceremonial burial of a weapon signaled that a period of war had come to an end.

Perhaps jokingly, it came to be said that when conflict ended a warrior would cover his weapon with earth so he wouldn't be tempted to use it on the skull of a foe.

No tomahawk was remotely like a metal hatchet of the white man, and Indian weapons were given ceremonial interment only among a few cultures. Yet when an opponent ceases to fight or a spouse stops battling with words, he or she is still said to "bury the hatchet."

Cracked Up

SITTING around the cracker barrel in a general store and swapping yarns, some idlers always evoked laughter. Others who told stories got only stares in response—the listeners didn't crack a smile.

Since hearty laughter constitutes a signal that a tale—or its teller—has hit the bull's eye, cracked faces came to signify "first class." Once that usage was established, it was an easy step to label anything inferior as "not what it is cracked up to be."

Dicker

TAX structures and levels being what they are, more and more people are engaging in unreported barter. In order to prosper in this activity, a person has to be able to dicker.

Merchants of imperial Rome were the first to spread this term throughout Europe. Well supplied with cheap trade goods, many an entrepreneur sent an expedition into the region of barbarians where trinkets were swapped for native produce, of which furs were the most valuable.

Traders found it inconvenient to try to secure individual pelts, so they adopted a practice of buying them only in lots of ten. In Latin, *decuria* means "a set of ten" and the European natives transformed it into *dicker*. Which shows that furs have affected life and speech in ways no one would suspect without looking beneath the surface of everyday words.

Dud

ANYTHING can fail. Consequently, an enterprise ranging from an amateur play to an offering of high-priced homes around a golf course can be a *dud*.

Pioneer aviators who ushered the world into the era of aerial bombing saw their targets burst open at times. Often an explosive charge was delivered precisely, but a defective fuse caused it to have no effect except a dull thud. The instant a bomb hit, an experienced pilot knew whether or not it was a dud.

So many duds hit enemy positions without exploding that the term born in World War I came to designate any failure or ineffective action.

Feel One's Oats

SOME mornings, you drag out of bed and wonder whether or not you will make it through the day. A week later you may bounce out full of energy, "feeling your oats" and ready to take on all comers.

When that happens, you are more or less like a fine-blooded horse who got only the best food in the early 18th century. Plow horses and ordinary plugs seldom received any grain except leavings and scrapings from the wheat crop. A splendid racer or a member of a team that pulled an ornate carriage was given oats at every opportunity. Something about this grain seemed to have an invigorating effect. After eating a belly full of it, a horse stepped high and seemed full of vim, vigor, and vitality.

Today, we can feel our oats without having to actually consume any of the grain.

Go Bananas

WHAT makes a person who is normally calm and quiet suddenly "go bananas"? Why do we specify this fruit instead of Granny Smith apples or Bosc pears?

No one knows exactly why a person will go wacko in a given situation. But there's a good reason for saying that anyone temporarily out of control has gone bananas. Actions of such a person are a lot like that of a caged monkey in a zoo. The sight of a keeper approaching with a bunch of bananas can make the animal freak out, or *go bananas*.

Go to the Wall

LOTS of ordinary folk gloated when they heard that Donald Trump's empire was about to "go to the wall." With the self-proclaimed billionaire facing possible bankruptcy, why did headlines say he might go to the wall instead of maybe going into the drink?

Because a person facing a firing squad is almost always backed up against a wall while executioners prepare to do the honors.

So many condemned men and women have gone to so many

walls in real life and in fiction that a trip to the wall came to mean the end of the road.

Hacker

INITIALLY regarded as being on the goofy side but harmless, the computer hacker became a menace when viruses began to appear in major systems.

Such a person has to be a dedicated enthusiast in order to stay at the keyboard for hour after hour. Why not use a time-honored label like *zealot*?

One possibility is that the term originated from the use of MIT students of the word *hack* to refer to a prank—in that technical milieu, it was soon applied to computer mischief also. Or it may refer to the patience that some computer experts exhibit. Slashing with a keyboard instead of a machete, the enthusiast hacks slowly through a jungle of symbols with a determination only a genuine hacker can comprehend.

Have Someone's Number, to

ANYTIME you are sure you have someone's number, you are confident that you know a lot about that person. What is more, the information you hold probably isn't generally available.

In recent decades, the idea of possessing inside information as a result of having a person's number has been linked with our social security system. The IRS aside, you cannot function in modern American society without one of these nine-digit identifiers.

But in the early days of the telephone—before printed directories came into use—it was a person's telephone number that was all-important. In many communities, operators refused to ring unless a number was supplied. Since numbers weren't made available to the general public, anyone who had another's was possessed of almost magical access. Once that secret number responded, the ensuing conversation provided enough inside information for the caller to know the respondent in a special way.

Heart in the Right Place

ANCIENT Egyptian priests who prepared bodies for mummification knew a great deal about anatomy. During Europe's long Dark Ages, much of this lore was lost. Peasants who knew little about the body's internal organs were impressed by the rhythmic throbbing of big blood vessels—which often varied from person to person and even from time to time in the same person's arm or leg.

Variations in rate and intensity of throbbing were attributed to wandering of the heart from its proper location. This literal belief produced a host of fanciful metaphors; an easily offended person was said "to wear his heart on his sleeve," and anyone mortally afraid was described as "having his heart in his mouth."

All of which means that a person whose heart is in the right place is properly constituted—and as a result is filled with good intentions.

Hell on Wheels

EVEN though it involves no vehicle, some of us are likely to say that a really bad situation is "hell on wheels." Tradition offers a logical explanation for this vivid expression.

Western lore has it that as soon as a transcontinental rail line was started, laborers and fortune hunters flocked westward. Just behind them were fellows determined to separate them from their fortunes.

Many long stretches didn't have a single outpost. That didn't stop canny operators from the East. They rented flatcars and used them to haul tiny brothels and mini-casinos. Pushed to the railhead, or halted anywhere else that potential customers could be found, one of these makeshift rigs literally constituted hell on wheels. Spreading slowly back to civilization, the vivid expression that seems all but meaningless proved just right to label any truly awful place or event.

Today the meaning has expanded and has become complimentary—used to label incredible skill as well as extremely rapid movement, whether on a basketball court or at the keyboard of a computer.

Hype

ON the surface, there seems to be no logical reason why we should use *hype* to designate high-pressure advertising. But ballyhoo from Madison Avenue or anywhere else is designed to affect behavior and decisions. That gives it a lot in common with mood-altering drugs.

During the 1920s, relatively mild narcotics were the most commonly available drugs for street use. Abbreviation of the hypodermic needle used to administer a drug created *hype* as a name for both an illegal drug and a state induced by it.

A carefully crafted promotional campaign is designed to alter attitudes and purchasing habits. Just as being "hyped up" by drugs might make one feel larger than life, so are a lot of ads just *hype*—exaggerated claims.

Inside Track

ANYTIME you're known to have the "inside track," a rival or competitor will acknowledge that you have the best of it. At least in its earliest usage, the expression had nothing to do with hidden or inside information.

As might be expected, the phrase comes from the racetrack.

Most contests of any length were held on oval or round tracks. Contestants waited for the signal to begin while spaced out along the starting line. Everyone knew that the person having the slot closest to the middle of the course had a good chance of running a shorter distance than rivals.

In a footrace the inside track was a major asset, and logically came to mean a strong advantage in any situation.

Know the Ropes

IF you "know the ropes" at your place of work, you may be a candidate for the job of helping new employees to learn their way around.

Generations ago, ships' masters knew that a fellow fresh from land was little help at first. A full-rigged vessel had a seemingly insoluble tangle of ropes with which to set sails and it took time and help to learn how to handle them. No man could hope to know the ropes until he had weathered the sun and salt spray for some time.

Long used literally aboard ship, the phrase expanded to describe an experienced person in any area of activity.

Loose Cannon

ANY business or industry or neighborhood plagued with a loose cannon is a place in which to be constantly on the alert, as someone could get hurt.

Crewmen aboard an old-time man-of-war expected danger. They signed on knowing that they'd probably be subjected to gunfire from enemy vessels. A broadside at 200 yards was bad enough, but every veteran knew that the worst thing a sailor could face was a loose cannon.

Enemy fire, the pitching and tossing of a ship, and damage caused by hurling explosives sometimes caused the gigantic weapon to break loose from its mounting. Rolling and sliding around the deck, such a piece of naval artillery might smash anything or anyone it encountered.

That is often the case with a human who seems neither to know nor to care about holding a steady position. Rumbling and tossing through a force of workers or an organization, a two-legged loose cannon is a likely cause of major damage even when the ship of life is sailing in calm waters.

Mexican Standoff

NOTHING in the saga of Mexico matches the U.S. story of the gunfight in the O.K. Corral. As depicted in countless movies and TV dramas, the Old West was a place where a cowpoke's gun was often his only friend. If shoot-outs had been as common as imagination makes them, the population of the whole region would have been wiped out.

Sometimes belligerents threw down on one another at the same split second. When that happened, they realized that both were about to go to Boot Hill. So they swapped insults instead of bullets.

In his prime, John Wayne would have preferred being dead to taking part in such a fracas. It reflected on a fellow's manhood to shove his gun into its holster and walk away from a standoff. Since everything and everyone from south of the border was considered inferior, the shoot-out that didn't happen was labeled a *Mexican standoff.*

Influence of cowboy lingo caused it to enter common speech to signify any stalemate between belligerents.

Nit-picker

MANY groups of people include a nit-picker, prone to concentrate upon insignificant matters and complain about them. Belly-aching about trifles might be reduced or stopped if such a person knew the source of his or her title.

Middle English, a language almost as distinctly different from Old English as from modern English, modified an old term and called the egg of any parasitic insect a *nite*. With the final letter omitted in contemporary usage, the word is most often employed to label an egg of a body louse.

Such an egg is so minute it is too small to be seen except with keen eyes. But because of its shape and texture, it is fairly easily discovered by probing with the fingertips. Frontiersmen who didn't like to be lousy learned to find nits and pick them off the skin so they wouldn't produce insects. Many caged monkeys, incidentally, exhibit great skill in this activity.

A person or a monkey busy trying to find and remove the tiny eggs doesn't have time or energy for big and important things. As a result, anyone who concentrates upon discovery of very small errors and faults is disparaged as a *nit-picker.*

Over a Barrel

UNLESS you have suddenly found yourself over a barrel, you can hardly imagine how dreadful such a situation can be. Financial reverses, a love affair, and pressures on the job are only a few of many things that can make a person feel absolutely helpless.

That is precisely how mobs of yesteryear wanted some of their targets to feel. A person considered too guilty to escape with tar and feathers was often publicly whipped. To prevent wriggling while the lash was being applied, a victim was tied to an overturned barrel. Though the feet remained firmly on the ground, the upper body was bent to follow the curve of the barrel.

Which is why anyone figuratively bent over a barrel while waiting for the worst to come is in a dreadful fix with little or no hope of escape.

Pipe Down

BIG sailing vessels required large crews, since most work was done by hand. Noise of winds and waves made it difficult to transmit orders by shouting. So the boatswain used a special pipe whose notes could usually be heard even in a storm.

When a master wished to give special instructions or give a crew an opportunity to voice complaints, the boatswain piped "All hands on deck." Another signal was used to send men to their quarters below deck. Sometimes a harsh captain would break off discussion and signal the boatswain to pipe the crew down. Failure to obey could be interpreted as mutiny, so rebellion was rare.

Long used literally in the lingo of the sea, the expression was adopted and modified at the U.S. Naval Academy. About 1890 it became customary for a man in his third or fourth year to command a plebe, "Pipe down!" Instead of being an order to go to quarters, this was a demand for silence, and today we treat it as slightly milder but nearly equivalent to "Shut up!"

Plug-ugly

BALTIMORE, famous for having been the site of the first bloody confrontation of the Civil War, was long a leader in the movement to save buildings by work of volunteer fire departments. Each such group was supposed to service a specific area of the city, but boundary lines were sometimes vague. The territorial imperative being what it is, rival bands of volunteers often scuffled with one another for use of a fireplug.

Our insatiable appetite for rhyming words led the fellow who put up an ugly scrap around a plug to become known as a plug-ugly. At least, that is the best explanation uncovered to date, a supposition that has won acceptance from some specialists in the development of language.

Powwow

UNLESS it is strictly formal and conducted under parliamentary rules, a conference or discussion is likely to be called a powwow.

Among the Algonquin Indian tribes, a *powwow* was the medicine man who heard voices and saw visions. The powwow frequently presided over councils and rituals, and was known as the dreamer.

Europeans learned that such men were often in charge of tribal talk sessions, but stumbled over their native title. Garbled into the form of powwow, that title was adopted by whites to designate any gathering that involves an idea person.

Security Blanket

CHARLES M. Schulz is famous as creator of the "Peanuts" comic strip and its characters. One of his claims to fame stems from coinage of the phrase *security blanket* to name any tangible object that soothes nerves and confers confidence.

As initially used by the writer-artist, the expression was literal. Linus, one of his characters, often appears holding a corner of a blanket that drags behind. While absence of that blanket means nervous apprehension, its presence symbolizes confidence and poise.

It is probable that, long before "Peanuts," lots of mothers and fathers noticed that toddlers felt insecure without their favorite blankets. So the concept behind the phrase may be as old as the family. Still, the word pattern that identifies positive emotional effects of having a familiar object in hand may be strictly 20th century in origin.

Small Fry

OUR use of *small fry* as a label for children memorializes, in a fashion, speech patterns of long ago. For in eras when most people lived close to the land, animals, birds, and fish were of vital importance. Dependent upon them, humans devised separate names for the stages of life cycles.

A few words from this specialized vocabulary have survived. As a result, first-time visitors to New England see numerous T-shirts proclaiming: "I CAUGHT SCROD IN BOSTON." That notice seems vaguely suggestive of venereal disease, until an outsider learns that a young codfish is a scrod.

Fishermen long referred to immature fish of all kinds as *fry*. Which meant that small fry were tiny swimmers indeed. With its background lost in obscurity, the phrase *small fry* is most often-applied to small children or unimportant events.

Stonewall

ANY person subjected to questioning may decide to be difficult and stonewall. This particular expression has undergone more than one transition.

Step one occurred among cricket players. Contestants lauded a successful batsman by congratulating him on having blocked everything as effectively as though he had been a stone wall.

Step two involved Confederate general Thomas J. Jackson. Lauded for having failed to yield ground when under heavy attack by Union forces at Bull Run, Jackson was nicknamed Stonewall.

A stonewall batsman doesn't let opponents score and Stonewall Jackson didn't yield under pressure. Therefore, contemporary usage includes *stonewall* as a designation for a delaying tactic such as refusal to answer questions.

Swat Team

MANY acronyms, formed by combining initial letters, are all but forgotten after having been in the news for a period. Not so the title of a modern police unit that operates much like a military assault team.

The rise of terrorism, marked by an increased holding of hostages, caused U.S. authorities to take a new look at ways of dealing with it. Several national conferences were held, and as a result some cities formed Special Weapons And Tactics units.

Soon it was found that a swat team equipped with high-powered weapons and elaborate communications devices was useful in many kinds of crises. Perhaps because such a group tends to strike swiftly and swat the opposition firmly, the artifically formed word that names it has become firmly entrenched in modern speech.

Sweetheart

DURING the era when the longbow was the ultimate weapon, even physicians knew little about human anatomy. Pumping action of the heart caused it to be regarded as the seat of personality. Expressions paying tribute to this notion were probably literal rather than figurative. A person could be hard-hearted, soft-hearted, light-hearted, or heavy-hearted.

In this climate of thought and speech, it was natural for a lover to refer to one who made the heart beat faster as "swete hert." Separate terms were hyphenated for two or three centuries before sweetheart entered modern talk to label the sweet person who makes the heart throb.

True Blue

CLOTH, made by hand, was long dyed in the household. Berries, bark, and a few blossoms yielded most of the coloring matter used. Even when synthetic dyes came on the market, most of them were of inferior quality. Consequently, cloth often faded after a few washings.

Artisans of Coventry, England, discovered and kept secret a formula for the manufacture of a blue dye of superior quality. This Coventry blue—or true blue—remained bright after many washings.

For generations, true blue was absolutely the best that could be bought. From chatter of those who labored over dye vats and washtubs, the term entered general speech to stand for faithfulness and reliability of every sort.

Wrong Side of the Bed

NEARLY everything we use is shaped for right-handed people. Even a dexterous southpaw may sometimes seem awkward. As a result, among the ancients the left side of the body or anything else was considered to be sinister—mysterious and dangerous, maybe even evil.

Old-time innkeepers often pushed the left sides of the bed against the walls so that guests could get up only on the right side.

Many who sleep in king- or queen-size modern beds attach little or no importance to the side that is used. But when a person shows unusual irritability or clumsiness, it may be called the result of having started the day by getting up on the "wrong side of the bed."

BIBLIOGRAPHY

More detailed information concerning most words and phrases in *Why You Say It* may be found in one or more of the following volumes. For the roots of standard English and American words, consult etymological dictionaries. By all odds the most valuable single work in print is the revised edition of the *Oxford English Dictionary*. Yet even this monumental work of scholarship omits numerous contemporary expressions that are American, rather than British.

Words and phrases not yet accepted as standard speech are treated in volumes dealing with slang. Many of these, but not all, appear in the *American Heritage Dictionary* where brief hints concerning their origins are often included.

Adams, James T. *Dictionary of American History*. 7 vols. New York: Scribner's, 1940.

American Heritage Dictionary of the English Language. Rev. ed. New York: American Heritage, 1989.

Ammer, Christine. *Have a Nice Day—No Problem!: A Dictionary of Clichés*. New York: Dutton, 1992.

Ayto, John. *Dictionary of Word Origins*. New York: Arcade, 1990.

Barrere, A. *Argot and Slang*. London: Whittaker, 1887.

Bartlett, John R. *Dictionary of Americanisms*. Boston: Little, Brown, 1877.

Berliner, Barbara. *The Book of Answers*. New York: Prentice Hall, 1990.

Berrey, Lester V. and Melvin Van Den Bark, *The American Thesaurus of Slang*. New York: Crowell, 1962.

Bodmer, Frederick. *The Loom of Language*. New York: Norton, 1944.

Chambers, Robert. *The Book of Days*. Philadelphia: Lippincott, 1899.

Chapman, Robert L. *New Dictionary of American Slang*. New York: Harper, 1986.

Dickson, Paul. *Dickson's Word Treasury*. New York: John Wiley and Sons, 1992.

Evans, Bergan and Cornelia. *A Dictionary of Contemporary American Usage*. New York: Random House, 1957.

Farmer, John S. *Americanisms Old and New*. London: Poulter, 1889.

Farmer, John S. and W. E. Henley. *Slang and Its Analogues*. 7 vols. New Hyde Park: University Press, 1966.

Flexner, Stuart B. *I Hear America Talking*. New York: Van Nostrand, 1976.

———. *Listening to America*. New York: Simon and Schuster, 1982.

Funk, Charles E. *Heavens to Betsy!* New York: Warner Paperback Library, 1972.

———. *Hereby Hangs A Tale*. New York: Warner Paperback Library, 1972.

———. *A Hog on Ice*. New York: Warner Paperback Library, 1972.

———. *Horsefeathers*. New York: Warner Paperback Library, 1972.

Goldin, Hyman E. *Dictionary of American Underworld Lingo*. New York: Twayne, 1950.

Granville, Wilfred. *A Dictionary of Sailors' Slang*. London: Deutsch, 1962.

Grun, Bernard. *The Timetables of History*. New York: Simon and Schuster, 1975.

Hargrove, Basil. *Origins and Meanings of Popular Phrases and Names*. Philadelphia: Lippincott, 1925.

Hendrickson, Robert. *The Dictionary of Eponyms*. New York: Dorset, 1972.

Hollander, Zander, ed. *The Encyclopedia of Sports Talk*. New York: Corwin, 1976.

Holt, Alfred H. *Phrase and Word Origins*. New York: Dover, 1961.

Hunt, Cecil. *Word Origins: The Romance of Language.* New York: Philosophical, 1949.

Lass, A. H.; Kiremidjian, D.; and Goldstein, R. M. *Dictionary of Classical, Biblical, and Literary Allusions.* New York: Facts on File Publications, 1987.

Manser, Martin. *Get to the Roots: A Dictionary of Word and Phrase Origins.* New York: Avon, 1990.

Matthews, Mitford M., ed. *Dictionary of Americanisms.* 2 vols. Chicago: University of Chicago Press, 1951.

Mencken, H. L. *The American Language.* 3 vols. New York: Knopf, 1936–48.

Morris, William and Mary. *Dictionary of Word and Phrase Origins.* 2 vols. New York: Harper, 1962–67.

Onions, C. T. *The Oxford Dictionary of English Etymology.* Oxford: Oxford University Press, 1966.

Oxford English Dictonary. 10 vols. Oxford: Oxford University Press, 1888–1935.

Oxford English Dictionary. Supp. 4 vols. R. W. Burchfield, ed. Oxford: Oxford University Press, 1987.

Oxford English Dictionary. 2d ed. 20 vols. J. A. Simpson and Edmund S. Weiner, eds. Oxford: Oxford University Press, 1989.

Partridge, Eric. *A Dictionary of Slang and Unconventional English.* New York: Macmillan, 1961.

———. *A Dictionary of the Underworld.* New York: Macmillan, 1961.

———. *Name Into Word.* London: Routledge, 1949.

———. *Origins.* New York: Greenwich House, 1983.

Roback, Aaron A. *Dictionary of International Slurs.* Cambridge: Sci-Art, 1944.

Shipley, Joseph T. *Dictionary of Word Origins.* New York: Littlefield, 1967.

Skeat, Walter, W. *An Etymological Dictionary of the English Language.* Rev. ed. London: Oxford University Press, 1963.

Sorel, Nancy C. *Word People*. New York: American Heritage Press, 1970.

Webster's New World Dictionary of American English. 3d. coll. ed. New York: Webster's New World, 1988.

Weekley, Ernest. *Concise Etymological Dictionary of Modern English*. New York: Dutton, 1924.

————. *The Romance of Names*. London: Murray, 1922.

————. *The Romance of Words*. New York: Dover, 1961.

Wentworth, Harold and Stuart B. Flexner. *Dictionary of American Slang*. New York: Crowell, 1934.

Weseen, Maurice H., ed. *Dictionary of American Slang*. New York: Crowell, 1934.

INDEX